Hg2|Cape Town

Cape Heritage

A Hedonist's guide to…

Cape Town

Written by
Keith Bain &
Pippa de Bruyn

A Hedonist's Guide to Cape Town

Written by
Keith Bain &
Pippa de Bruyn

Photographed by
Keith Bain and Joe Botha

Managing director – Tremayne Carew Pole
Marketing director – Sara Townsend
Design – Nick Randall
Maps – Amber Sheers
Repro – Advantage Digital Print
Printer – Leo Paper
Publisher – Filmer Ltd

Email – info@hg2.com
Website – www.hg2.com

Published in the United Kingdom in June 2010 by
Filmer Ltd
17 Shawfield Street
London SW3 4BA

ISBN – 978-1-905428-47-2

Icon Villas

Hg2|Cape Town

How to…

A Hedonist's guide to Cape Town is broken down into easy to use sections: Sleep, Eat, Drink, Snack, Party, Culture, Shop, Play and Info. In each section you'll find detailed reviews and photographs. At the front of the book is an introduction to Cape Town and an overview map, followed by introductions to the main areas and more detailed maps. On each of these maps the places we have featured are laid out by section, highlighted on the map with a symbol and a number. To find out about a particular place simply turn to the relevant section, where all entries are listed alphabetically. Alternatively, browse through a specific section (e.g. Eat) until you find a restaurant you like the look of. Surrounding your choice will be a coloured box – each colour refers to a particular area of the Cape Town. Simply turn to the relevant map to find the location.

Book your hotel on Hg2.com

We believe that the key to a great Cape Town break is choosing the right hotel. Our unique site now enables you to browse through our selection of hotels, using the interactive maps to give you a good feel for the area as well as the nearby restaurants, bars, sights, etc., before you book. Hg2 has formed partnerships with the hotels featured in our guide to bring them to readers at the lowest possible price. Our site now incorporates special offers from selected hotels, as well information on new openings.

The concept

A Hedonist's guide to Cape Town is designed to appeal to quirky, urbane and the incredibly stylish traveller. The kind of person interested in viewing the city from a different angle – someone who feels the need to explore, shop and play away from the crowds of tourists and become part of one of the city's many scenes. We give you an insider's knowledge of Cape Town; Pippa and Keith want to make you feel like an in-the-know local, and take you to the hottest places in town (both above and under ground) to rub shoulders with the scenesters and glitterati alike.

Work so often rules our life, and weekends away are few and far between; when we do manage to break away we want to have as much fun and to relax as much as possible with the minimum amount of stress. This guide is all about maximizing time. The photographs of every place we feature help you to make a quick choice and fit in with your own style.

Unlike many other nameless guidebooks we pride ourselves on our independence and our integrity. We eat in all the restaurants, drink in all the bars, and go wild in the nightcluubs – all totally incognito. We charge no one for the privilege of appearing in the guide, and every place is reviewed and included at our discretion.

Cities are best enjoyed by soaking up the atmosphere: wander the streets, partake in some retail therapy, re-energize yourself with a massage and then get ready to revel in Cape Town's nightlife until dawn.

Hg2 Cape Town author

Pippa de Bruyn
Durban-born and Johannesburg-bred Pippa de Bruyn knew she had to move to Cape Town from the first time she sat watching the waves break over the Clifton boulders aged 8. A decade later she did, and has now lived there for 25 years. She travels extensively in Africa, Europe and the East on writing assignments, but no matter how exotic the destination is always grateful to return to her home on the slopes of Table Mountain.

Keith Bain
A perennial wanderer and persistent wonderer, Keith Bain has lived in each of South Africa's three major cities, but long ago lost his heart to Cape Town. Here, too, he has moved around and explored, having made a home in more than a dozen different neighbourhoods, and played in many more. Although he has a doctoral degree in drama, Keith now spends the majority of his time travelling and writing, having worked on guidebooks to such diverse destinations as India, Romania, Slovenia, Ireland, and East Africa.

Cape Town

Prepare to be seduced by the sexiest, most sophisticated city on the continent, and one of the most beautiful on the planet. One of only two urban centres in the world with a national park running through it, the city fringes a vast natural playground, and offers that rare combination of mountain and sea, the proximity such that the slopes drop perpendicularly into a coastline lined with crescents of white sand.

Table Mountain National Park measures only 22,000 hectares yet includes more plant species than the entire British Isles or those of New Zealand. Aside from that well-trotted out fact, where else can you can drive along a major highway and spot wildlife grazing on the mountain slopes and, within 20 minutes of the city's compact, bustling centre, drink glorious wines in historic wine estates, surrounded by vineyards and craggy peaks?

The Cape of Good Hope was born as a garden in 1652, when the Dutch East India Company established it as a victualling station for ships passing between Europe and the East. There was never any real intention of transforming it into a perma-nent colony, but the abundance of fresh water, arable soil and temperate climate (not to mention the gentle nature of the nomadic San and Khoi who combed the beaches at the time) saw it not only flourish, but become a much desired outpost, fought over by the Dutch and the English, even as the German and French settled on its slopes, along with slaves from Indonesia, Mozambique, Angola, and India. In fact, by the end of the 17th century, slaves outnumbered the Europeans, and their influence remains to this day: their mixed race descendents, known locally as 'Coloureds', comprise the majority of the population, and provide the city with a unique cultural tone.

Like the juxtaposition of city and wilderness, Cape Town is a place of contrasts, some of them quite unsettling – such as the clash of freewheeling opulence against heartbreaking poverty. Thousands of the city's inhabitants still live in shacks, most of them rising pre-dawn for the laborious commute into the city to service the needs of the well-to-do in their sprawling homes. Airconditioned SUVs share the asphalt with jam-packed minibuses, all whizzing along new highways that link the social playgrounds of the city centre and its residential suburbs with the

prosperous, impeccably groomed winelands. In other respects, the contrasts are a delight, such as the rambunctious fishermen who ply their trade with a toothless cackle to bronzed surfers and antique dealers in Kalk Bay; the muezzin's call to prayer drifting down over the city's burgeoning aperitif scene, or the hot sun on your back, tingling from the viciously cold waters of the Atlantic.

Historically, Cape Town's restorative beauty has always been a magnet for illustrious visitors, and a favoured bolthole for celebrities, yet it has always had a perception of itself as a small, slightly parochial city. But things are changing rapidly. With the announcement that South Africa was to be the first country in Africa to host the FIFA World Cup in June 2010, the city embarked on the most concentrated effort to improve and prettify its streetscape yet. Construction projects have been immense and the gentrification and modernisation has made the city feel cutting edge and youthful, filling many with a renewed sense of pride and anticipation.

Cape Town may draw criticism for lacking the type of African identity that's recognisable in, say, Johannesburg or Durban, but it is hard not to appreciate the cosmopolitan nature of the country's oldest city. Cape Town has always had a distinctive creolised culture that reflects influences from just about every corner of the globe, and even today the city remains in flux, attracting African immigrants from as far afield as Somalia and the Congo, as well as a large flock of European swallows, here to nest far from their northern winters, or set up shop in the city's prime real estate belts, opening restaurants, bars and guest houses, their presence bringing a modern sensibility to the African beat. Like them, whether you've come to worship the sun, undertake a new adventure in the shadow of Table Mountain, or simply party up a storm, your stay here will transform you not simply into an enthused visitor, but a lifelong fan.

Cape Town Overview

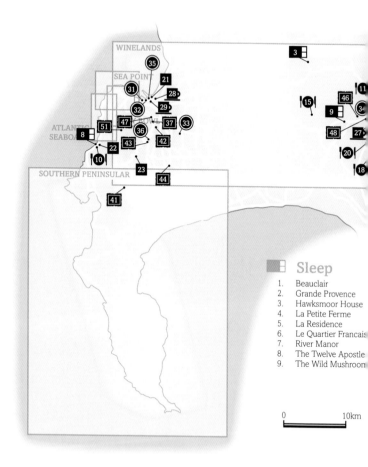

WINELANDS
SEA POINT
ATLANTIC
SEABOARD
SOUTHERN PENINSULAR

Sleep

1. Beauclair
2. Grande Provence
3. Hawksmoor House
4. La Petite Ferme
5. La Residence
6. Le Quartier Francais
7. River Manor
8. The Twelve Apostle
9. The Wild Mushroom

0   10km

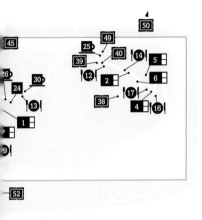

🍜 Snack

25. Fyndraai
26. Man'oushe
27. Milla The Cake Shop
28. Neighbourgoods Market
29. Suprette
30. Tokara DeliCatessen

◉ Party

31. Albert Hall
32. Decodance Underground
33. Galaxy / West End
34. The Hidden Cellar
35. House of Rasputin
36. Kirstenbosch Summer
    Sunset Concerts

🍴 Eat

10. Azure
11. The Big Easy
12. Bread & Wine
13. Delaire Graff
14. Grande Provence
15. Jordan Restaurant
16. La Petite Ferme
17. Le Quartier Francis
18. Overture
19. Rust en Vrede
20. Terroir

🍷 Drink

21. aMododa! Braa
22. Leopard Room Bar
23. Martini Bar
24. Wijnhuis

🎞 Culture

36. The Baxter Theatre
37. Boekenhoutskloof
38. Franschhoek Motor Museum
39. Graham Beck
40. Groot Constantia
41. Irma Stern Museum
42. Kirstenbosch Botanical Garden
43. Maynardville Open Air Theatre
44. Muratie
45. Oude Libertas Amphitheatre
46. Rhodes Memorial
47. Rupert Museum
48. Solms Delta Wine Estate
49. Taal Monument
50. Table Mountain
51. Vergelegen

City Centre & City Bowl

Capetonians are creatures of habit – once in a suburban groove they enjoy, they tend to dig in for life, allowing one to make sweeping statements about the kind of company certain suburbs attract, and keep. The exception to this is the city centre, which pulls by far the most cosmopolitan crowd, gathering together surfers and collar-and-tie execs (though the two are not mutually exclusive), hippies and model hipsters, Rastafarians and trustafarians, students and street kids, the Bohemian and bourgeois – all within a city centre so compact you can walk its breadth.

Built more or less on a grid system, the city's major arteries –Adderley, Long, Loop, Bree and Buitengracht – run parallel to each other, connecting the upmarket city bowl suburbs and Camps Bay with downtown Cape Town (where the majority of the city's high-rises are clustered), and the Foreshore: the result of a massive land reclamation project during the early-20th century, the Foreshore is a relatively barren area with flyovers cutting the city off from its docks. In recent years there has been a great deal of effort to further reconnect the city to its surrounds, with the semi-pedestrianisation of Waterkant Street making it possible to walk from Cape Town station to the Greenpoint Stadium, the upgrading of public squares, the canal network linking downtown to the Waterfront, the installation of CCTV cameras, and the general gentrification of the streetscape encouraging both locals and visitors to re-engage with the city. And what a delightful city.

The oldest urban centre in southern Africa, Cape Town's centre has collected some excellent examples of colonial architecture during it's 350-year history, and you'll see an agglomeration of styles – from Cape Dutch and French Rococo to Georgian, Victorian and Edwardian, as well as some fine Art Deco (don't miss the Mutual Heights building in Darling Street) and Apartheid-era Brutalist blocks such as the Civic Centre. And at its heart is the green lung that is the Company Gardens – a great place to stroll, play chess, or have a picnic. But most visitors are not here to gawk at buildings or wander garden paths, but to party, drink and shop – if that's you, head straight for Long Street, the city's most delightful browsing street (including its extension, Kloof, which stretches all the way up the mountain's lower slopes), and the place where Cape Town's most hedonistic like to gather after dark. But don't just stop in here – new cafes, cool boutiques and galleries are luring people to explore other parts of the central city, like Heritage Square on

Bree Street, and the East City, where The Assembly rocks with live bands, and The Fugard is revitalizing theatre.

Abutting the East City is part-industrial, part-residential, part run-down Woodstock, slowly but surely regenerating, as every month sees a new art gallery, shop or café open up, especially along Albert Road. Certainly the weekly Neighbourgoods Market (see Snack), started in a disused biscuit factory, is one of the top highlights for anyone interested in hanging with a cool crowd and digging into an assortment of culinary treats. The same duo have since opened Superette and the Whatiftheworld Gallery a few blocks from the Market; their dream – to bring community back into the neighbourhood – is fast being realised.

If you want to be walking distance (or near as dammit) from your playground, then the city centre has some excellent places to stay, but if you want to combine proximity along with sparkling city and harbour views, look to the pretty residential belt that fringes the city – fanning up the lower slopes of the surrounding mountains, these are locally referred to as the 'city bowl' suburbs.

On the western edge of the city, ranged along the eastern flank of Lion's Rump (or Signal Hill), is the traditional Muslim quarter of Bo-Kaap, a community that was formed by liberated slaves after the British finally banned slavery in the 1800s, and today still a colourful bastion of an era that was elsewhere destroyed. Moving southwards, as the swell of Signal Hill merges into the upwards sweep of Table Mountain, are the suburbs of Tamboerskloof, Higgovale, Oranjezicht and Gardens. Of these the most sought-after is Higgovale – protected from the wind (as evidenced by the many mature trees) it is akin to being surrounded by a mountainside forest, despite being just a short drive from the CBD. Opposite, on the south-east side of the city, in the shadow of Devils Peak, lies Vredehoek – you can spot it easily by looking out for the three Le Corbusier-inspired towers that were erected in the 1960s: disparagingly referred to by Capetonians as the 'Tampon Towers', the circular eyesores are actually named Disa Towers, and afford some unbelievable views of the city whilst interrupting the otherwise unfettered view of Table Mountain you enjoy from most anywhere in the city bowl and nearby Waterfront.

City Centre & City Bowl

0   1km

🍜 Snack

47. Biesmiellah
48. Birds Boutique Café
49. The Café (aka The Showroom Café)
50. Cheyne's
51. Depasco
52. Eastern Food Bazaar
53. Freida on Bree
54. High Tea at the Nellie
55. Jardine Bakery
56. L'Aperitivo
57. Lola's
58. Lazari Food Gallery
59. Liquorice & Lime
60. Manna Epicure
61. Melissa's Café
62. Noon Gun Tea Room & Restaurant
63. Nzolo Brand Café
64. Rcaffe
65. Rhubarb Room
66. Vide e Caffé

⚫ Party

67. The Assembly
68. Bang Bang Club
69. Cape Town International Jazz Festival
70. Chrome
71. Club Chevelle
72. Fez Club
73. Fiction DJ Bar & Lounge
74. Hemisphere
75. House of Kink
76. Mercury Live Lounge
77. Zula Sound Bar & Restaurant

🏛 Culture

78. Artscape
79. Bo-Kaap Museum
80. Castle of Good Hope
81. Coffeebeans Routes
82. Company Gardens
83. District 6 Museum
84. The Fugard
85. Labia
86. The New Space Theatre
87. On Broadway
88. Parliament of South Africa
89. The Pink Flamingo
90. South African National Gallery
91. Vaudeville

Atlantic Seaboard

For many visitors the Atlantic Seaboard—the sunset coast that stretches from Bantry Bay's cliffs, through picture-perfect Clifton and jazzy Camps Bay to the marvellously isolated enclave of Llandudno—is the essence of Cape Town. Overlooking the city's most beautiful beaches, the coast is home to the most flamboyantly wealthy, slowly edging out the lucky few who moved into the 'hood long before the value of an ocean view had been fully appreciated.

Bantry Bay, bordering Sea Point, is the most established, and where you'll find our favourite city hotel, The Ellerman, as well as Salt, a restaurant with views that are as fine as the dining. It's the steepest, most developed enclave, culminating in a rocky coastline with no public access. If it's a beach locale you're after, Clifton is the number one choice: a small cliff-hugging village of charming bungalows, most of them reached via winding steps. Enormous natural granite boulders divide the beach below into a string of four wind-sheltered coves: Blue-Flag status Fourth Beach is the most accessible, Third Beach is popular with (mostly male) models, while tucked away Second and First Beaches see the least traffic.

Spilling down the Twelve Apostles, palm-lined Camps Bay has, despite its undeniable glitz 'n glam (and exorbitant pricing), acquired a certain degree of tackiness, thanks to the proliferation of overpriced, substandard restaurants that flaunt their god-given views while ignoring any investment in their kitchens, and the LA-style posers who seem not to care. Still, if you can secure lodgings in one of the luxurious, intimate guesthouses on its slopes, you'll experience the best of what this

rapidly changing suburb has to offer—a blazing African sunset from the privacy of your own terrace, after which you can slip into the suburb's happening nightlife; the next morning you'll be one of a privileged few to awaken to an empty view. If the crowds get too much (and in peak season this beach is clogged thick) and you're looking for a more local spot, don't miss Glen Beach: right next to Camps Bay, but cut off by massive boulders, this tiny cove is often dotted with surfers and other board sports enthusiasts, and is usually missed by tourists. Alternatively, if you're looking for real seclusion, (or just a sunny place to get your kit off) take the winding coastal route to Llandudno, a scenic 15 to 20 minute drive away, on the self-same road carved out by Thomas Bain in 1848. Llandudno is within easy striking distance of Hout Bay, but the lack of amenities (there are no shops, no restaurants, no bars, and very little parking) keeps numbers on the beach to a minimum. Aside from the main beach (which is pretty but tiny), there's hidden-away Sandy Bay (walk from the parking lot on the south-western edge of the village) — one of the few city beaches that isn't overlooked by houses, and the only one where a costume is strictly optional.

There's no denying that each of these beach enclaves has a mesmeric beauty… From gazing up at the jagged peaks of the Twelve Apostles, to staring out at the ocean, glittering like a snakeskin in the sun, or surreptitiously taking in the hot young things playing and reclining along its length, the Atlantic Seaboard is a turn-on—though one brief dip in its freezing waters should cure you of that.

Atlantic Seaboard

Sleep

1. Atlantic House
2. Atlantic Suites
3. Ebb Tide
4. Ellerman House
5. Ellerman Villa
6. Lion's View
7. O On Kloof
8. Sea Five

🍴 Eat

9. Grand Cafe
10. Paranga
11. The Roundhouse & Rumbullion
12. Salt

■ Drink

13. Cafe Caprice
14. Sapphire Cocktail Lounge
15. St Yves Beach Club

☕ Snack

16. Sandbar
17. Vida e Caffe

● Party

18. Karma Lounge

■ Culture

19. Theatre on the Bay

BANTRY BAY
Queens Rd
Fir Ave
Beach Rd
Victoria
Ravine Rd
De Wet Drive
Maina Ave
Ocean View Drive
Arcadia Rd
Top Way
Road
Kloof
Nettleton Road
Road

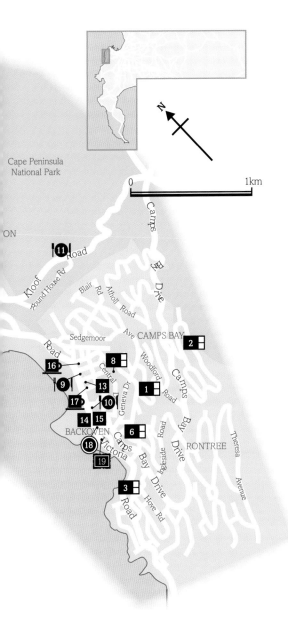

Cape Peninsula
National Park

ON

Camps Bay Drive

Kloof Road

Round House Rd

Blair Rd

Atholl Road

Sedgemoor

Ave

CAMPS BAY

Road

Woodford Road

Central

Camps Bay Road

Geneva Dr

Geneva Rd

BACKOVEN

Camps

Victoria

Ingleside Road

RONTREE

Theresa Avenue

Bay Drive

Hove Rd

Road

0   1km

11

2

16

8

9

13

1

17

10

14 **15**

6

18

19

3

Sea Point, Green Point, & V & A Waterfront

Draped over the ocean-facing flanks of Signal Hill, the residential neighbourhoods of Sea Point and Green Point create the most densely populated Atlantic seaboard suburb, with high-rise apartments interspersed with quaint Deco blocks and Victorian terraced housing creating a seamless blend with Mouille Point, the sea-side strip that wraps itself around Green Point, ending abruptly in the Waterfront.

Sea Point in particular has an almost inner city feel: an area that has seen its fortunes rise and wane, it is centred on the conglomeration of upmarket and seedy shops, cheap restaurants and neighbourhood bars, all plying their wares along Main Road, while just a short stroll west the fresh sea breeze whips over the Promenade that snakes along the coast. Stretching from Mouille Point to Sea Point (where cliff-hugging Victoria Road links to Camps Bay) the Promenade is one of the most popular places in the city to walk the dog, jog, rollerblade, play soccer or just imbibe the scene, occasionally sprayed by the waves that crash against the manmade seawall below.

Having always felt somewhat cut-off from the city centre thanks to the heavy traffic that flows up and down heavy-duty Buitengracht Street (constantly fed by the national highway that spills into its bottom end), Green Point is now linked to the inner city by a pedestrian fly-over bridge - part of the Fan Walk route, linking the station with the new Green Point Stadium - which lands at the site of the new Prestwich Memorial, an ossuary dedicated to the hundreds of unmarked graves unearthed during the 2003 excavations for the Rockwell complex, one of the many developments that have sprung up in this area in the past decade. Apart-

ment, retail and hotel developments aside, what has altered the Green Point sky-line for good is the city's new stadium— spread over 57,000 square meters, Green Point residents fought tooth and nail to stop it being built in their view, but since the dust has settled it's hard to find anyone not in favour of this sleek new addition to the suburb's varied attractions.

Connecting Green Point to the city is the small, charming but very busy De Wa-terkant, a tiny cobblestone village much favoured by the gay community, with the majority of the city's gay-friendly restaurants, bars, clubs and saunas (as well as a number of accommodation options but we find it a little too noisy and claustro-phobic to overnight here). These days, too, De Waterkant—a mere two-by-three blocks in size and comprising rows of quaint, semi-detached houses on narrow streets—is the preferred destination for shoppers who find the selection of inde-pendent outlets in the Cape Quarter more interesting than the international brands and chain stores at the Victoria & Albert Waterfront.

Originally built in 1860, and named for Queen Victoria and her son, Prince Alfred, a section of Cape Town's working harbour was transformed into one of the world's most successful waterfront leisure and shopping complexes in the early 1990s. It has since been extended by new owners Dubai World, which probably goes some way to explaining the bland, insular atmosphere of the main shopping mall. That said, the actual harbour —still working—and its tidy marinas are worth strolling around, taking in the stunning views of Table Mountain—time your visit for sunset to catch a cruise and offer a 'salut' to the glittering city at its base.

Sea Point, Green Point, & V & A Waterfront

Sleep

1. Cape Grace
2. Dock House
3. One & Only Cape Town
4. Sugar
5. Victoria & Alfred Hotel
6. Villa Zest

Eat

7. Anatoli
8. Baia
9. Den Anker
10. Grand Cafe & Beach
11. Il Leone Mastrantonio
12. La Boheme/La Bruixa
13. La Perla
14. Nobu
15. Signal
16. Sloppy Sam
17. Tank
18. Wakame
19. Willoughby & Co.

Drink

20. Alba
21. Bascule Whisky
22. Beaulah Bar
23. Belthazar
24. Wafu

Table Bay

24

18

Beach Road

MOUILLE POINT

10

Granger Bay

Granger Bay Road

phen Way

Green Point Common

Peters

Vlei Road

Fritz Sonnenberg Road

Drive

28

ern Blvd

Main

Clyde Rd

Wigtown Road

York Rd

32

Level

6

16

Road

37

30

7

29

22

26

11

36

ed St.

25

31

33

V & A WATERFRONT

19

8

23

14

Portswood Road

2

5

20

39

Port Road

9

3

Western Road

1

21

WATERFRONT

4

Port Road

15

Boulevard

34

Prestwich

38

Dock Rd

Duncan Rd

S Arm Road

Victoria Basin

17

35

● Party

36. Bar Code
37. Bronx/Navigaytion
38. Crew Bar
39. Jade

🍴 Snack

25. Andiamo
26. Beefcakes Burger Bar
27. Caffe Neo
28. Giovanni's Deli World
29. La Petite Tarte
30. Lazari
31. Loading Bay Cafe
32. Miss K Food Cafe
33. Origin
34. Table Thirteen
35. Truth. coffeecult

0   1km

The Southern Peninsula

Jutting into the Atlantic Ocean like a beckoning finger, the Southern Peninsula is ranged around a mountainous spine that separates its various coastal villages both geographically and atmospherically—hard to believe that the city centre lies just 40 minutes from the quaint fishing village of Kalk Bay, or 60 minutes from the laid-back naval enclave of Simons Town and its protected colony of penguins, or 80 minutes from where Chacma baboons browse for food on the cliffs of Cape Point and the odd unsuspecting tourist.

Certainly no trip to Cape Town is complete without driving its length in an easy circular route that starts (or ends) in Hout Bay, heading from here along the spectacular Chapman's Peak Drive—a winding 10km road carved into cliffs that plunge straight into the ocean—to Noordhoek. Popular with creatives, hippies and surfers, and now somewhat of a culinary destination (two of the city's best restaurants literally face one another at the Noordhoek Farm Village), Noordhoek is also famous for Long Beach —an 8km stretch of sand that ends at the sleepy village of Kommetjie. Beyond lie Misty Cliffs and Scarborough, an idyllic laid-back coastal enclave with pristine and empty beaches. From here it's a short hop to the sharp rocky outcrop that is Cape Point - pummelled by an unremitting ocean and wild winds, the surrounding Cape Point Nature Reserve is home to baboons, zebras, elands, red hartebeests, ostriches and bontebok.

The villages ranged along the eastern slopes of the Peninsula—the first to see the sun rise— overlook the waters of False Bay (so named by the early sailors who regularly mistook its embrace for that of Table Bay). Unlike newly developed Noordhoek or even the shiny Atlantic Seaboard, there is a real sense of history here —False Bay was once the preserve of the wealthy randlords, such as mining magnate Cecil John Rhodes, who chose to build their coastal mansions

overlooking the warmer waters and balmier temperatures of False Bay, spurning the harsher Atlantic Seaboard. From the nostalgic atmosphere of Simons Town, a naval base since the early 1800s, where a 3000-strong colony of penguins commune around the beaches, to the charming fishing village of Kalk Bay, lined with Victorian-era shop fronts displaying antiques and vintage collectibles; from the rows of colourful bathhouses of tiny St James, where the tidal pool still draws old-timers for their early morning dip, to scruffy Muizenberg's easy-going surfer culture, this side of Cape Town is a world away from the big sunglasses and pneumatic breasts of the Atlantic seaboard posers.

Proof that fashion is indeed fickle, the False Bay suburbs are, despite their obvious benefits, tagged as relatively cheap. If you need to be near the action rather than surrounded by nature, you'll probably find the area a little too far from the city. But with a warm, eminently swimmable ocean, historic atmosphere, and a generally non-materialistic approach to life, the area has nurtured an artsy, warm community, one that is more in tune with the movements of the moon than the stock exchange. If this sounds like you, look no further.

Note: When Capetonians refer to the "southern suburbs" the term denotes a far larger area than covered here, and includes the land-locked middle-class suburbs of Rondebosch, Newlands (where Kirstenbosch Gardens are located), Claremont, Wynberg and Kenilworth, as well as fancy Bishopscourt (Cape Town's embassy district), and lush Constantia —the latter is the closest wine-producing area to the city centre, some 30 to 40 min. away, and attracts an equally affluent but more discreet 'old-money' type than the brasher Atlantic Seaboard (see Winelands for more on Constantia).

The Southern Peninsula

m

8

22

18

Silvermine
National
Reserve

4

15
26
16
10
11

Peter Boyle's

21
20

d

False
Bay

p

Main

23

le Mountain
ational Park

Main

CASTLE
ROCK

Rd

Main

Road

ood Hope
Reserve

The Winelands

Stretching from the slopes of Table Mountain to the semi-arid plains of the Klein Karoo, the wine farms of the Cape number more than 550 – a vast area divided into some 15 wine regions, of which only three are touched on here, namely: Constantia, Cape Town's oldest wine producing area and so close that it is in fact a city suburb; Stellenbosch (46km from the city), the country's finest wine-producing area, and Franschhoek (83km from Cape Town), the most beautiful wine valley on the continent, with a sophisticated dining scene that sees it regularly lauded as the 'gourmet capital' of the country.

Over and above the delicious wines being produced amid splendid vistas – with experimental winemakers extending the vineyard-carpeted valleys ever higher up the mountain slopes – there is much by way of cultural diversion, including the distinctive Cape Dutch architecture of the estates (particularly in Franschhoek where regulations about building aesthetics are strictly monitored), as well as museums and galleries, and alfresco cafes along oak-shaded streets that have retained much of their historic atmosphere.

This is particularly true of Stellenbosch, South Africa's second-oldest town and home to a vivacious (and occasionally obnoxious) student crowd, who inject their energy into the late-night scene. Until just a few years ago, the 'village of oaks' was something of a backwater for urbanite Capetonians, with little beyond wine-tasting to lure them here, but – as elsewhere – things have been moving apace, and today there are a plethora of chi-chi shops and street cafes clamouring for your time and money; the Stellenbosch wineries too, have started flexing their culinary muscle and provide strong competition to Franschhoek's status as the number one fine dining destination in the Cape.

But if what enters your eye is as important as what lands on your palate, there's little to beat Franschhoek. Originally known as Oliphantshoek (Elephants' Corner) after the elephant cows who chose to calve in this lush, protected valley, Franschhoek (French corner) is where the French Huguenots, fleeing religious persecution in 17th-century Europe, settled in 1860, bringing their winemaking skills with them. Although the village thoroughfare, with its faux-French feel, is a bit touristy and twee, the valley – dwarfed by the embrace of the Great Drakenstein Mountains, which flanks it on three sides – remains astonishingly fertile and pretty; it's retail heart, jam-packed with dining options, quaint and compact.

While Franschhoek is ideal for the gourmand hedonist looking to feast on food and wine in style, there are few pubs, and absolutely no clubs or late-night hangouts here; although it does host the occasional jazz evening or concert (The Killers played on a polo estate here towards the end of 2009), it's very much a rural sophisticates hangout. If it's a party you're after, but like the idea of living among vines, the best winelands area in which to base yourself is Constantia – with only seven producers, this is the Cape's most compact wine route, offering all the usual sybaritic pleasures of the Cape winelands (views, Cape Dutch architecture, great dining) but a mere 20 to 30 minutes from the city centre and Atlantic Seaboard. Aside from this, Constantia is short hop from the unmissable Kirstenbosch Botanical Gardens, as well as the relaxed villages and beaches of the Southern Peninsula, making decisions (Swim with the penguins at Boulders? Parade with the body beautiful at Clifton? Swig another bottle of wine?) that much more difficult...

sleep…

Despite the temptation to party non-stop in this headily gorgeous city, you will need, at times, to sleep. And finding a good bed in which to do so is no chore. Variety and value abound in a lodging scene that is as diverse as the city's spectacular enclaves, and in many instances you'll be blown away when you step into your room.

Views are key. With the mountainous peninsula wearing the city like a glittering halter necklace draped along its slopes, you are well within your rights to demand a captivating scene from your bedroom window, be it twinkling harbour lights, vineyard valleys, or the Atlantic ocean at your feet. Note however that the orientation of your room can impact quite heavily on your pocket – the more widescreen your private vista along the Atlantic Seaboard, the more privileged you'll be made to feel, while on the slopes of the aptly named City Bowl, or down at the Waterfront, a full-on view of the city's iconic table-top mountain comes with a top-dollar price tag. Once you move beyond the city itself, into the Winelands especially, the pull is being surrounded by wide-open space in semi-rural surrounds, and for many opening your terrace door to be greeted by a vast carpet of plush green vineyards is more soothing than a bracing sea view. You'll find yourself amidst just such a scene at La Petite Ferme, La Residence, and Grande Provence, all impressive addresses in the 'gourmet capital' of the Cape, Franschhoek Valley, around 80km from the centre of Cape Town – an easy 40 minute drive away.

Bear in mind, though, that nobody spends all day indoors in Cape Town, and many hotels feature lounges, pool decks and bars that afford mesmerising views that a few guests are paying extra to have private access to. And as important as a great view is, the availability of a sociable host or well-grilled staff to bring you up to speed on what's going down in the city cannot be underestimated. Up-to-date recommendations about where to dine and where a good party is brewing is likely to have a better impact on your stay than whether or not you can see the top of the mountain from your shower. And come June, during the aptly named 'Green Season', when rates drop along with temperatures, you'll be grateful for the hot water bottle that the kindest hoteliers tuck under your sheets. You won't get that kind of treatment from the larger establishments, but in many smaller guesthouses, the level of intimacy and care is quite astonishing, and often it'll feel as if you've stumbled into your very own private travel agency, with your hosts ever-ready to dispense local knowledge.

Hout Bay Manor

Sea Five

For those who prefer the anonymity of large hotels, we have included our top-rated five-star establishments sporting international logos, such as the cosseting One&Only (Africa's first), the Orient Express' authentically historic and gracious Mount Nelson, and the new-but-old Taj, recently opened in the centre of the city. These combine great locations with stellar services, but no more so than independent hotel brands, such as Cape Grace, our favourite Waterfront option, or the spectacularly located Twelve Apostles, with an award-winning spa attracting hydrohedonists from every corner of the globe.

Rates tend to be a fairly accurate reflection of what's on offer, with location, level of exclusivity, and degree of luxury determining how much you're likely to fork out. Breakfast is always included in the rate, although note that many smaller establishments do not have their own restaurant. Prices, traditionally, increase over the busy summer season: Dec-Feb is peak (book well in advance), though it's worth knowing that the more temperate (and far less busy) months of March-April are rated by many locals as the best time to sample the city's delights. Lastly, with the World Cup-related launch of so many new hotels, there's every chance that competition will perhaps drive room rates down; 2010 is likely to be a benchmark year as prices are tested in the market and finally settle at some kind of standard…

Regardless of where in the city you decide to base yourself, there is a room waiting with your name on it. We trust it suits your pocket, expresses your style, tickles your fancy and let's you sleep tight!

Forthcoming Attractions

It's worth mentioning that at the start of 2010, even more dreamy-looking hotel projects were lined up to open imminently. Amongst these, if the rendered computer images are to be believed, is Camps Bay's super-slick **Pod** (www.pod.co.za; Tel: 082 600 9438 or 083 459 7707). Within spitting distance of Camps Bay beach, this brand new boutique establishment – not to be confused with the The Pod Hotel in New York – is a design-crazy modernist's dream, with the most compact (but marvellously chichi) rooms going for as little as R1,650 in winter. Their top suite will reach just over R7,000. And, in the Winelands, on the spectacularly-sited **Delaire Graff Estate**, 10 super-luxurious suites are set to launch even as this book rolls off the press; with a Banyan Tree Spa, and a restaurant that has been making waves for several months already (see Eat), it's destined to be the most magical place to stay anywhere in the region.

Ellerman House

the best hotels

Top ten:

1. Ellerman House
2. Cape Grace
3. Boutique Manolo
4. La Residence
5. Alta Bay
6. Kensington House
7. Hawksmoor House
8. Atlantic Suites
9. Dock House
10. Mount Nelson

Style

1. Boutique Manolo
2. Ellerman Villa (Icon Villas)
3. La Residence
4. Cape Heritage Hotel
5. Dock House

Atmosphere:

1. Ellerman House
2. La Residence
3. Alta Bay
4. Mount Nelson
5. Cape Grace

Location:

1. Boutique Manolo
2. Ellerman House
3. La Petite Ferme
4. The Long Beach
5. Cape Grace

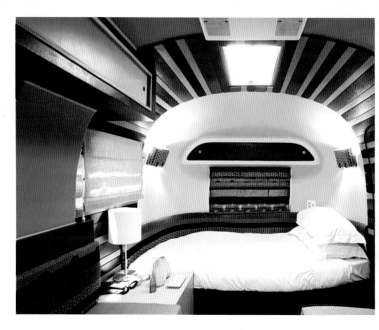

▮ Airstream Trailer Park *(left)*
▮ at The Grand Daddy
38 Long Street, City Centre
Tel: 021 424 7247
www.granddaddy.co.za
Rates: R1,750–2,450

Hock damn! the owners of this funky inner-city experience-hotel have got balls. It may not be to everybody's taste, but if you're hip to trying out the new and unusual, then bed down in this world-first: a vintage collection of Airstream trailers parked on the inner-city rooftop of Cape Town's oldest hotel. Each shiny, metal-surfaced caravan was given an artist's make-over and designed according to quirky themes, such as retro-sweet "Pleasantville" polka-dotted *Wizard of Oz*-themed "Dorothy" or "The Ballad of John and Yoko" an all-white love-nest, stocked with musical instruments. Besides the limitations on space (they're not for the claustrophobic; bathrooms are truly tiny), light sleepers might have a problem with noise drifting up from the streets below, and in summer you're forced to have the A/C flicked on full blast. Still, if you stay here, you're almost certainly in town to party, and you're a doorstep from the hotel's rooftop bar; below is the ultra-bling Daddy Cool bar (see Drink), and the delights of Long Street. Nothing in Cape Town (except perhaps sister hotel, Daddy Long-Legs; www.daddylonglegs.co.za) comes close in conceptual outrageousness, and this really is nothing like any caravan experience you might have had before.

Style 8, Atmosphere 7, Location 5

Alta Bay *(right)*
12 Invermark Crescent,
Higgovale, City Bowl
Tel: 021 487 8800 www.altabay.com
Rates: R1,500–3,300

Alta Bay's suave Portuguese proprietor, Ariel Glownia, has done an enviable job of converting an old, enormous mansion – located high above the city, on Table Mountain's slopes – into a space of seemingly effortless luxury. A bit like finding yourself in a stylish, architecturally-modified secret garden, it's built on different levels with huge windows adding to the sense of space, privilege and spectacular elevation: even lounging around the pool area, you're eye-level with treetops. Ivy clings to the outside walls, and beneath the well-established canopy of trees the garden offers wooden walkways

and discreet areas where you can relax in tranquil solitude – there's even a secluded massage deck. Each room (of which there are only seven) is a chic yet cushioning space in which neutral hues are off-set by eye-catching works of art; even the 'smaller' bedrooms are very spacious, with kingsize beds, monogrammed linens and bathrooms that range from good to spectacular. And rising up right behind you is the hulking, incredible mass of Table Mountain; if you're up for it, it's possible to hike to the cableway, and once you're on top of the Table, you can stare back down, looking for Alta Bay amidst the dense greenery.

Style 9, Atmosphere 9, Location 9

An African Villa   *(left)*
19 Carstens Street,
Tamboerskloof, City Bowl
Tel: 021 423 2162
www.capetowncity.co.za
Rates: R990–1,600

Comprising three interconnecting
Victorian terrace houses that now
share a pretty courtyard with pool,
this 13-roomed guesthouse is cool,
comfortable and excellent value. Without ignoring the original architecture
and fittings, owners Jimmy and Louis
have cleverly combined contemporary
furnishings with ethnic elements in a
tasteful blend that draws on African art
and design. Bedrooms are categorized
according to the view (or lack thereof)
and relative sumptuousness of what's
on offer – it's definitely worth bag-
ging a Platinum, with a personal balcony facing Table Mountain, while the
street-level Bronze rooms may pick up
noise from the road alongside. Jimmy
and Louis are superb hosts and you're
encouraged to make yourself totally at

home, with free rein to traipse through
the kitchen, where you can chat with
the staff or help yourself at the well-
stocked honesty bar. In winter, you
can share a spot at the dining table,
warmed by a cosy fire. And, beyond
the front door, you are walking distance
to a wide variety of neighbourhood
restaurants and drinking venues.

Style 8, Atmosphere 7, Location 6

Atlantic House   *(middle)*
20 St Fillians Road,
Camps Bay, Atlantic Seaboard
Tel: 021 437 8120
www.atlantichouse.co.za
Rates: R1,500–3,200

Unless you make it down for breakfast,
you hardly ever see another guest at
this handsome, understated five-bed-
room guesthouse built on two levels,
and tucked into the heart of residential
Camps Bay. It's the kind of ultra-relax-
ing space where you'll feel tempted to

hole up in your room, perhaps ordering in a meal and making a selection from the intelligent DVD collection. The large, unfettered spaces offer room to manoeuvre, laze, luxuriate, and contemplate, while the huge frame-box windows transform epic ocean views into ever-changing artworks. The sophisticated approach to design owes much to Oriental minimalism; bedrooms are done out in shades softer than beige and brought to life with strips of dark wood and shards of silk in ravishing colours. You can fall in love with the sea-view rooms, from where you can toast the setting sun, or make the less obvious choice and select the superb garden room where you can check out Table Mountain whilst soaping up beneath your private alfresco shower.

Style 8, Atmosphere 7, Location 8

Atlantic Suites *(right)*
30 Hely Hutchinson Avenue,
Camps Bay, Atlantic Seaboard

Tel: 021 438 9455
www.atlanticsuites-campsbay.com
R3,295–3,995

Another beautiful day in Africa, and whereas most temporary Camps Bay residents will be dashing off to the beach for the day, you'll probably find yourself wanting to lounge about in one of these elegant, pared down spaces, taking it all in from a distance. Chic and understated, this solid family home – appealingly reincarnated as an exclusive guesthouse accommodating just eight guests – is like an auditorium for showstopper views of the seemingly infinite Atlantic Ocean that spreads out below. Although there's a cosy, contemporary lounge with books and decorative detail, the breakfast room above is entirely empty of excess, with Starck's Louise Ghost Chairs floating like real ghosts in the blue landscape of sea and sky. Each bedroom is the size of a suite (the two upstairs enjoy especially fine views, even from the bathroom) and flawlessly executed in hushed tones and

43

such considerate luxuries as a complimentary mini-bar, spa-grade toiletries, and living breathing plants, orchids and lilies, that not only complement and soften the room design, but signal some serious eco-consciousness.

Style 8, Atmosphere 8, Location 9

Beauclair *(top)*
1 Coetzenburg Road,
Stellenbosch, Winelands
Tel: 021 886 7662
www.beauclair.co.za
Rates: R1,260–2,500

Situated right near Stellenbosch's famous rugby grounds, amongst gnarled, ancient oak trees, is this square-shaped manor house, with a small herb garden and fragrant lavender, roses bushes and a fountain spilling into a small koi pond out front. You step inside a space that conveys the idea of an earlier, ageless, period. Chandeliers help fill the double-volume spaces and heavy drapes accentuate the French windows. Out back, a wooden deck is poised towards a small, tailored lawn and a stone pool. Back inside, antiques have been re-upholstered with updated, textured fabrics; oil paintings in chunky gold frames hang on the walls. For smokers, a cigar bar with leather sofa. For sleeping, all-white cloisters combining a fresh classicism with clean, no-nonsense lines. Signs of modernity – TV, DVD and safe – are all discreetly hidden in wardrobes; crystals dangle from chandeliers and the fat, plush mattresses are bedecked with soft white linens while delicately embroidered chiffon curtains shape-shift in the breeze.

With just seven rooms, your hosts can afford to pamper you with little luxuries – fresh baked rusks, homemade breakfast muesli, and hot water bottles slipped under the covers in winter. In the spirit of grown-up relaxation, children are not typically accepted.

Style 8, Atmosphere 7, Location 7

Boutique Manolo *(right)*
33 Leeukloof Drive,
Tamboerskloof, City Bowl
Tel: 021 426 2330
www.boutique-manolo.co.za
Rates: R1,800–4,500

Stationed up here, you can't help feeling like a god. Hovering above the city, this small, exclusive, and very chichi guesthouse is located high up in the most discreet and undiscovered part of Tamboerskloof, and affords spellbinding vistas of Table Mountain – an

absolutely head-spinning sight from this vantage point. Cast your eyes downwards, and the city bustle reveals itself in extraordinary detail, while at night, the twinkling lights below spark off decadence. Inside the house, everything's been slickly honed to appeal to contemporary tastes – guests tend to be younger, and of the urban sensualist tribe who appreciate hand-picked artworks, ultra-modern amenities and the clever use of stark colours against an almost monastic palette of pure white. There are numerous spaces for lolling about in and you're encouraged to sink into one of the sofas overlooking the city, traipse around the secret, lush garden, and drift into a peaceful reverie at the edge of the spectacularly located blood-red swimming pool. If ever there was a perfect city sanctuary, this is a solid contender.

Style 10, Atmosphere 9, Location 10

Cape Grace *(top)*
West Quay, Victoria & Alfred Waterfront
Tel: 021 410 7100
www.capegrace.com
Rates: R4,510–17,450

Perched at the edge of one of the Waterfront marinas, this stately harbourside hotel looks not unlike a large Victorian-era renovation, but was in fact built purpose-built in 1996. It's a wonderful bit of faux vintage much augmented by the recent revamp, which provides an unbridled, intense sense of place. The decorator – who clearly has an eye for the theatrical – has sourced a collection of antique artefacts from the Cape's colonial era, and commissioned everything from hand-painted drapes to iron-forged lampstands and the most outrageously flamboyant chandeliers. All of this creates a decadent pastiche-museum atmosphere that cannot help but leave its impression – though admittedly it is not to everyone's taste. What is, are the absolutely impeccable service levels, arguably the best in the city, with every guest remembered by name and engaged by discreet and intelligent staff. There is a daily city orientation and wine-tasting (don't miss the excellent whisky bar here, either; see Drink); fantastic child-minding services; additional in-room facilities such as an X-Box or Wii and a magical, discreet spa that's open to residents only. The best option by far in the Waterfront.

Style 9, Atmosphere 9, Location 9

Cape Heritage Hotel *(bottom)*
Heritage Square,
90 Bree Street, City Centre
Tel: 021 424 4646
www.capeheritage.co.za
Rates: R1,950–4,080

This 17-bedroom hotel – an imaginative revamp of one of Cape Town's original Georgian houses – is our favourite inner city pad, offering a great sense of history (parts of the house date back to the 1780s), a strong individualistic style, and a delightful cobbled courtyard winebar-restaurant, Caveau (see Drink), where the oldest grape-producing vine in the country still grows. The hotel, now in its 10th decade, was integral to the steady revitalisation of Bree Street and today its neighbours include some of the hippest and best-dressed shops, bars and dining establishments. Although it can be slightly noisy during the day, it's the ideal base if you want to be walking distance from the action, and a great showcase of local decorative design. It's very much an authentic heritage building, so every room is unique in terms of shape and size, and the designers have followed through by imbuing every space with a personality all of its own, combining sassy contemporary elements without detracting from original architectural elements (high ceilings, exposed wood beams, and sash windows overlooking the street). There's no pool, but a rooftop Jacuzzi offers mountain views peeking out between the high buildings around you.

Style 9, Atmosphere 8, Location 7

Constantia Uitsig *(left)*
Spaanschemat Road,
Constantia, Winelands
Tel: 021 794 6500
www.constantia-uitsig.com
Rates: R1,750–7,600

It's hard to believe that this enchanting wine estate is a mere 20 minutes from the city centre, yet here you are, completely and utterly removed from city life, amid oak avenues, vineyards, horse paddocks, craggy mountain peaks and a short stroll from a selection of three formidable restaurants (see Eat and Snack), one of which features annually in South Africa's top 10. Accommodations on this working wine farm comprise a handsome collection of cottages beneath trees that fan out behind the original manor house. Inside it's old-school style: dignified, comfortable and relaxing, surrounded by mature gardens that are a delight to butterflies

and visitors alike. Wander off in any direction and you're enjoying another astonishing vista: Uitsig (literally "view") is a perfect base for exploring Constantia, the nearest wine route to the city (and manageably small), and ideal for trips around the Peninsula – there's a nifty shortcut to Hout Bay, and from there, the Atlantic Seaboard beaches, or Chapman's Peak Drive. And, awaiting your return, a spa, followed by yet another restaurant experience to delight you.

Style 8, Atmosphere 8, Location 8

....

Dock House *(top-right)*
Portswood Close, Portswood
Ridge, Victoria & Alfred Waterfront
Tel: 021 421 9334
www.dockhouse.co.za
Rates: R4,125–8,245

Looking at the unadorned Victorian-era exterior of the former Harbour Master's residence overlooking the Waterfront, you'd never guess there were rooms for rent. Inside, the ambience is that of a private home where you're waited on by a pleasant, idiosyncratic staff dressed in long Indian-style *kurta* tunics. The unadorned exterior and bare carpet-like lawn only heighten the Rococo impact of the rooms, all six of them dressed up in an appealing version of contemporary mock-baroque that is neither too heavy on the frills nor too pared down to suggest any lack of effort. The muted colour palette shows up the glittery chandeliers and silken drapes, whilst the original architectural details – vintage plasterwork and fireplaces – are a great contrast to the state-of-the-art bathrooms, modern art collection, and technological enhancements. It's all very personal, from the complimentary mini-bar (pre-stocked to your desire) to a spa that'll stay open late should you require after-hours pampering. There are occasional setbacks – ground floor rooms are hounded by early morning noise by the staff, and they sometimes get things wrong – but on the whole, this is an exercise in class.

Style 9, Atmosphere 9, Location 9

Ebb Tide *(bottom-right)*
Victoria Road, Camps Bay, Atlantic Seaboard
Tel: 083 719 5735
www.ebb-tide.co.za
Rates: R4,300–8,900

Brand spanking new, these four über-modern villa-apartments offer all the privacy and contemporary gizmos a city slicker could wish for. Park your car in the basement and, in true VIP-style, a secure elevator takes you directly to your super-sleek pad. Sophisticated state-of-the-art techno-wizardry (intelligent lighting, single panel electronic control for everything from surround sound to air-conditioning) augments the modern design aethestic, while double-glazing works hard to keep traffic noise at bay: Bang on Victoria Road (along which there is a constant flow of traffic during the summer), the duplex penthouses in particular have fabulous views over one of Camps Bay's pretty tourist-free coves, and you're a short stroll from the miniature beaches of Bakoven. Open-plan design and the use of gleaming white surface, natural fabrics in shades of grey and pale wood underfoot gives the apartments a cool gallery-like sensibility – it's an Austin Powers glamour fantasy, a showy space for schmoozy, decadent parties, where you'd half expect scantily clad models to emerge from the bedrooms at any moment.

Style 9, Atmosphere 7, Location 7/8

Ellerman House *(left)*
180 Kloof Road, Bantry Bay,
Atlantic Seaboard
Tel 021 430 3200
www.ellerman.co.za
Rates: R4,500–14,500

If you're ready to be treated like the blue blood you are, book here. Epitomising the thinking hedonist's notion of well-positioned luxury, this gracious Cape Edwardian mansion lords it over the curvaceous boulder-strewn coastal enclave known as Bantry Bay, immersing you in a world of sophisticated old world style, hyper-dramatic views, and kid-glove pampering – a hip rendition of early-Twentieth Century taste and refinement. Once the summer residence of shipping magnate Sir John Ellerman and his wife, Lady Esther, this cliff-hugging property was

restored in 1992 and transformed into the Atlantic Seaboard's most elegant lodgings, an exclusive retreat with only 11 guest rooms. It's also a repository for one of the country's finest collections of local art, and in 2009 a new contemporary gallery was carved into the rock beneath the large, manicured garden. Each room has a distinctive personality – the best, of course, also have sea views. The spa, which features its own infinity pool, is available exclusively to Ellerman guests, as is the phenomenal in-house dining. Our number one choice on the Atlantic seaboard, and one of our favourite hotels in the world.

Style 10, Atmosphere 10, Location 10

Four Rosmead *(middle & right)*
4 Rosmead Avenue, Oranjezicht, City Bowl
Tel: 021 480 3810
www.fourrosmead.com
Rates: R1,400–2,950

Your stay in this meticulously restored listed monument will not only be supremely comfortable, but will provide you with an insider view into 'real' Cape Town. Owner David Shorrock is not only a keen outdoorsman, but has his finger on the city's more offbeat cultural pulse, and more than willing to share his knowledge with you. He also understands the boutique hotel ethos, and the atmosphere is at once discreet and personal. The eight individually-decorated rooms are all soothing, comfortable spaces; pared down rather than over-the-top, with interesting objets and artworks, many of them for sale. Rooms are categorized and priced according to size and the type of views you'll enjoy – the best (deluxe) rooms have private balconies and views either over the city or towards Table Mountain, or both; all feature considerate touches (a ready-packed beach bag with towels and Frisbee, iPod docking station). It's a grown-up kind of place, offering restrained comfort and luxury, with lots of space and attractive, mellow lounge areas that open out onto a terrace overlooking the intimate garden, a heated saltwater pool, and large honeymoon cottage. You really couldn't ask for a smoother, more agreeable introduction to the Mother city.

Style 8, Atmosphere 9, Location 9

....

Grande Provence *(top)*
The Owner's Cottage,
Main Road, Franschhoek,
Winelands
Tel: 021 876 8600
www.grandeprovence.co.za
Rates: R12,000–50,000

Between the vines of one of Fran-schhoek's most celebrated and his-toric wine estates (the deeds to the 47-acre farm date back to 1694), this romantic country cottage has got to be your number one choice to host a wine-fuelled house party. Interior de-signer Virginia Fisher has celebrated the history of the region with care-fully-selected objects that include oil paintings and antique, yellowed books, creating an unpretentious hide-away that offers cleverly concealed modern comforts (such as the TV and DVD hidden away in a crocodile-skin folding desk at the foot of the bed). The cottage has its own private gar-dens and a Mediterranean-style pool; there's also a loggia for shaded out-door lounging and a smaller spa pool. Five rooms – all similarly in design but differing in size and position – are serviced by a round-the-clock butler; most drinks are included in the rate, as are breakfast and dinner, served either in The Restaurant (see Eat), or

at the Cottage itself. There are more wine farms in the immediate vicinity than you'll have time to sample, and if the pleasures of the grape become too much, head off for a spot of shark cage diving along the nearby Whale Coast.

Style 9, Atmosphere 8, Location 8

....

Hawksmoor House *(bottom)*
Majieskuil Farm,
off the R304 near Klipheuwel,
approx. 20km from Stellenbosch,
Winelands
Tel: 021 884 4815
www.hawksmoorhouse.co.za
Rates: R1,250–1,750

Bliss. That's the word that comes to mind when you check into this beguil-ingly rustic Cape Dutch manor house, perhaps the most perfect romantic es-cape in town (though this depends on how much of a princess your partner is). Located on a wine farm near Stellen-bosch, Hawksmoor occupies a restored historic homestead that's been given a second lease of life with an eclectic assortment of antiques and a bright, appealing palette. It's as much working farm as guest house, with the delightful aromas of fresh countryside to draw you outdoors, and – on a clear day – silhou-etted views of Table Mountain in the distance. A help-yourself liquor cabinet is well stocked, feisty cheese platters with bottles of the wine made on the farm can be served if you're too lazy to head for one of the Winelands restau-rants, and a simple breakfast is served on the garden terrace overlooking the delightful garden; later on, cookies and

cakes will emerge from the oven to accompany peppermint tea. It's barefoot laid-back luxury – a place where the occasional power cut or sudden lack of running water is forgiven, because that's the price you pay for being in this kind of paradise.

Style 8, Atmosphere 9, Location 8

Hout Bay Manor *(top)*
Baviaanskloof,
off Main Road, Hout Bay
Tel: 021 790 0116
www.houtbaymanor.co.za
Rates: R1,920–10,500

Interiors, executed by Boyd Ferguson (one of the SA's most celebrated designers), are the principal reason to stay at this heritage hotel, a stone's throw from Cape Town's dramatic Chapman's Peak Drive. Exteriors are pretty dull, but step inside and it's packed with drama. A brilliant home-away-from-home lounge, a sexy bar and relaxing sitting areas, all with lots of bold red accents and a strong collection of African art and craft (the owners are from Europe, so thoroughly in love with the textures, vivid colours, and creative pizzazz of local cultures). At night the house, with its polished wooden floors and clever adornments (a collection of hats decorates one wall, whilst assorted locally-painted landscapes are assembled on another) becomes a moodier, more romantic proposition, with mellow tunes and flickering candles. One drawback is the wavering service, which tends to be genuinely welcoming and warm in one instance, and so roughshod and careless the next, it's enough to drive you to drink.

Style 8, Atmosphere 8, Location 7

Icon Villas *(bottom)*
all across Cape Town and beyond
Tel: 021 424 0905
www.iconvillas.travel
Rates: Vary considerably depending on size, location and season, but a 3-bed Atlantic Seaboard villa starts from around R2500 (Ellerman Villa: R38,300–R67,000)

If you're looking for a private pad to blow out with friends, Icon Villas is a collection of 'handpicked and gorgeous' sole-use residences located in the city's most glamorous suburbs, all offering space and luxury, with the best villa concierge services in town. Of these, our favourite is the high-altitude Ellerman Villa (pictured here, and rated below). With multiple teak terraces, floor-to-ceiling windows, its own infinity pool, assorted lounges, and a master bedroom affording showstopper views across the Atlantic, you'd be forgiven for imagining yourself in some kind of glorious IMAX reality show. Every room features South Africa's most sought-after artists, and the entire house is wired to the max, making just about anything – even the curtains – jump at the touch of a button. Included in the rate (which scales up or down according to the number of rooms you occupy) are your private butler and chef, use of the Ellerman Spa, most of your drinks, breakfast and airport transfers. If, however, you'd prefer to wake up on the beach, there is

gorgeously unpretentious Villa Blanc, another favourite, or stylish Llundudno Beach Villa. Or take a look at Villa Yvette, Gorge Villa, Bridge House, and many more…

Style 10, Atmosphere 10, Location 10

....

██ **Kensington Place** *(left)*
38 Kensington Crescent,
Higgovale, City Bowl
Tel: 021 424 4744
www.kensingtonplace.co.za
R1,850–3,410

With Leeuwenkloof, residence of the Western Cape Premiere, across the road, you'd expect this to be one of the most luxurious and exacting places to stay in Cape Town. And you'd be right. While the glamorous good looks are straight out of *Wallpaper**, they're accompanied by not the least bit of pretence or snobbishness. It's a blissful little charmer that cushions guests from the hubbub of the city, yet is just a short walk to the nearest cafes and restaurants at the top end of Kloof Street.

Sleek and sophisticated, the Kensington's rooms are topped up with every sort of luxury, including personal laptops, emergency supplies of condoms, and beach gear. You can play at being a sun-worshipper in the chiffon-walled gazebo alongside the wood-terraced pool, or stretch out on one of the super-luxe sofas near the sexy little bar, or simply unwind on your private terrace to scope the city views. Wherever you choose to station yourself, both staff and space are designed to cosset while maximising your sense of total escape.

Style 9, Atmosphere 8, Location 8

....

██ **La Petite Ferme** *(right)*
Pass Road, Franschhoek,
Winelands
Tel: 021 876 3016/8
www.lapetiteferme.co.za
Rates: R1,600–3,200

High above Franschhoek village and overlooking much of the valley that earns the South African winelands

such high praise, this really is one of the most enchanting hideaways in the country. Your cottage-style suite is the epitome of countryside class with a contemporary colonial atmosphere in hushed, natural hues that focus your eyes on the magnificent green of the vineyard-covered valley sweeping down from the edge of your verandah (the Vista Suite, especially, is unparalleled). The look is gracious and grown-up, and there's a no children policy in consideration of maintaining absolute decorum. Although one of the Cape's finest restaurants (see Eat) is just a moment from your doorstep, it's only open during the day, and at night you're pretty much left to fend for yourself – arrange Franschhoek dinner reservations well in advance, or settle in for an evening of pure, unadulterated romance, watching a sky of glittering stars from your private plunge pool, or warming yourself in front of the fire with bottle after bottle of the estate's own wine. You'll need several days to properly work your way through all their vintages. In 2010, five new 'Manor House' suites, in the owner's original home, will become available. These will be ultra-luxurious, although they'll share a communal pool.

Style 8, Atmosphere 7, Location 9

La Residence *(middle)*
Elandskloof Road, Franschhoek, Winelands
Tel: 021 876 4100
www.laresidence.co.za
Rates: R8,200–8,530

Wham, glam, thank-you, Ma'am.... Grab a bottle of wine from your complimentary stock, settle on your terrace, and let your eyes drift across the velvety vineyards, sweeping up to meet the craggy valley walls... We defy you not to vote for Franschhoek as the most beautiful winelands destination on the planet! And the most beautiful place to experience it ensconced in Liz Biden's lavish boutique hotel, the kind of place you can't help but keep picking up your camera to capture the sense of awe her magpie eye inspires. Each suite is an opulently themed coccoon – from

the classically-sophisticated Huguenot and chic Armani, to the Indian ornamentation and step-up porcelain bed in Maharani (Elton John's favourite), and the smouldering Oriental boudoir atmosphere of Tang – there's hardly a space that doesn't benefit from the eclectic combination of authentic, re-invented antiques, contemporary artworks and pretty, shiny things. Access to numerous historic wine estates is easy, as is the gastronomic fanfare of Franschhoek's main drag, but you'll be hard-pressed to leave at all. And when it's time to check out, you'll be forgiven for kicking and screaming.

Style 10, Atmosphere 10, Location 9

Le Quartier Français *(left)*
16 Huguenot Road,
Franschhoek, Winelands
Tel: 021 876 2151
www.lequartier.co.za
Rates: R3,950–R8,900

Steering clear of the froufrou look you might expect from a place that takes its Gallic-inspired identity quite so seriously, this is a magically upbeat place to come home to after a day of serious wine-tasting. Smack dab in the heart of Franschhoek village, this über-upbeat *auberge* (as sassy world-wise owner, Susan Huxter, insists on calling it) is set back from the main road behind its two sensational restaurants (see Eat) and an exuberant flower-filled garden. Bedrooms are either arranged in Victorian-style cottages around the

handsome pool in the central garden or, if you're splashing out at the even more exclusive Four Quarters, on ether side of a more private and modern solar-heated pool. The latter suites (there are just four) are of the over-generous variety – enormous, with lovely extra luxuries (including a sweet-tempered private butler named Mr T). Susan decorates each room personally, marrying classic and modern elements to her exacting standards; including the regularly-changing artworks (which you can plunder after due negotiations). The wonderfully relaxed atmosphere will, in all likelihood, ease you into a coma. If that doesn't do it, a session in the spa probably will.

Style 8, Atmosphere 8, Location 8

Lion's View   *(right)*
4 First Crescent, Camps Bay, Atlantic Seaboard
Tel: 021 438 0046 or 083 719 5735
www.lionsview.co.za
Rates: R3,900–5,900 (2-bedroom penthouse), R8,250–15,000 (5-bedroom villa)

Utterly desirable, this first-class villa enjoys a near-secret location on one of those Camps Bay roads that doesn't get constant through-traffic. Little wonder it's been the object of such praise by leading international architectural and design digests. Open plan living areas with gigantic glass sliding doors lead on to a fabulously sleek and sexy pool deck that in turn gives rise to mesmeric views of Lion's Head and Camps Bay below. It's not as high up as Atlantic

Suites, but there's the advantage of being within relative walking distance of the shore (yet still a decent distance away from the non-stop bustle that besieges the Sunset Strip during summer). The house works as either two separate full-hire private units – there are five rooms in the main house, and a two-bedroom penthouse apartment above – or as a single-use villa. Like the rest of the house the downstairs master bedroom is a masterpiece in stripped back minimalist design – it's a big open-plan space focused on massive picture windows, with azure seaviews above which green-dappled Lion's Head rears up that will have you perpetually pinching yourself.

Style 9, Atmosphere 8, Location 9

The Long Beach *(left)*
1 Kirsten Road,
Kommetjie, Southern Peninsula
Tel: 021 783 4183

www.thelastword.co.za
Rates: R2,700–5,950

It's an irony that in a city this blessed by ocean-frontage, there aren't too many places where you can roll out of bed and onto the beach, or fall asleep with the sound of the waves a few meters from your feet. That's why we love The Long Beach, set directly on the beach in the tiny hamlet of Kommetjie, known for its crayfish and happy hippie vibe. With only six rooms, you'd expect to feel like an exclusive guest, and you do, with a small but warm staff complement. Kommetjie is a little cut off from the action but even the most ardent hedonist needs a little R&R and if the eight kilometres of sandy beach doesn't turn you on, you can always unfurl your towel next to the solar-heated swimming pool or chill out on your private deck with a pair of binoculars in case the whales show up. Or, if you're feeling more adventurous, suit up for a spot of surfing, or summon the horses

for a gambol next to the gentle-breaking waves. There's a chauffeur ever-ready to show you the sights or help you explore the burgeoning restaurant scene in this neck of the woods.

Style 9, Atmosphere 9, Location 10

Mount Nelson   *(right)*
76 Orange Street,
Gardens, City Bowl
Tel: 021 483 1000
www.mountnelson.co.za
Rates: R4,714–17,090

Cape Town's unopposed matriarch, the Nellie is a big (201 rooms) sprawling colonial-era hotel that looms at the top end of the Company Gardens and lingers in local mythology as a hang-out of the elite. Sure, heads of state and countless celebrities choose this genteel charmer as their preferred address, but that doesn't make this a snobbish choice; barefoot and tattooed

gentlemen cruise through the lobby en route to the large pool (best in the city), passing members of the shuffleboard generation lazing on antique sofas in cravats and garden hats. Complementing the elegant historic rooms and enchanting Old World public spaces is Planet, one of the sexiest and most happening bars in town (see Drink), and nine acres of manicured gardens with two delicious pools (one is adults only). Aside from this it's easy walking access to Kloof Street and the city, and the paradoxical combination of fine eating and drinking venues, an ultra-pampering spa and close proximity to a clinic means this is the ultimate place for a detox-retox combination holiday (just ask Robbie Williams). High tea, too, is an institution (see Snack).

Style 9, Atmosphere 8, Location 9

More Cape Cadogan *(top)*
5 Upper Union Street,
Tamboerskloof, City Bowl
Tel: 021 480 8080
www.capecadogan.com
Rates: R1,715–R4,100

Fat white columns—hinting at Georgian grandeur—dominate the white-shutter façade of this Victorianized monument on a residential road just off bustling Kloof Street. Inside it's all soothing white, perfumed with the sweet smell of ever-present St Jospeh's lilies and sensual lounge music; sink deep into one of the beautifully re-textured antique sofas and admire the thoroughly modern design of a driftwood sculpture, or be distracted by the shining baubles hanging off the nearby chandelier. The juxtaposition of vintage collectibles and minimalist cool is quite sexy, and the guest house enjoys the restricted intimacy of just 12 rooms. Bag a luxury room for maximum comfort and oodles of space (number 8 has plenty of it, coupled with a superb view of Table Mountain from the tiny terrace), not to mention exhilarating bathrooms with enormous showers built for two (at least). It's all very good value, and well located if you prefer to walk; at the upper-end of the price spectrum, you can rent the adjacent Owner's Villa, a chic private nest with a lavish, compact design that's perfect if you're the solitary sort or simply prefer to have everything all to yourself.

Style 9, Atmosphere 8, Location 7

More Quarters *(bottom)*
2 Nicol Street, Gardens, City Bowl
Tel: 021 487 5660
www.morequarters.co.za
Rates: R1,810–R6,250

From the same team that runs the aforementioned Cape Cadogan, here's a clever idea for hip travellers looking for a similar location but with more privacy. Ranged along the old cobbled sidestreets just off hectic Kloof, a small flotilla of semi-detached Victorian houses has been given a cool contemporary make-over. Although some original character has been retained, the new look is 100% chic, with masses of mirror and other gleaming light-reflective surfaces, and absolutely no holding back on those modern-day conveniences, either – plasma TV, surround sound music system, a proper little kitchen, and big, tap-dance routine rainshowers are all designed to make you feel rather happy with your new Cape home. Choose number 10 for the most romantic ambience – the big, sensuous bathroom includes a freestanding central tub. Although there's a communal check-in venue with an upstairs breakfast room (and views of Table Mountain), these cottages allow you to feel completely self-sufficient; for the rest, it's a simple walk to Kloof's endless dining possibilities, galleries, and a parade of able-bodied Capetonians strutting their stuff.

Style 9, Atmosphere 8, Location 7

One&Only *(bottom-left)*
Cape Town
Dock Road,
Victoria & Alfred Waterfront
Tel: 021 431 5888
www.oneandonlyresorts.com
Rates: R5,500–55,000

South Africans tend to equate hotel magnate Sol Kerzner with the kind of Byzantine finance that builds enormous faux-wonderland resorts with plush accommodations. Predictably then is this manmade lagoon, complete with its own palm tree-laden islands. Large, looming, and unappealing from the outside, the agoraphobic may be overwhelmed by the voluminous expanse of the lobby lounge, its clubby oval-shaped island-style bar bookended by two celebrity restaurants. But things soon settle as you step into a plush Modernist gallery of smart sofas, oversized lamps and elegant, Sino-inspired minimalism; in front of you, huge floor-to-ceiling windows frame Table Mountain and the manmade marina-style waterway outside. Rooms are clean-lined and state of the art, with mammoth beds (Cape Town's fattest mattresses), sleek entertainment systems, bedside mp3 docks, espresso machines, lavishly-stocked minibars (with classy single malts, zingy energy drinks, and health concoctions), two kinds of bathrobes, and super-ergonomic bathrooms; the massive hulk of Table Mountain (sadly foregrounded by apartment blocks) and the city itself, are visible from your private balcony. Serious shoppers will be grateful for the walking-distance proximity to Cape Town's flashest shopping mall.

Style 9, Atmosphere 7, Location 7

O On Kloof   (right)

92 Kloof Road, Bantry Bay,
Atlantic Seaboard
Tel: 021 439 2081
www.oonkloof.co.za
Rates: R2,130–4,250

A dark chocolate-coloured house on
Kloof Road, the busy road that links
Sea Point with Camps Bay (not to be
confused with Kloof Street, the restaurant strip that runs into Long Street in
town), this is one of the most sump-
tuously designed boutique hotels in
Cape Town. Funky tunes give soul to a
large open-plan space that's dressed to
impress – in one corner there's a comfortable lounge nook with a library of
books you'll want to thumb; there's a
TV and DVD here, too. But our favourite corner is the bar – suitably stocked,
its mosaic tile counter glimmers in anticipation of having your elbows polishing it. Knock back a few then head
up the steps to your lavish suite – only
room number 5 will do, so insist on
this – where the awesome, enormous
space strikes just the right balance
between contemporary clean lines
with pure sensual comfort. There's
everything you could want, including
a private terrace where you can scope
the Bantry Bay rooftops, with loungers
to soak up the sun. Pop your iPod in
its dock, crank the tunes and order up
some bubbly, then fire up the Jacuzzi,
because you're probably going to want
to settle in for the night.

Style 8, Atmosphere 8, Location 6

River Manor *(middle)*
Boutique Hotel & Spa

6–8 The Avenue, Stellenbosch,
Winelands
Tel: 021 887 9944
www.rivermanorguesthouse.co.za
Rates: R780–2,600

River Manor is for old school romantics who want to be right in the heart
of historic Stellenbosch. At night, fairy
lights sparkle in the fragrant garden, a
great spot to toast the day with a few
of the prize bottles you've gathered
during your tour of the famed Stellenbosch winelands. Inside the feel
is vintage colonial, with antiques and
collectibles – from old travelling trunks
to leather-bound journals, even an
18th century Flemish Bible – serving
as visual prompts to your time-warp
fantasy, along with crystal chandeliers,
French doors and sash windows. Roses
add a feminine touch, and in winter, the
fireplace turns even the coldest and
wettest evenings very cozy. It's not all
Out of Africa, though – modern fabrics brighten up the rooms (superior
numbers 15 and 16 are the ones to
book), the spa is pure contemporary
indulgence, and there are two pools
in which to refresh yourself between
outings to nearby restaurants – these,
along with Stellenbosch's quaint shops
and cafes, are walking distance away.
Or you can opt to idle away the day
beneath the heavy-scented guava trees
and order from the in-house deli.

Style 7, Atmosphere 8, Location 8

Rodwell House *(left)*

Rodwell Road, St James,
Southern Peninsula
Tel: 021 787 9880

www.rodwellhouse.co.za
Rates: R2,000–10,000

According to the proprietor, a super-charged meridian runs right through this property. This bit of whimsy might in fact explain the positive energy that prevails within this grand old mansion that sits, like a mellowed aristocrat, in a prime spot along the millionaires' Mile of St James (a speck-sized enclave with it's own train station and famous Victorian-era beach). Built in the 1930s by billionaire mining magnate J.B. Taylor, the house has seen its fair share of important and notable guests; you'll get some sense of that history and social pomp as you explore its well-proportioned rooms. In its redesign, spaces have been mildly contemporized with sleek new bathrooms, but the original period furniture and even some naff floral textiles have remained alongside

the plasma TVs. The house benefits from a lovely position – overlooking a formal garden and a pool fed by crisp mountain spring water, it's separated from the ocean by just the road and railway line. The house also shelters an epic wine cellar, and walls showcase a great collection of South African art. Get up early to dip in the tidal pool, and spend the better part of a day observing the spunky surfer tribe that makes nearby Muizenberg such a delight.

Style 9, Atmosphere 8, Location 8

Rouge on Rose   *(right)*
25 Rose Street,
Bo–Kaap, City Bowl
Tel: 021 426 0298
www.capetownboutiquehotel.co.za
Rates: R900–1,200

Rooms this decent at prices this affordable are downright unbelievable this close to the city centre. But it's true, and Ursula, the pioneering spirit who owns and runs this little Bo-Kaap retreat, is determined to make all her guests feel like they've struck gold. Ultimately, it's less a hotel than a collection of suite-size rooms above a bite-size reception area, and a small, very appealing café offering breakfast and all-day light dining. The curving stairways and landings on each floor feature quirky ghostlike murals with deep red accents; somehow they help transport you to a gentler mindspace as you head up to your sleeping quarters. The nine rooms and suites have fresh, boho appeal, decorated with random antiques and objects and bits of decorative junk collected by Ursula from all corners over the last 35 years. Staying here is very different to any other city bowl suburb: you're in a unique part of historic Cape Town, where the call to prayer rings out from nearby mosques and the rows of colourful little houses are traditionally home to the so-called Cape Malay (Muslim) community descended from colonial-era slaves. In short: one of the best bargains south of the equator.

Style 7, Atmosphere 6, Location 6

. . . .

Sea Five *(top)*
5 Central Drive,
Camps Bay, Atlantic Seaboard
Tel: 021 438 0743
www.seafive.co.za
Rates: R1,600–8,000

With just six bedrooms and one magnificent penthouse, this is the ultimate Camps Bay beach house, handsomely turned out and just 300 metres from the bars and restaurants of its sought-after sunset strip. Clad in bungalow-style clapboard wood, the contemporary Cape Colonial interiors are the work of local designer François du Plessis (responsible for the restaurant and whiskey bar at the Cape Grace; see Eat and Drink). He has chosen a palette of soothing, comforting colours, pure Milanese linen, judicious use of local artworks and subtle references to African design, all of which work perfectly in this milieu. There's loads of space and light, in-room luxuries are optimal (including premium aged whiskies, Voss mineral water, and handsome beachbags), and bathrooms are sleek. Downstairs rooms give you direct access to the garden, but the views from the junior suites and penthouse are no doubt what you're in Camps Bay for, so bag 'em. Although you're a short drive from The Roundhouse (see Eat), one of the city's top restaurants, you can always opt to stay in for a night or two, collaborating on a menu with Jean Paolo, the lovely Italian chef who keeps a herb garden here, and knows where to find the freshest ingredients in the city.

Style 9, Atmosphere 8, Location 8

. . . .

Sugar *(bottom)*
1 Main Road, cnr Main and
Boundary roads, Green Point
Tel: 021 430 3780
www.sugarhotel.co.za
Rates: R1,390–1,930

Giles, the tall and dapper owner, gutted the rundown backpackers formerly

known as 'Brown Sugar', and set about transforming the building into something special – an urban hideaway rated in one poll as the Best Designer Retreat in Africa. While this is perhaps a little overstated, Sugar sure is sweet, comprising just seven luxurious rooms, with a chic open-plan lounge-bar-dining room that opens on to a terraced pool, and very friendly rates. Giles' has stuck to a strict, dramatic palette of grey and black, underscoring a love of the modern, cloistered look, with each room accented in a vibrant single hue (red, blue, green or silver), with colour-coded curtains and cushions, beaded bedside lamps, tinted glass basins and underfloor lighting effects in the bathrooms; even the toiletries are colour-themed. Geared up with a full complement of mod-cons, from plasma screens and DVD players to Playstation consoles, the rooms are true urban sanctuaries, although even the toughest double-glazing battles with traffic noise from the busy Main Road (light sleepers might want to opt for one of the two rooms at the back). That said, this scores a home run with anyone wanting to be a stone's throw from the new Green Point stadium.

Style 7, Atmosphere 7, Location 6

Taj Cape Town   *(left)*
Wale Street, City Centre
Tel: 021 819 2000
www.tajhotels.com/capetown
Rates: R3,500–35,000

Don't be surprised if you're overcome by the scent of old money as you wheel into the surprisingly intimate lobby of this grand new city centre hotel. This was after all the original banking hall of the Reserve Bank, an elaborately crafted space in which four majestic marble columns support a dazzling barrel-vaulted skylight that has – along with many of the original fittings (chandeliers, heavy timber doors, he-

raldic crest) – thankfully been incorporated into this otherwise very modern, very chic hotel. Located diagonally opposite Parliament at the bottom end of the Company Gardens, walking distance from most of the city's cultural offerings, Cape Town's newest kid on the block is the result of more than two years of reconstructive surgery at a cost of R500 million, and – given what the 5-star Taj hotels offer in their native India – is poised to raise the bar on inner city hospitality. To make space for the 176 rooms (offering every conceivable luxury), a completely new 17-floor block has been grafted onto the original heritage buildings, and the result is a rather unusual piece of inner city design. And if all of the above isn't enough to persuade you, there are the astounding views, especially from mountain-facing rooms near the top.

Style 9, Atmosphere 8, Location 8

Tintswalo Atlantic *(right)*
Chapman's Peak Drive,
Hout Bay, False Bay
Tel: 087 754 9300
www.tintswalo.com
Rates: R7,000–22,000

Perched – literally – at the edge of the ocean below Chapman's Peak Drive, this hidden away lodge-style retreat within the Table Mountain National Park is the ultimate hideaway for anyone who savours the solitude of nature amidst the crash and roar of the ocean. Designed a bit like a tiny upmarket and exclusive seaside village, the 10 little cottages (each one named and styled in honour of a different island) hang on the lip of the ocean – very much safari lodge meets ocean locale. Each cottage is individually decorated in a mix of vibrant colours (lots of silver and predictable ocean-themed azures) and splashes of rustication, coupled with rather heavy-handed hints of glamour – elaborate chandeliers, Persian rugs,

and all possible amenities to make you feel pampered. Each cottage has a balcony from where you can get lost in the tumult of the waves below or keep lookout for whales that are frequently seen in this part of False Bay.

Style 8, Atmosphere 8, Location 10

The Twelve Apostles *(left)* Hotel and Spa

Victoria Road, Oudekraal,
Camps Bay, Atlantic Seaboard
Tel: 021 437 9000
www.12apostleshotel.co.za
Rates: R4,310–20,760

The only building along the gorgeous coastal road that connects the beach enclaves of Camps Bay and Llandudno (and running along the base of the mountain range known as Twelve Apostles), this hotel grew out of an original 1920s Herbert Baker-inspired house, known as 'The White House'. There's little left of this other than the double-gabled façade but the hotel – now comprising 70 guestrooms – remains gleaming white, as it still serves as a navigational landmark. Aiming for old world luxury, the hotel was recently given a thorough make-over, and rooms and public spaces are looking a lot more lavish, with fabric wallpapers and white marble floors, and agreeable clutter from huge vases filled with proteas; jars of sweets and marshmallows; and walls covered with prints, paintings and etchings. Behind the hotel, pathways lead to the Table Mountain reserve, and there are gazebos and hammock for you to stretch out on amongst the trees. The Sanctuary Spa is cut into the surrounding rocks and offers hot and cold plunge pools, a Rasul chamber, a hydrotherapy bath, and various fynbos-infused treatments – a combination that recently lead to it being named Leading Spa Resort in Africa.

Style 8, Atmosphere 8, Location 9

2inn1 Kensington *(middle)*
21 Kensington Crescent,
Oranjezicht, City Bowl
Tel: 021 423 1707
www.2inn1.com
Rates: R1,580–2,500

A guesthouse with five-star aspirations, 2inn1 combines smart, well-considered rooms with a sexy vibe around the long, skinny saltwater pool and requisite views of Table Mountain from the outdoor Jacuzzi. High Victorian pressed ceilings, original wooden floors, and large sash windows are offset by modernist touches like leather sofas and oversized snakeskin light fittings. The look is fresh and vibrant – in the main house, lime green accents perk up the long, narrow all-white breakfast room, while the adjacent lounge features zebra skin contrasted against white wooden floors, with antelope horns and the century-old fireplace a counterpoint to the contemporary furniture. Classy bedrooms, too, and – for such a small place – packed with extras, including

a local cellphone, underfloor heating, dimmable lighting, sound system (with docking station), and a complimentary soft bar. There's even an on-site spa room if you're in need of massage.

Style 8, Atmosphere 7, Location 8

....

Victoria & *(right)*
Alfred Hotel
Waterfront Pierhead,
Victoria & Alfred Waterfront
Tel: 021 419 6677
www.vahotel.com
Rates: R2,950–4,650

The first hotel to open in the heart of this working harbour-cum-shopping mall, the V&A Hotel offers a comfortable central base from which you can shop, dine, sample wines (and local and imported beers), take in some great jazz (in the adjacent Green Dolphin) and be lulled to sleep by the sound of seals playing in the water. Forget the television – designers have had the

Style 7, Atmosphere 7, Location 8

▪ **Villa Zest** *(left)*
2 Braemar Road, Green Point
Tel: 021 433 1246
www.villazest.co.za
Rates: R1,490–2,990

good sense to position a pair of plush velveteen armchairs facing directly towards that fantastic view (so do be sure to book a mountain-facing room). There's something very authentic about this Waterfront hotel – perhaps due to the care the architects took to retain the original facade of the warehouse which the hotel occupies – and while it may not be as luxurious and fanciful as some of its competitors, if offers the best value in the Waterfront, not least now that you have access to the spa and pool at the nearby Dock House (see page 46), an exclusive sister hotel which overlooks the entire V&A complex.

How Kevin Gerlach and his staff keep this ultra-white four-level house as clean and spiffy as they do is a matter for serious speculation. Sleek, compact, and packed with showy, memorable details, this is a very flashy, very slick ode to the era that produced Barbarella, American Graffiti and Studio 54. Which are the names of three of the seven rooms Kevin has on offer in this out-of-the-way corner of Green Point, down the drag from the city's brand-new stadium and not too far from De Waterkant's trendy shops at the two

Cape Quarter developments. In a way, it's like a glammed-up disco club, only without the crowds and, as yet, no mirror ball (and definitely no rollerskates on those gleaming white floors!). Retro wallpaper and classy designer furniture make the place look and feel very Austin Powers, while the relaxing spaces in the poolside garden and the little rooftop lounge give you space to prepare yourself emotionally for a night on the town, away from all of this.

Style 8, Atmosphere 8, Location 6

The Wild Mushroom *(right)*
39 Digteby Estate, Vlottenburg Road, Vlottenburg, Stellenbosch, Winelands
Tel: 021 881 3586
www.wildmushroom.co.za
Rates: R2,280–2,400

On the quirky side, this hotel's six rooms have each been stylistically inspired by the colours and textures of different kinds of mushrooms – and, yes, one in honour of the magic mushroom, known here by its Latin name. The scientific nomenclature is fitting, perhaps, since the look is serious and level-headed, so rather than tawdry toadstool references, designer George Velissariou has used inspiration from the colours and textures of the eponymous fungi – some brilliant and unexpected hues used to good effect. He's studiously modernized the restored original Digteby manor house, first built in 1890 – much of the original building has been retained, so the final result is a very clever amalgam of old and modern. To deepen the impact of the world's first mushroom-inspired hotel, the manager isn't a hotel school graduate, but a former science professor

75

(who taught for two decades at Stellenbosch University) whose knowledge of fungi is staggering. Then, to cap things off, there's a fine little in-house restaurant run by the impossibly young and talented chef whose enthusiasm in the kitchen means that you start your day at the most sumptuous breakfast table in the Winelands.

Style 8, Atmosphere 7, Location 7

....

Zensa Lodge Sport *(bottom)*
534 Egret Street,
Scarborough, Southern Peninsula
Tel: 021 780 1166
www.zensalodge.com
Rates: R700–2,500

With just seven refreshingly white rooms in the oldest house in Scarborough, Cape Town's most laid-back coastal village, Zensa is a real sanctuary – the perfect place to cast away your shoes. You're expected to slip into an altered state while here, lounging by one of the pools, dangling in a hammock, strolling the beach, or more productively honing your surfing skills or diving for crayfish. Established by a Belgian couple back in 2007, the original Zen atmosphere has recently been tweaked thanks to the arrival of new owners, also from Belgium, who've introduced more African elements into the mix. So, set against the all-white palette you'll find artefacts from all over the continent as well as whale bones and newly-commissioned furniture by a couple of Cape Town creatives. They've also added a bistro-style eatery (with a Brazilian chef) in the black clapboard house that stands

in the garden near the enormous new swimming pool. And, if you're in any way worn out by trips to the beach or to the must-see Cape Point Nature Reserve nearby, there's now a massage therapist too.

Style 8, Atmosphere 8, Location 8

eat…

Cape Town may be a part of Africa, but you'd never guess based on your dining experiences here. You could spend weeks eating out, not once encountering anything approaching so-called South African cuisine. The reality is that South Africa's multicultural heritage – and its social make-up to this day – means that influences are many and tastes, broad. This makes the very notion of 'South African cuisine' a slipperly, much-debated, one: the ubiquitous *braai* (barbeque) hardly constitutes a culinary style – it's rather a particular lifestyle, a highly social event that involves long hours of gregarious drinking. That said, the barbeque experience is one that's shared among white and black communities, with the latter often gathering en masse at neighbourhood *shebeens* (traditionally, an illicit drinking den) or 'butcheries', were communal feasting and drinking happens at ridiculously low prices. In Cape Town, the most famous of such butcher-style gatherings is Mzoli's Place (Tel: 021 6381355) in Gugulethu, an experience most visitors seem to thoroughly enjoy, including Jamie Oliver. Most foreigners who end up there (and it has become very touristy) do so as part of a scheduled tour, so it's not quite the bastion of authentic township life it once was, but is still your best bet if you become bored with how very 'white' Cape Town seems. Closer to town, aMadoda! Braai (see Drink) draws a remarkably well-heeled and wonderfully mixed gathering to Woodstock's semi-industrial quadrant three nights a week, and offers a chance to fraternise with an all-local crowd.

The *braai* aside, the only truly authentic local cuisine is so-called Cape Malay, an amalgam of imported influences which arrived here with slaves and settlers from as far afield as Indonesia, bringing to our shores an affinity for aromatic curries, pickled fish, *samosas*, and a love of spices. A fair number of restaurants and cafés will feature at least one traditional Cape Malay dish, such as *baboti*, on their menus, whilst fewer places actively specialize in the local cuisine: head for Bo Kaap Kombuis (7 August Street, Tel: 021 422-5446;) or Biesmiellah, both in the Bo-Kaap (2 Upper Wale street, Tel: 021 423-0850) if you prefer authenticity over good looks, otherwise book a table at Cape Malay (Tel: 021 794 2137) at the Cellars-Hohenort hotel in Constantia. For a more innovative take on these imported tastes, book a table at the upmarket Signal (see page XX) at the Waterfront's Cape Grace, or head out to the new Fyndraai restaurant on the Solms Delta Wine Estate (see Snack), where you can try out examples of a slow-to-emerge South African cuisine that's based on pre-colonial (as well as later) culinary influences, including the use of endemic *fynbos* (literally 'fine bush'). And, if you find yourself feeling adventurous while in Stellenbosch, there's the chance to try out traditional (and sometimes updated) examples of *boerekos* (farmers' food), associated with the white Afrikaans community. Try De Volkskombuis (Aan-deWagen Road, Tel: 021 887 2121, www.volkskombuis. co.za) for a staid, formal peek at traditional Cape dishes, or Cognito (137 Dorp Street, Tel: 021 882 8696) for a more contemporized approach to tradition.

Naturally there are, as in any city, plenty of establishments showcasing the cuisines of Italy, Thailand, India, China and Japan – the best of which are reviewed in this chapter. We have not covered any African restaurants as these unfortunately end up being something of a tourist-only preserve, with cuisine very much of the pan-African variety, which is as exotic here as it would be in Europe. If you want to sample it, Africa Café (108 Shortmarket Street, Cape Town, Tel: 021 422 0221) is the most popular, while Addis in Cape (41 Church Street, cnr Long Street, Tel: 021 424 5722) gets the thumbs up as somewhere you can try the dishes of a legitimate cuisine from this continent.

A *New York Times* journalist once made the comment that the dining culture here in the Cape is defined by it's fusion approach, and it's probably an apt nomenclature – even "Cape Modern" refers primarily to fusion cuisine, a global mishmash of influences, including of course the chef. Some of the city's finest restaurants are the work of foreigners who've settled here, bringing their own cuisine styles and mingling it with fresh local produce. And what produce…

Our Karoo lamb is phenomenal, our beef cuts beautifully proportioned (insist on free range), and our range of game meats quite astonishing. We grow virtually every fruit and vegetable known to man, and our 2,500km coastline produces an abundance of seafood. Here, as elsewhere, the plunder of the seas has become the subject of raging debate, and there's a massive drive to cut down on restaurants selling endangered species; you're able to check if a particular species is considered sustainable, by SMSing the name of the fish to the SASSI hotline (Tel: 079 499 8795). A reply message will tell you just how endangered the fish you're considering is believed to be; if it's on the 'red list' it's illegal and definitely shouldn't be on the menu.

As per accommodation, dining with a view – at least once a day – is not an outrageous prerequisite. Ironically there are precious few quality restaurants that afford the privilege of a genuine waterside location, with those located within spitting distance of the Atlantic tending to skimp on the details – such as preparing a half-decent meal, and serving it to you with genuine warmth and skill. Thankfully there are exceptions, such as Wakame, Harbour House, The Roundhouse and Salt, all reviewed here. But the most innovative kitchens tend to be located in the winelands, on exquisite estates where the quality of the meal (and wine) is matched with extraordinary views across vineyard-clad valleys surrounded by craggy mountain ranges. If you value your surroundings as much as what's on your plate, then here – on farms in and around Franschhoek and Stellenbosch – is where you'll find the most seductive restaurants on the continent.

the best restaurants

Top ten:

1. Overture
2. Nobu
3. Aubergine
4. Savoy Cabbage
5. The Roundhouse
6. Bizerca Bistro
7. Sidewalk Café
8. Opal Lounge
9. La Colombe
10. Delaire Graff

Food:

1. Overture
2. Aubergine
3. La Colombe
4. Bizerca Bistro
5. Nobu

Service:

1. Nobu
2. Opal Lounge
3. Kitima
4. The Roundhouse
5. Delaire Graff

Atmosphere:

1. Opal Lounge
2. Delaire Graff
3. The Roundhouse
4. Kitima
5. Constantia Uitsig

95 Keerom *(left)*
95 Keerom Street, City Centre
Tel: 021 422 0765
www.95keerom.com
Open: noon–2pm Thurs–Fri,
7–10.30pm Mon–Sat
Italian   **R260**

Occupying a suave-looking townhouse
tucked away deep in the city, this is
among the most reliable places for
classic Italian anywhere in the country.
Milanese owner Giorgio Nava, from
whom you can usually expect a personal visit to enquire about your meal,
not only believes in simple sophistication (evident in the pared down glamour of the interiors; downstairs décor
consists almost exclusively of a single,
scene-stealing indoors olive tree) but
goes all the way to ensuring the success of his dishes by growing and
catching many of his own ingredients.
On offer are Nava's legendary carpaccio dishes, ultra-authentic pastas, and

always a nod to local tastes in the form
of some kind of game meat, treated in
the Italian way – just a dash of oil with
suitable herbs. Like the stark, striking
interior of the restaurant itself, nothing on the plate is too complicated,
and regulars take comfort in the con-
sistency of what's served: a menu that
never, ever seems to change, at affordable prices that remain relatively stable
despite its overwhelming popularity.

Food 8, Service 8, Atmosphere 8

Anatoli *(middle)*
24 Napier Street, Green Point
Tel: 021 419 2501
www.anatoli.co.za
Open: 7–10.30pm Mon–Sat
Turkish   **R235**

Step into the renovated hull of this century-old Victorian warehouse, and you
immediately relinquish the glam of the

city's nearby Cape Quarter in favour of an atmosphere that's exotic and filled with the scents and sounds of Anatolia – ancient Turkey, with a sizeable hint of bazaar. Like most converted warehouses the space is vast, and would be awkward were it not for the uninhibited use of gigantic rugs and drapes – everywhere you look, there's another piece of Turkey assembled over the 25 years since Anatoli opened for business. The three interconnected rooms are warm-hued, lantern-lit, and stuffed with Turkish paraphernalia, but the best part is that it isn't in the least bit stuffy or pretentious. You can stick to just ordering the multiple *mezze* (served on a large wooden tray, with at least 22 different kinds to choose from), combined with freshly-baked Turkish flat bread that's delivered, piping hot, to your table. Sharing is of course essential. If you have space for more, think about lamb shanks cooked in orange juice; sword-fish kebabs (exceptional but not always available) or lamb prepared in yoghurt. End with proper *baklava* or similarly flaky *kadayif*, and a tot of Tayfun's specially imported aniseed liqueur, *raki*.

Food 7, Service 7, Atmosphere 8

....

Aubergine *(right)*
39 Barnet Street, Gardens,
City Bowl
Tel: 021 465 4909
www.aubergine.co.za
Open: noon–2pm Wed–Fri,
Modern Cape   R330

Many consider Harald Bresselschmidt the best chef in Cape Town. His impeccably classy yet unstuffy bistro and lounge-bar arrangement occupies the 19th-century home of the first Chief Justice of the Cape, which was once an extensive estate; today, the enclosed courtyard is where you can dine beneath the stars, while the modern interiors work reasonably well within the historic framework. Certainly the venue serves as an elegant backdrop to some downright avant-garde culinary creations; Harald (a German import from the Luxembourg border region) likes to play, and – when it comes to sauces – reduce, reduce, reduce, until he's uncovered a taste that's worth showing off. Yet, while he experiments with combining medallions of springbok with foie gras, or pork and pancetta pralines, he's equally adept at creating uncomplicated dishes, such as his rare fried ostrich medallions. Whatever you do, don't miss his exceptional signature aubergine soufflé with marinated goats milk cheese. Aubergine is tucked away in a city bowl residential neighbourhood that tends to get very quiet after dark, but don't let that put you off – there's good reason it's such a consistent draw for well-travelled gourmands.

Food 9, Service 9, Atmosphere 7

Azure *(left)*
Twelve Apostles Hotel, Victoria Road, midway between Camps Bay and Llandudno, Atlantic Seaboard
Tel: 021 437 9029
www.12apostleshotel.com
Open: daily, 7–10.30am, 12.30–3.30pm, & 6–9pm
Modern Cape R450

Despite the opulent beauty of the interior, you'll probably want to book a table on the outside terrace, where the real azure of the Atlantic opens up before you, and you can watch seals basking on the rocks. Come in a cel-

ebratory mood, and feast on Roberto de Carvalho's clever reinventions on traditional dishes, such as Durban-style lamb curry, chicken pot-pie, and an interesting *fynbos* vegetable curry, all served in miniature three-leg black pots (known colloquially as *potjies*). The *fynbos* theme is Roberto's signature, having worked for years to come up with a menu that's truly SA-unique, making use of the highly specialized and fragrant plants that are endemic to the Cape. The grass-fed Natal Midlands beef goes incredibly well with *fynbos* flavours, and don't miss the delicately-flavoured *rooibos crème brûlee*. There's also a separate vegetarian menu, and a few superb renditions of classic sea-food dishes, including a great salmon and tuna carpaccio, served with a wild *dagga* (a relative of marijuana) pesto,

and Parmesan shavings. One of Cape Town's lesser-known surprises that combines perfectly with a lazy drive along the Atlantic Seaboard.

Food 8, Service 7/8, Atmosphere 8

Baía *(right)*
upstairs at the Victoria Wharf, Victoria & Alfred Waterfront
Tel: 021 421 0935/6/7
www.baiarestaurant.co.za
Open: daily, noon–3pm &
6.45–10.30pm
Seafood   **R450**

The name of this Waterfront establishment refers to the gorgeous bay over which it looks, whilst alluding to its primary raison d'être – unfailingly good

seafood. Frankly, this is about as touristy as things get in Cape Town, and its mammoth proportions and shopping centre location are unlikely to drum up support from locals (who usually blanch at the bill), or those tourists in search of venues with authenticity. Still, the quality of the seafood is faultless – wide in reach, the menu also encompasses plenty of red meat for those with no love for pescatore, though it would a be pity to come here to dine on this alone. Waiters are polished and well-spoken, acclimatized to dealing with the varied international clientele; elegant interiors are also sufficiently refined, although you'd be hard-pressed to say this place has any personality to call its own – which makes the steady stream of rich, famous, or simply gorgeous, diners an essential atmospheric ingredient.

Food 8, Service 8, Atmosphere 6

The Big Easy *(left)*
La Gratitude, 95 Dorp Street, Stellenbosch, Winelands
Tel: 021 887 3462
Open: daily, noon–10pm, 8–11.30am Fri–Sun
International   **R290**

Behind the elegant façade of this grandiose Cape Dutch mansion, first built in 1798 and now imaginatively refurbished in a flash, luxurious contemporary style, you'll discover a choice of different personalities, depending on which room you decide to dine in (avoid the sleek, semi-casual bar, with its (least-appealing) sports channel TV and lame photographic shrine to golfing legend Ernie Els, the owner, hence the moniker). Given the mostly elegant surrounds, the menu is an unexpected assortment of comfort food and high-end café fair, e.g. the Big Easy burger – apparently enjoyed by local

billionaires, who pair it with an ultra-expensive bottle of cabernet franc – that takes pride of place. Half the waiters are candidates for the catwalk; the other half ooze charm and the kind of easy-going personalities the name hints at. Better still, all appear proficient at matching wines (which they appear to taste regularly) with what's on the menu – settle in for a night of fun, and let your waiter take charge rather than try to make sense of the Biblically-proportioned wine menu. What fun.

Food 7/8, Service 9, Atmosphere 8

Bizerca Bistro *(righ)*
Jetty Street, Foreshore,
Tel: 021 418 0001
www.bizerca.com
Open: noon–3pm Mon–Fri,
6:30–10pm Mon–Sat

French bistro   **R285**

Laurent Deslandes is another contender for finest chef in Cape Town. Cool, calm, exceptionally easy on the eye (although the restaurant's huge gay following really does come because of the gorgeous cuisine), and – above all – a humble genius who dreams up exceptional flavours. Having him here is a stroke of romantic good fortune. He met Cyrillia, his Afrikaans wife, two decades ago in Paris; their return to South Africa came amid protestation from friends who called them "biserca" (berserk) – and the name stuck. Laurent's style has been honed over more than 30 years (he started cooking when he was 15), and is probably best described as French with an Asian influence, developed during a stint in Sydney, producing such delicacies as his much-loved salmon salad, duck spring rolls, and squid stuffed with locally-grown snails. In an unattractive downtown location that you need to make a little extra effort to track down, Bizerca is astonishingly bare-bones considering its reputation: a simple space with cement floor, patterned white veneer tables sans table cloths, and an open kitchen overlooked by a simple bar counter.

Food 9, Service 6, Atmosphere 7

Bread & Wine *(top)*
Môreson Wine Farm,
Happy Valley Road, Franschhoek
Tel: 021 876 3692
www.moreson.co.za
Open: daily, noon–3pm; (Jan–Mar 6.30–8.30pm Thurs–Sat, but call ahead to check)
Mediterranean-influenced   R245

A one-page menu and a vine-covered courtyard with tables under umbrellas – the simple life. Then peruse that menu, and you realize that the lazy farm setting is a ploy – Chef Neil Jewell's creative imagination produces some of the Franschhoek Valley's rarer taste sensations. Among his notorious (and delicious) creations is his famous charcuterie antipasta plate (don't miss this starter); grilled swordfish; a truffle risotto finished with Auriccho cheese, and his unmissable tuna *boerewors* – first concocted for a competition the latter turns the traditional South African 'farmer's sausage' on its head, and works exceptionally well served with *pap*; it's worth calling ahead to see if he's willing to prepare this on the day you're here. With an attached farm grocer store stocking home-cured meats, fudge, free range eggs, mushrooms, ol-

ives, spicy aubergine dip, and all kinds of fresh farm produce, this is also be a good place to load a picnic basket (or ask them to do so for you) – or you can select from the deli-style counter and order from a smaller menu at one of the shop tables.

Food 9, Service 7, Atmosphere 8

Bukhara *(bottom)*
33 Church Street, City Centre
Tel: 021 424 0000
www.bukhara.com
Open: daily, noon–3pm, 6–11pm. Closed Sunday lunch.
North Indian   R320

Regularly vaunted as the best Indian restaurant in Cape Town, Bukhara has undergone a recent facelift that now makes it one of the city's most impressive-looking restaurants, fragrant with spices, simmering curries, and smoky flavours drifting from the tandoori oven. You can watch the entire, marvellous spectacle through the massive glass wall that separates the elegant dining room from the kitchen, a dramatic space that beats any cooking channel hands down. As dozens of celebrity guests, including the King of Jordan, a regular, will attest, Bukhara's dining combines authenticity with a careful nod to a more international palate; when Bono flies in to Cape Town he apparently calls in to check they're open. Although staff can come across as a tad arrogant, it's easy enough to ignore them and get caught up in the exquisiteness of the décor – a sultry mix of dark wood, vibrant red walls, green marble floors, beautifully patterned bamboo screen trellises – not

to mention the magic on your plate. Caveat: Acoustics can be problematic when it's full.

Food 8, Service 7, Atmosphere 8

■ **Café Chic** *(left)*
7 Breda Street,
Gardens, City Bowl
Tel: 021 465 7218
www.cafechic.co.za
Open: 7am–2am Mon–Sat
French   **R310**

A gorgeous Victorian house in the hub of mainstream residential Cape Town has been refashioned into a prettily tailored venue equipped for winning, dining, and decidedly late-night adventures. With no qualms about things turning a touch raucous, former Parisian restaurateur Francoise Queyroix has imported a young French chef (from Michelin-starred stock) and infused each room with a distinctive personality – a likeable blend of bordello and art gallery. Open from early, with tables on the outdoor terrace, the indoor breakfast room is probably the best-looking space in which to dine, whilst the cosy whisky bar and chic (but clumsily-named) Hip & Happening Bar (see Drink) are both good places for pre-dinner drinks. Classic French fare is balanced by modern inspiration and a hint of local influence – homemade ravioli works well with

prawn and pesto; salmon is deliciously marinated. Prices are higher than you might expect from such a new and relatively undiscovered spot, but we love the exceptionally easy-going and fun-loving attitude that makes this as much a place for drinking as for dining.

Food 7, Service 7, Atmosphere 8

Café Gainsbourg   *(right)*
64 Kloof Street,
Gardens, City Bowl
Tel: 021 422 1780
Open: 7.30am–10.30pm Mon–Fri;
9am–10.30pm Sat–Sun
Belgian   **R220**

Just two images of Serge Gainsbourg stare down on the relaxed interior of Belgian native Martine Drake's eponymous bistro. An unassuming cream-coloured space faces busy Kloof Street in a part of town dominated by fairly uninspiring restaurants that tend to blag their credentials rather loudly. Armed with a love of cooking (and Gainsbourg's music), Martine left Europe for a more laid-back life, and she maintains a similar respect for calm in her café, encouraging the lost art of lingering for hours over a meal fuelled by hearty food, conversation, and fine wine (sourced here from only top South African wineries). The Gainsburger – served, of course, with Belgian frites – is a good all-day din-

ing choice but lunch and dinner are the times to sample fresh, authentic home-style Belgian cooking such as mussels cooked in garlic and white wine, genuine fillet *bleu*, and tasty *voul e vont* (chicken stew). This is also one of the city's lesser-known picks for a perfectly seared tuna steak.

Food 7, Service 7, Atmosphere 7

live band and lunchtime spills over into the early evening, whilst on Thursday, there's a *braai* (barbeque) night where you're expected to kick back and chill the South African way. And, if you find you just don't want to leave, it's good to know that the bar stays open into the night. Unmissable.

Food 9, Service 9, Atmosphere 8

Café Roux *(top)*
Noordhoek Farm Village, Village Lane, Noordhoek, Southern Peninsula
Tel: 021 789 2538
www.caferoux.co.za,
Open: daily, 8.30am–5pm
Bistro/Café **R165**

After the exhilarating views of Chapman's Peak Drive, this is a hugely rewarding stop as you gently ease your way around the Southern Peninsula. A major draw for surfers (who come to break their hunger with the famed 'Earl's All-Day Breakfast'; also salvation from a serious hangover), Café Roux has a decidedly cosmopolitan atmosphere, and you'll be surrounded by a cross-section of Capetonians mellowed out beneath the oaks. There's also a fenced-off, supervised play area for children, which means the dining area stays tranquil and parents' stress-free. Huge emphasis is put on fresh ingredients, so the menu – on portable A-frame chalkboards – changes daily, and you soon discover that even the simplest-sounding dishes (like beef fillet with bone marrow, or crispy butternut and goat's cheese salad) tend to look (and taste) extraordinary. On Sunday afternoons, there's usually a

Carne SA *(bottom)*
70 Keerom Street, City Centre
Tel: 021 424 3460
www.carne-sa.com
Open: daily, 6.30–10.30pm
Steakhouse **R240**

For committed carnivores, heaven is this crisp, sleek two-level space right across the road from Milan restaurateur Giorgio Nava's well-established 95 Keerom, where nothing but superb meat is served. Downstairs, you'll discover a smartly pared down room with light bouncing off the brushed-charcoal walls and wood-beam ceiling. Upstairs, the counters display various cuts of meat and charcuterie, and the ambience is a little less rigid. The man from Milan owns a farm in the Karoo where much of his meat is grown in the natural way, i.e. nothing force-fed or confined to too-small barracks. The result is meat of outstanding quality, and Nava insists that the authentic product, never overwhelmed with sauces or elaborate reductions, be allowed to show through. So, whether you're opting for beef, lamb, ostrich, or a more adventurous cut of game, chances are it'll be served pretty much *au naturelle*, with as little interference from the kitchen as possible – perfectly

grilled to order, a dash of oil and a sprinkling of herbs.

Food 7, Service 7, Atmosphere 7

| ![] | **Constantia Uitsig** | *(left)* |

Constantia Uitsig,
Spaanschemat River Road,
Constantia, Winelands
Tel: 021 794 4480
www.constantia-uitsig.co.za
Open: daily, 12.30–2.30pm
& 7.30–9.30pm
International   **R300**

While the food may not inspire quite the same levels of hyperbole as sister restaurant La Colombe (located on the same wine estate; reviewed later), the gracious atmosphere of Uitsig's original Cape Dutch manor house is a great deal more gratifying than you'll experience next door. Dishes can be a bit hit and miss (with more hits than misses) but what you're really here for is the jaw-dropping views of the vine-yard-clad mountains, so either get here early, or make sure this is a luncheon stop. The menu is not particularly creative but you can't go too far wrong with offerings such as grilled springbok loin with a honey and lemon sauce, or roasted lamb with juniper jus. Laze in the garden or flop down on the private cricket oval before or after your meal,

and imbibe the wholesome country goodness of this beautiful estate along with another bottle of wine – preferably Vin de Constance, the famous dessert wine produced by the same valley.

Food 7, Service 8, Atmosphere 10

Delaire Graff Estate *(right)*
Helshoogte Pass,
Stellenbosch, Winelands
Tel: 021 885 8160
www.delaire.co.za
Open: daily, noon–2pm, 7–9.30pm
International   **R300**

Hands down the most impressively positioned restaurant in the country, this is a mind-blowing venue, dressed with an amazing art collection, and augmented by very sexy cellars. A humungous renovation that began in 2003, when diamond dealing billionaire Laurence Graff bought this beautiful estate, the massive spend is hugely evident and appreciated. At lunch, you sit on a large, beautifully constructed terrace, built around a row of ancient oak trees facing the vine-covered slopes of Simonsberg mountain and the steep, craggy rockface of Groot Drakenstein; reserve a seat on the lip of the deck and the vineyards start just beyond your table. At night, after drinks out

here on the deck, you move inside for the more formal, sumptuous and decadent atmosphere of a space inspired by the early William Kentridge portrait study that hangs above the fireplace. The food is rich, comforting and varied – seafood is excellent: the West Coast oysters are spectacularly fresh, as is the seared tuna. Bordeaux-born Tatiana, possibly the country's top-rated sommelier, is on hand to pair you up with the best possible vintages.

Food 8, Service 8, Atmosphere 10

Den Anker (top)
Pierhead, V&A Waterfront,
Tel: 021 419 0249
www.denanker.co.za
Open: daily, 11am–4pm, 6–10.30pm
Belgian **R 220**

Arguably the least pretentious Waterfront restaurant, this perennial favourite has been here since the start; located in a disused boatshed, originally used for trawlers. Some famous individuals have dined here and, in Den Anker's laid-back spirit, they've added their autographs to the graffiti-covered patches of wall around the bar, itself capped by an upturned rowing boat. For the rest, the décor is a comforting blend of exposed wooden rafters, a fireplace, and a swath of wrap-around windows framing wonderful views of the harbour and Table Mountain. As famous for its beer as it is for its home-style preparation of Belgian specialities such as pepper steak, rabbit, steak tartare, and fillet béarnaise, they've also retained such quirky traditions as handing the barman your left shoe

when you order a Kwak beer, served in a tall, bauble-bottomed glass (your shoe hangs in a basket above the bar until you return the glass). Whatever you do, don't pass on the legendary *moules marinières*, Belgian-style mussels (from Langebaan) cooked in beer, served in a black pot, and accompanied by little bowls overflowing with skinny *frites*. For something a little offbeat, try the marrow bones; the salmon tartare is a beautiful starter.

Food 7, Service 7, Atmosphere 7

Five Flies (bottom)
Rembrandt House,
14–16 Keerom Street, City Centre
Tel: 021 424 4442   www.fiveflies.com
Open: noon–3pm Mon–Fri, 6–11pm Mon–Sat
Modern French **R285**

Tucked away in the belly of the city's legal district, close to the Company Gardens and close enough to Parliament, this white-washed colonial monument formerly housed an exclusive Dutch members' club, and takes its name from a famous 1920s Amsterdam restaurant, *D'Vyjff Vliegen*. They do meat and fish commendably, with very generous servings (in response to the T-bone, a typical reaction is: "Where's the plate?") and full-on tastes (some sauces a bit too rich, perhaps). The grilled ostrich fillet with red wine jus is particularly memorable, while desserts are probably worth skipping in favour of time in the upstairs bar, a leathery, clubby lounge-style space with striking checkerboard tiles at the end of the white marble stairway. In

summer, try for a table in the gorgeous cobbled courtyard – the oldest part of the restaurant – adjacent another bar. No less romantic, though, are the jumble of dining rooms upstairs, a beguiling mix of antique, uneven floors and walls doubling as art gallery.

Food 7, Service 9, Atmosphere 8

The Foodbarn *(left)*
Noordhoek Farm Village, Village Lane, Noordhoek
Tel: 021 789 1390
www.thefoodbarn.co.za,
Open: noon–2.30pm daily and

7–9.30pm Tues–Sat (in winter closed all day Mon, and Tues for dinner)
French/Innovative   **R295**

While most restaurateurs dream of being named chef of the year, Franck Dangereux – who created La Colombe – earned the title six times and then gave up the limelight to start the type of laid-back unpretentious restaurant he wanted to dine in. In Noordhoek he found the perfect venue: a traditional A-frame thatched roof with exposed bricks (originally a farm stall), and asked his wife to decorate it – the result is an airy space with lots of personal elements, and an upbeat French

blueberries come from locals who arrive on his doorstep. The exception (weakness?) is for hugely expensive scallops from the USA; these he serves seared, with avocado and blood orange butter sauce and a salad of baby mesclun and sunflower sprouts. A truly special experience Time called the best-value fine dining experience in Africa (just how Franck feels about the 'fine dining' label?).

Food 9, Service 8, Atmosphere 8

Fork   *(right)*
84 Long Street, City Centre
Tel: 021 424 6334
www.fork-restaurants.co.za
Open: noon–11pm Mon–Sat
Fusion Tapas   **R175**

A novel way to eat, with every freshly-prepared dish served in ready-cut bite-size morsels (no knives needed, hence the name), and designed to be mixed, matched and shared – not easy, given that just about every bite is seriously delicious, so make sure you order plenty. It's ideal for those of us who suffer from 'plate envy', or long for varied tastes but hate buffets. It's also a rather lovely venue – an old 18th century two-storey townhouse, now sandwiched between Long Street's high-rise business blocks. Exposed brick walls, creaking floorboards, an antique fork collection at the base of the stairs and red lampshades dangling from exposed wood-beam ceilings create a rustic atmosphere; even the simple wooden chairs are a throwback to another era, while the dishcloths on the tables are another no-frills touch.

jazz soundtrack you can move your shoulders to. Franck, in the meantime, has gone to work once again making magic in the kitchen. Only now he does it without all the bells and whistles (or outrageous prices) typically associated with fine dining (seated here, you're not expected to wear shoes – or even a shirt). Franck has taken the 'little baskets and other bits of fluff' that irritate him, and there's no deconstructive or molecular gastronomy here either. What you get are amazing flavour combinations using fresh ingredients bought locally; fish comes from within 50km of Cape Town; beef is free range ('happy meat', he calls it); herbs, salads,

The simple, unfettered décor is a welcome counterpoint to the mushrooming craze for monochromatic Modernism and natty artfulness, but the real reward is on the end of your tine.

Food 8, Service 7, Atmosphere 7

Ginja *(top)*
70 New Church Street (entry via Buitengracht Street), City Centre
Tel: 021 426 2368
Open: daily, 7–11pm
Innovative **R325**

The jury is still out on whether or not Ginja, relocated in late-2009 to a more sophisticated venue that affords stunning views of Table Mountain (something surprisingly few restaurants here can boast), will ever again achieve the high-flying culinary status it achieved in its altogether
unprepossessing location in an old warehouse at the edge of the Bo-Kaap. The earlier, grunge-cool label no longer flies, and perhaps Mike Bassett's rather showy, complicated dishes, combining tastes and flavours that not everyone can get a handle on, are simply less fashionable. When his dishes work (and they tend to work better when he's actually in the kitchen; difficult since he has another restaurant, Myoga, in Newlands) they work very well indeed, but this is not guaranteed. Aside from this Cape Town tends to punish venues that appear to be too popular, too over-subscribed, and ultimately too good to be true: this may well be the new Ginja's fate, as early reports have been vicious. Early days, however…

Food 8, Service 7, Atmosphere 7

Grand Café *(bottom)*
35 Victoria Road,
Camps Bay, Atlantic Seaboard
Tel: 021 438 2332
www.thegrand.co.za
Open: 12.30–11pm Tues–Sun
International/Seafood **R290**

By far the sunset strip's 'prettiest' venue, the Grand is a balancing act of Bohemian fun and sophisticated sensuality, a mix 'n' match of borrowed bits and pieces, collected artworks and artefacts, casual clutter, studied antiques and bowls of overblown roses. The whole may be greater than its parts, but it sure is romantic, and a great place to schmooze away a summer evening, having witnessed an inevitably gorgeous sunset (book a table upstairs with a view through the picture-frame windows). A starter of cold crayfish with mayonnaise might empty your pockets before you move on to the rather staid mains: grilled calamari, grilled crayfish, grilled prawns, or – heaven help us – grilled chicken breast with a yoghurt dressing. The grilled fillet is however a showstopper, and generally the kitchen is competent albeit unimaginative. Being gorgeous, the Grand is understandably popular, and in peak season you might find yourself completely ignored – in the most obvious manner – several times before you're shown to your seat, and you'd do well to follow up on any reservation twice before arriving.

Food 6, Service 4, Atmosphere 8

Grand Café & Beach *(left)*
Haul Road, off Beach Road,
Granger Bay, Waterfront
Tel: 021 425 0551
www.thegrand.co.za
Open: daily, noon–11pm
International/Pizzas **R290**

A huge abandoned warehouse from which a mammoth wooden deck juts out, separating it from the manmade beach which, in turn, edges onto a wide swath of ocean that curves out from Cape Town's harbour and the Waterfront, the new Grand Café (younger sister to the Camps Bay outlet) was hands down the most talked about Cape Town restaurant during the 2009/2010 summer season. Tables bedecked with flamboyant candles, a 50-metre marble-topped bar counter decorated with baroque white-painted cherubs and backed by a wall of neatly arranged wine bottles, and at one end a massive brick pizza oven at the entrance to the open kitchen are all very chichi but on a summer's day you'll want to be outside on the 'beach' in your most expensive Gucci sunglasses, watching the moon cast its glow across the water. Balancing praise for its innovative on-the-beach setting in the otherwise concrete harbourside is deep criticism for the direo door policy and thoroughly kack, snooty service. To guarantee you're not treated with an air of condescension, email beach@thegrand.co.za or send an SMS to 072 586 2052, and don't go without a booking confirmation.

Food 6, Service 3, Atmosphere 9

Grande Provence *(right)*
The Restaurant, Main Road,
Franschhoek, Winelands

Tel: 021 876 8600
www.grandeprovence.co.za
Open daily, noon–2:30pm and
7–9:30pm (out of season, closed Sun
night)
Modern French   **R370**

Located on a historic wine estate
situated just beyond the main strip of
Franschhoek's little village, Grande
Provence – The Restaurant is considered one of South Africa's top 10 restaurants, and not to be missed if you're
up for a spot of truly fine dining. In a
formal dining space attached to beautiful gardens, and right alongside a magnificent cellar (the mildew-covered underground brick cellar, in fact, is where
Prince Edward and Sophie held private
dinners when they were here), the atmosphere is hushed and old school,
despite the fresh, contemporary seating arrangement of throne-like white
leather high-back chairs. It's a well-lit
dark-walled space that alludes faintly
to the farm setting, but is in no way
rustic or casual – the kitchen is just
about as large as the dining room, and
service is as friendly and unassuming
as it tries hard to be gracious. You decide how many dishes you want from
the menu (from R280 for three courses,
without wine), with no distinction between starters and mains – if you're
hungry, you'll want to go for at least
four dishes, the approach to plating
being that you shouldn't burn out after
tasting just two courses. Sunday lunch
is accompanied by entertainment by
an excellent Marimba band featuring
an angel-voiced lead singer.

Food 9, Service 7, Atmosphere 7

Haiku *(left)*
33 Church Street, City Centre
Tel: 021 424 7000
www.bukhara.com
Open: daily, noon–3pm and 6–11pm
Asian Tapas **R320**

Step into this moodily-lit modern space and you're struck by the three kitchens that run its length: here Asian speciality dishes, from dim sum, Thai wok, Japanese *teppanyaki*, sushi and tempura, are produced by a team of mostly handpicked Chinese imports preparing meticulously-crafted tastes below the diaphanous amber glow of handmade Japanese rice paper. Facing this are the tables, perhaps all a fraction too close together (a built-in design flaw meant to encourage a sense of communal eating), where a myriad dishes arrive according to a jumbled schedule – sharing meals is definitely the way to go. You can dodge the evening's two-session seating poli-

cy by grabbing a seat at the solid gran-ite kitchen counter and enjoy a close-up view of the theatrical performance as the team cooks for an inevitably capacity-packed restaurant. This is mix and match dining at its most up-market, with a tome-like menu, which may account for the many repeat vis-its. As the night progresses, the lounge beat soundtrack steadily progresses – a quirk that tends to divide the romantics from the urban hipsters, sending one group scurrying and another summon-ing their waiter for another round from the bar.

Food 8, Service 6, Atmosphere 7

Harbour House *(middle)*
Kalk Bay Harbour,
Kalk Bay, Southern Peninsula
Tel: 021 788 4133
www.harbourhouse.co.za
Open: daily, noon–4pm, 6–10pm

Designed a bit like a beach bungalow set on the landward end of Kalk Bay's concrete pier, Harbour House has one of the best seaside locations in Cape Town; literally right on the ocean, you have a perfect vantage from which to watch the waves frothing against the rocks right outside the windows. Cocooned against the elements by wraparound glass, you're likely to spot seals and seabirds chasing after fish just meters from your table (reserve a window seat – although, if things get rough, there's no guaranteeing you won't feel the spray). You can either choose from a selection of chalked-up fish, caught from their very own boat, or scan the compact menu for calamari (pan-fried with paprika), prawns, crayfish or the seafood platter. If you're not a seafood lover but like the idea of being close to the ocean, there is also a selection of non-seafood dishes such as rack of lamb or grilled fillet. It's a pretty,

mood-enhancing space, best enjoyed at a relaxed pace. Neither you nor the waiters are likely to be in a hurry, so go with the flow and settle in for a very romantic sojourn.

Food 7, Service 6, Atmosphere 9

Headquarters *(right)*
Heritage Square,
100 Shortmarket Street, City Centre
Tel: 021 424 6373
www.hqrestaurant.co.za
Open: 11.30am–10.30pm Mon–Sat
(bar open till late)
Steakhouse **R215**

Wandering through HQ's slightly surreal tunnel-like entrance, lit with paper-and-wire animal sculptures, you arrive in a space with charcoal-hued walls, exposed brick-and-ceiling ducts and all-embracing leather sofas that make it feel almost like a nightclub. Which

is a good thing, because Cape Town's hot-to-trot turn up here in their droves (especially on Wednesday and Friday nights), working the bar before and after their meals. This is the ultimate place for carnivores who struggle to make up their minds, with 'choice' limited to free-range sirloin steak (sirloin, apparently, being the most underrated cut of meat, preferred by genuine connoisseurs, and always the most consistent cut), sourced from Namibia and aged for 35 days. The meat is like butter, very tender, and accompanied by chips and a salad. Since you don't need to look at the menu, you can spend time soaking up the atmosphere and appreciating the design of one of the most exciting looking spaces in Heritage Square, a quintessential part of the steady revitalisation of downtown Cape Town.

Food 8, Service 7, Atmosphere 8

▨ Il Leone Mastrantonio *(left)*
22 Cobern Street
(cnr Prestwich Street), Green Point
Tel: 021 421 0071
Open: noon–3pm &
6.30–10.30 pm. Closed Mondays.
Italian   **R270**

Away from the limelight of Green Point's Main Road, Il Leone occupies a two-level building dating back to a time when this was an oceanfront hotel named 'The Thistle'. Three hundred years on, and thanks to Cape Town's extensive land reclamations, 'The Lion' is nowhere near the sea, and in its slightly tucked away location certainly doesn't rely on passing trade or tourists. Instead, there's the regular flow of informed locals – always an eclectic crowd – who return time and again so that they might succumb to the Mastrantonio recipes, recreated here each night by Daniel Toledo, who is not only a bit of a perfectionist, but also a dead-ringer for a young Tom Hanks. You'll

meet him as he takes a break from the kitchen engaging in friendly riposte while checking reactions to his perfectly al dente pasta and flawless sauces, always authentic enough to keep even the fussiest local Italians satisfactorily in awe. Having tasted the real deal – no fuss, no pretence, no over-the-top decor – you're unlikely to leave without booking for another night.

Food 9, Service 8, Atmosphere 8

Jordan Restaurant *(right)*
Jordan Wine Estate,
Stellenbosch Kloof Road, off the
M12, outside Stellenbosch, Winelands
Tel: 021 881 3612
www.jordanwines.com
Open: noon–3pm Tues–Sun, from
6.30pm Thurs–Fri

Contemporary European   R250

George Jardine, amongst Cape Town's most celebrated and (despite being relatively low-key) sought-after chefs, has refocused his attentions from his brilliant eatery in the centre of the city (if he's in residence, we highly recommend you also try Jardine, 180 Bree Street, City Centre, Tel: 021 424 5640, www.jardineonbree.co.za) and taken up operations on one of the country's top wine estates. Here he's trying his hand at country cooking, apparently working at simplifying his style over a vine-fired oven alongside a custom-designed grill. 'Simple' isn't quite the right word, however, because Jardine refuses to let up on complexity and elaborate coaxing of delicate and elusive flavours – you dine with him to 'experience' his food and savour rich, robust, perfectly-executed tastes and textures. Order anything that's slow-cooked or wood-fired, and you'll know this man means business. As for the venue – well, like so many of the Winelands spaces, you're here to drink in the views along with the magnificent wines.

Food 9, Service 7, Atmosphere

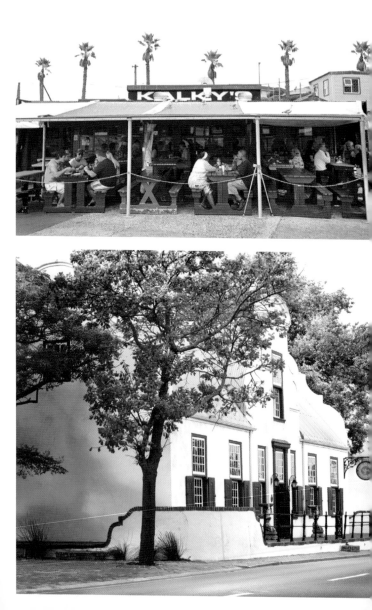

Kalky's *(top)*
Kalk Bay Harbour, Kalk Bay,
Southern Peninsula
Tel: 021 788 1726
Open: daily, 10am–8pm (8.30pm
Fri–Sat)
Seafood **R40**

The most authentic harbourside fish 'n'
chips joint in town, and the one place
where you can be guaranteed that the
seafood hasn't been losing flavour at
the bottom of a freezer. It's straight off
the boat, and the boat belongs to the
owner, so any complaints about fresh-
ness should be directed to the ocean
itself. Chips, always fried in fresh oil,
are good too. Whether or not you're up
for lining up to place your order before
plunging into a rudimentary plastic
chair or timber bench at a potentially
grubby table stocked with cheap and
crusty tomato sauce is another story.
If you're looking for a more delicate
atmosphere, head over to Harbour
House (a skip away) – if, however,
you want to rub shoulders with a totally mixed assortment of Cape Town
'characters', from the Constantia types
swirling their sauvignon (you're not
charged for bringing you own wine)
to the cackling, toothless matriarch
dispensing lemon wedges, and the tattooed gangsters out for a family treat,
this is the best place to do so. Once
your food is ready, your number will be
yelled, so stay alert.

Food 7, Service 4, Atmosphere 7/8

Kitima *(bottom)*
Kronendal Estate,
140 Main Road, Hout Bay
Tel: 021 790 8004
www.kitima.co.za
Open: 5.30–11.30pm Tues–Sun,
noon–3pm Sun
Asian **R175**

Kitima is a top choice, and one of the
funkiest places to spend an evening in
Cape Town, regardless of where you're
based. Quartered within a brilliantly
renovated national monument called
Kronendal – a supposedly haunted
18th-century Cape Dutch manor house
– this stylish yet unpretentious restaurant is forever brimming with Mother
City socialites and a mixed, gregarious
crowd that knows how to have a good
time. And a good time is exactly what's
provided, in a provocative and exciting space that's a heck of a lot more
theatrical than most dining spaces in
the city, the opulent mix of wallpapers,
fabrics, and good-looking furniture
striking a good balance between aesthetic *joie de vivre* and a bottom-line
concern for your comfort. There's an
extensive selection of Asian dishes, in-
corporating Chinese, Vietnamese and
sushi along with Thai specialities, all
good enough to warrant making a reservation. Kick off the night in the gold
and pink Raya Lounge (see Drink) before being escorted to your particular
dining venue – there are several rooms,
each done up in a distinctive style that
avoids clichéd period styling – where
you'll be taken care of by some of the
best serving staff in town.

Food 8, Service 9, Atmosphere 9

■ **Kyoto Sushi Garden** *(left)*
11 Lower Kloofnek Road,
Tamboerskloof, City Bowl
Tel: 021 422 2001
Open: 5.30–11pm Mon–Sat
Japanese   **R280**

Ultra-Zen. Impeccably understated. Small. Hushed. There's much here that contributes to the sense that Kyoto Sushi Garden is trying to remain anonymous, and stay well clear of the beaten track. From the outside – crammed into one of Cape Town's busiest corner intersections, right at the start of Kloof Nek's inevitable summertime bottleneck leading towards Camps Bay and the cableway, this looks to be a design store of sorts, or perhaps a disappearing act. Inside, things are streamlined and tiny, the design is elegant and bears a strong resemblance to what your imagination might tell you a genuine Japanese restaurant should look and feel like, yet there's a distinctly personal, homegrown look to the

place. There's the beechwood on beige colour scheme, freestanding bamboo poles, rice paper screens, a serene Buddha watching over the good-looking private dining room, and backlit boxes framing ultra-dainty bonsais. But it's the bottles of *Suntory* whisky, and cans of Asahi, Sapporo and Kirin which key you in on the overwhelming obsession with all thing Japanese – the tiny kitchen, presided over by a suitably serious Japanese wizard who not only turns out a brilliant selection of sushi – which extends to flying fish eggs and sea urchin – but prepares some authentic hot dishes that you won't find elsewhere in the city, such as sake steamed crabs, and scallop with octopus and fresh wasabi. The wasabi, incidentally, is the real deal freshly grated root flown in from Japan. A scan of the cocktail menu, too, lets you know you're in for a treat – try a dirty ninja sakatini, or a dangerous sounding Shinkansen (or 'bullet train') made with Japanese whisky and Red Bull.

Food 9, Service 7, Atmosphere 8

![] **La Boheme/La Bruixa** *(right)*
Address, Sea Point,
Atlantic Seaboard
Tel: 021 434 8497
www.labohemebistro.co.za,
La Bruixa 7.30am–11pm Mon–Sat;
La Boheme 12.30–11pm Mon–Sat
Mediterranean/Spanish   R135

This two-spaces-in-one-venue offers a genuine neighbourhood vibe – something that's mostly lacking in a city that caters overwhelmingly to the tourists and the trendy. La Bruixa ('the witch') is an all-day venue serving the only genuine Spanish tapas in Cape Town, not to mention mean paella. La Boheme is the more recent addition – Sea Point's only bistro-style restaurant and wine bar (with over 60 varieties by the glass) – a laid-back, yet slightly more glamorous, trattoria-style venue that spills out onto the sidewalk and fills up with locals out for no-nonsense good food that's carefully prepared and comforting. La Boheme's chalkboard menu changes daily, but always features six starters and 14 mains, based on what's good and fresh and available, so there may be chicken curry and rice, but beef tagine tomorrow, or rabbit (farmed in Stellenbosch, and brought in fresh); handmade pastas are always on offer, as is their signature balsamic beef fillet with risotto and mushroom sauce. The vibey outside section is prime people-watching territory, and the crowd that flocks here is a sexy cross-section of cosmopolitan Capetonians, with only a minor sprinkling of foreigners sent here by savvy hosts.

Food 8, Service 7, Atmosphere 8

La Colombe *(top)*
Constantia Uitsig,
Spaanschemat Road,
Constantia, Winelands
Tel: 021 794 2390
www.constantia-uitsig.com
Open: 12.30–2.30pm and 7.30–9.30pm
(closed Christmas night, New Year's
Day, and Sun evenings in winter)
French   **R500**

Bold flavours and exquisite presenta-
tion – that's the real allure of what is
considered one of the world's Top 50
restaurants, and rated number one in
the country by a local panel that seems
to care about such things. And it is true
that La Colombe should be experienced at least once during your time in
Cape Town. Whether you're seated beneath the vine canopy on the terrace,
or indoors soaking up the country
kitchen atmosphere, Luke Dale-Roberts' (who filled the enormous shoes of
Franck Dangereux; see The Foodbarn)
creations are exemplary. British-born,
classically trained in the French style,
and a veteran of such luminary London outfits as The Loft and Sugar Club,
his years in Asia did much to cultivate
his talent for fusion. A chalked-up a la
carte menu vies with a blowout seven-
course set menu that evolves according to Luke's creative whims (right now
he's dreaming up something with pine-
smoked veal tongue – maybe with a
touch of veal offal). The best time to
try out new creations is after March;
during the summer season he tends
to be a tad creatively drained when
everyone – from celebrity chefs to international culinary journalists – wants
a taste of La Colombe.

Food 9, Service 8, Atmosphere 8

La Perla *(bottom)*
Beach Road, Sea Point,
Atlantic Seaboard
Tel: 021 439 9538 www.laperla.co.za
Open: daily, noon–11pm
Italian   **R325**

This old-fashioned restaurant, located
on the Sea Point promenade, hasn't
changed a bit in over 30 years, and
exudes an Italian Riviera-style glamour. For nostalgia addicts and fans of
quirky service, this is an undisputed
Cape Town institution; for anyone interested in quality and a good attitude
(you can almost hear the gears turning
as waiters churn out much the same
fare they've been serving – in much
the same mechanized way – for decades), go elsewhere. Those who sing
its praises have, over the years, grown
accustomed to its Mafioso drinking
crowd (the retro bar tucked away at
the back of the restaurant is a discreet,
hidden gem that's great for a relaxing
drink) and shameless eccentricities of
the staff. Although views across Sea
Point's large public concrete seaside
swimming pool across the street don't
quite match the scene in Camps Bay,
the golden-hued sunset and women
with big hair walking their poodles
remains a classic sight, and takes the
edge off overpriced pasta and over-
done tuna steak.

Food 5, Service 6, Atmosphere 8

La Petite Ferme *(left)*
Pass Road, Franschhoek,
Winelands
Tel: 021 876 3016/8
www.lapetiteferme.co.za
Open: daily. noon–4pm
Rustic Contemporary   **R245**

Along with Uitsig and Delaire Graff, this 20-hectare farm, with an astonishing mountainside location, offers the best vineyard views in Cape Town – this time over the magical Franschhoek Valley. It has been operating for over three decades, evolving from its humble roots as a farm stall, selling homemade preserves made from the fruit that was grown here before it was transformed into a wine estate. Over the years Franschhoek has been transformed into the city's 'gourmet capital' but La Petite Ferme has somehow retained its unpretentious and rustic atmosphere with décor that is classic countryside eatery, and manicured lawns where you are welcome to sit and watch the sun go down long after last-orders. Food remains simple and nourishing, with a menu that changes four times a year and might include Peasant fish stew; springbok *babotie*; a classic rabbit dish with honey and mustard; the signature Franschhoek trout, and the aubergine wrapped lamb, slow-roasted over night. Chef Tamarin van Zyl hails from Paarl, another nearby wine district, but she's spent time training under Jamie Oliver – if you really like her fare, pick up a copy of the restaurant's latest recipe book, La Petite Ferme Rustic Contemporary Cuisine from Franschhoek.

Food 9, Service 7, Atmosphere 9

Le Quartier Français *(right)*
(The Tasting Room & iCi),
Le Quartier Français, 61 Huguenot Street, Franschhoek, Winelands
Tel: 021 876 2151
www.lequartier.co.za

Open: daily, 7–9pm (Tasting Room);
daily, noon–3.30pm and 7–9pm (iCi)
French (Innovative & Bistro)
The Tasting Room: **R550**; iCi: **R250**

It was arguably Le Quartier that transformed Franschhoek from pretty wine-
producing valley into the country's
foremost culinary destination. That
was more than a decade ago; step inside today and you have a choice between two extraordinary restaurants,
each quite different yet overseen by the
same dynamic chef. The internationally respected Margot Janse decided
some time ago to separate her ultra-
fine gastronomic venue, The Tasting
Room, from the more down-to-earth
bistro-style iCi. You'll need deep pockets and a reservation (unless you're a
guest at the hotel; see Sleep) to work
your way through the five- or eight-
course fine-dining experience served
in the stripped down, ultra-minimal-
ist exclusive confines of The Tasting
Room. Here Margot's enthusiasm for

slightly off-centre cooking means that
every dish sounds more than a touch
curious, but is ever-inspired by available, fresh, local ingredients, sourced
from small suppliers personally known
to her. If you're not up for making such
a substantial investment, book at iCi,
a modern, comfortable lounge-style
environment with a gorgeous terrace
looking onto the garden; sit in oversized leather armchairs and feast on
such simple brilliance as springbok
lasagne, wood-roasted chicken, or a
salad combining watermelon, goat's
feta and nasturtiums.

Food 9, Service 9, Atmosphere 8

Mezzaluna *(top)*
16 Loop Street, City Centre,
Tel: 021 421 6391
Open: 7.30am–4pm Mon–Fri, 7–11pm
Tues–Sat
Italian **R270**

In downtown Cape Town, among the business blocks and shadowy high-rises, Jimmy Fiore's uncompromisingly authentic and thoroughly relaxed little trattoria has grown from strength to strength with absolutely minimal hype or fuss. It started out, in fact, as a daytime-only venue, until popular demand dictated that it extend its hours after dark. There's none of the typically tawdry South African approach to pastas and pizzas here – the deal is to serve up food that's fresh and flavourful rather than prettied-up and glamorous. Like the simple venue, carved out of a corner space on the ground floor of an office tower, with small tables, chequered table cloths, and a gentle soundtrack alluding to an earlier era, the food lacks pretence (his overpriced lunchtime buffet looks downright sloppy), but when it comes to flavour, you won't go wrong here. Don't miss his *melanzane parmigiana*, or his saffron and bonemarrow risotto, or the mind-blowing sea urchin spaghetti (which truly puts the marinara at La Perla to shame). Hard to imagine that laidback Jimmy was, not so long ago, an investment banker, his sensational cooking known only to family and friends.

Food 9, Service 7, Atmosphere 6

Nobu *(bottom)*
One & Only Cape Town, Dock Road, Victoria & Alfred Waterfront

Tel: 021 431 5111
www.oneandonlycapetown.com
Open: daily, 6–11pm
Japanese **R450**

This may be an international brand but Nobuyuki Matsuhisa's first African restaurant is without any doubt in a league all of its own. Food is simply spectacular; service beyond reproach. Capetonians who haven't eaten here will make all kinds of excuses – particularly around price – but the fact is that anyone who is truly interested in Japanese fine dining must make the effort. An evening here is an event, and starts when you step onto the mezzanine level of a vast two-tier space done out in the classiest Modernist lines, with soaring columns, gigantic circular frames, and upturned pyramidal ceiling lights miles above your head. Upbeat tunes from the live DJ in the hotel's lobby bar create a fresh, contemporary vibe. Below you, the enormously proportioned dining space terminates in an open kitchen where sushi master Hideki Maeda and his team take time from their serious endeavours to chat to anyone who's perched at the sushi counter. While the menu is worth browsing, you'd do well to go straight for the chef's *omakase* ("from the heart") selection – a multi-course taste adventure, best enjoyed with a selection of paired sakes, served from beautiful bamboo flasks.

Food 10, Service 10, Atmosphere 9

Opal Lounge *(top)*

30 Kloof Street,
Gardens, City Bowl
Tel: 021 422 4747
Open: daily, noon–3pm and 6pm–late
(open for drinks throughout)

International Fusion **R325**

'Sexy' isn't close enough to describing the flash, sumptuous décor of what is the most visually arresting restaurant in town, where there's always something wonderful to look at. If it weren't located on bustling and ever-popular Kloof Street, you might call it a hidden gem. Owner Rochelle Bushell has flawlessly rendered each room of her precious dark-walled Opal to evoke a mood that's sultry, romantic, and quite unforgettable. Along with judicious use of antiques, there's much savvy emphasis of original Victorian architectural detailing along with many beautiful objects – Persian, Oriental, African-Colonial – that serve as the perfect background to a wonderfully romantic dining experience, and augmented by the good-looking wait staff. Embark first upon the bar. Here, engulfed by a palette of plush charcoal and ebony, accented by gold trim and flickering candles, sample The Opal Chill, a cocktail of champagne and lemon sorbet nectar, topped off with vodka, before being led to your table by your waiter. Mains – ingenious creations that are neither too elaborate nor lacking imagination – won't disappoint either, while desserts – by young, adventurous Steven Kruger (a chef to watch) – are simply extraordinary. A great experience, not oft repeated.

Food 8, Service 9, Atmosphere 10

Overture *(bottom)*

Hidden Valley Estate, Annandale Road, outside Stellenbosch, Winelands
Tel: 021 880 2721
www.dineatoverture.co.za
Open: noon–3pm Tues–Sun,
7–9pm Thurs–Fri

French **R300**

Yet another amazing location to drink in the pleasures of the vine at this lofty cellar restaurant, located among the vineyards that carpet the lower slopes of the Stellenbosch Mountains that stretch languidly towards Somerset West, and offering unbelievable value in the wine-paired fixed price menus. Here, a manly kitchen is run by top-rated chef, Bertus Basson, a workaholic who constantly updates and changes his 10-item-per-day menu to ensure that everything is fresh and nothing gets wasted, and explains the occasional appearance of unusual and little-known cuts on the menu such as *blesbok tartare* and soy-cured swordfish. It's possible to enjoy up to an eight-course blowout gastronomic experience – pausing between each one to imbibe one of the most sensational views anywhere in the vicinity of Stellenbosch (although not quite on a par with Delaire Graff; see page 94). Sadly, despite the views, the rigour of the kitchen and the brilliance of what's on the plate, service can feel a touch rushed and manic – it's not always easy to enjoy a relaxed meal when your server looks like he's involved in a gruelling marathon.

Food 9, Service 6/7, Atmosphere 9

Paranga *(left)*
Shop 1, The Promenade,
Victoria Road, Camps Bay,
Atlantic Seaboard
Tel: 021 438 0404
www.paranga.co.za,
Open: daily, 9.30am–10.30pm
Eclectic   **R350**

Aside from The Grand this is the classiest joint on the sunset strip, which means you're in prime posing territory here – more like a theatre stage for the mod-squad preppy-set than a legitimate restaurant, but that doesn't make it any less alluring if you're the type who likes to be in the royal box at a soap opera starring toned beachbound flesh on the white sands of Camps Bay beach. With a few steps leading up to the 'auditorium', you'd better make sure you've pre-booked a seat on the open-air terrace – you'd hate to be stuck at the back where there's nothing to be seen (and no-one can see you). An upbeat soundtrack of Buddha Bar-style lounge tunes takes the edge of the mediocre service, as does the range of decadent wines and champagnes. While nobody really comes here for the food, the salads and sushi are passable, and if you're a fan of decadent-looking spaces, you can take a look at next door sister establishments, The Kove (Tel: 021 438 004) and Bungalow (Tel: 021 438 0007),

both well-designed, but with middling food at inflated prices you are paying for a seat amongst the so-called mortal gods.

Food 4, Service 6, Atmosphere 8

....

Pure *(right)*
Hout Bay Manor, city area,
Tel: 021 791 9393
www.pure-restaurant.co.za
Open: 6.30–10.30pm Tues–Sat,
noon–3pm Sun
International **R280**

One of the most visually arresting restaurants in Cape Town, Pure feels more like a theatre set than a dining space, yet still manages to make you feel comfortable rather than a bit-part performer. What it does is set you up for some serious culinary razzle-dazzle, ideal as nothing served in an environment like this should be anything less than extraordinary. And Chef Alexander Mueller does everything possible to blow you away – his tasting-size portions are packed with flavour. It's a menu that sounds like furious hard work, and although there's nothing disappointing to distract from the experience, you somehow come away feeling perhaps a little hungry for more, the curious flavours feeling too much like a prelude rather than a satisfying

meal. Ultimately, that's a massive compliment: Maestro Alexander should simply put more of his genius on the plate.

Food 7/8, Service 9, Atmosphere 7

■ **The Roundhouse**   *(top)*
  & Rumbullion
The Glen, Kloof Road,
Camps Bay, Atlantic Seaboard
Tel: 021 438 4347
www.theroundhouserestaurant.com
Open: 6–11pm Tues–Sat (Roundhouse). 8am–8pm Tues–Sat and
8am–3pm Sun (Rumbullion)
The Roundhouse: **French**   **R595**
Rumbullion: **International**   **R250**

Two exceptional dining experiences rolled into one fabulous, magical location, lording it high over Camps Bay on the slopes of Lion's Head. Originally built as a guardhouse in 1786, and later used as a hunting lodge by a spoilt and apparently riotously decadent Lord Charles Somerset, The Roundhouse offers you an evening of French fine-dining, complemented by a brilliant selection of wines and imported single malts. Seating is in carefully renovated intimately proportioned rooms with stripped-down appeal; within the curvaceous (and in one case, completely oval) rooms, original wooden floors, kiaat Nguni chairs and starched white linen do little to detract from the main attraction. Gordon Ramsey-mentored chef P.J. Vadas is a whizz in the kitchen, concocting amazing degustation menus night after night, while pastry chef Vanessa Quellec prepares desserts to blow your good intentions. During the day, tables spill out onto

the lawns and a cheerful summery atmosphere is accompanied by a more relaxed selection of bistro-style meals ranging from burgers to roasted bone marrow on toast. A great early-evening cocktail venue, too, with sunsets over the Atlantic a formidable sight.

Food 9, Service 8, Atmosphere 9

■ **Royale Eatery**   *(bottom)*
  273 Long Street, City Centre
Tel: 021 422 4536
Open: daily, noon–11.30pm
Burgers   **R150**

This is probably the quirkiest restaurant on Long Street, awash with pretty young things, some of whom are the fresh-faced beauties who dispense menus, while others are those feasting on the awesome burgers and shakes. Like something Mia Wallace in *Pulp Fiction* would have dreamt up, Royale is Cape Town's long-standing burger champion, and the extensive selection of what can be squeezed between your buns – Thai fish; ostrich and beetroot; lentils, soya, chickpeas and hummus; even a supremely over the top 'fat bastard' – still sets this place apart from the competition (although quite a few Capetonians have now fallen for the homogenized New York ambience at Hudsons – *The Burger Joint*, farther up the drag, on Kloof Street, Tel: 021 426 5974). Besides the tantalising array of burgers, the milkshakes are the kind worth giving Uma Thurman a foot massage for – try the Jack Daniels and peanut butter concoction – and the ever-fresh retro-Bohemian décor is an instant spirit lifter.

Food 7, Service 7, Atmosphere 8

Rust en Vrede *(top)*
Rust en Vrede Wine Estate,
Annandale Road, Stellenbosch,
Winelands
Tel: 021 881 3757
www.rustenvrede.com
Open: for dinner Tues–Sat
Contemporary international R440

Yet another beautiful wine estate to have opened a restaurant that has been catapulted into the limelight, offering what is generally considered one of the country's best dining experiences. However, this can be a double edged sword with some feeling Rust en Vrede has perhaps alienated many potential diners because of its air of exclusivity. The estate is home to one of the Cape's truly iconic reds, the selfsame 315-year-old Stellenbosch estate that produced the wines chosen by Nelson Mandela for his Nobel Peace Prize dinner celebration. But don't let this put you off from experiencing a superb meal, choosing between a four-course menu with a la carte options, or the six-course set menu; for the full-on experience, the latter accompanied by paired wines from the country's diverse wine-growing regions. As you'll hear all across the Winelands, ingredients are typically fresh and seasonal, with the benefit of specially-matured meat homegrown on Rust en Vrede's very own Kalahari farm.

Food 8, Service 8, Atmosphere 8

Salt *(bottom)*
Ambassador Hotel,
34 Victoria Road, Bantry Bay,
Atlantic Seaboard
Tel: 021 439 7258
www.ambassador.co.za
Open: daily, 12.30–3pm & 6.30–10pm
South African Fusion R350

Occupying an elevated position in Bantry Bay, with grand-slam views through floor-to-ceiling windows of the mesmerising ocean and waves crashing against the rocks below (do book a window seat, or wait until you can), Salt has been wowing diners with its location since it's revamp a few years back; now it's tipped to soar to new culinary heights when Grande Provence chef Jacques de Jager takes over in 2010. At sunset, as if part of a theatrical performance, the glare-reducing translucent blinds go up and, if the weather's fine, the glass windows are folded away – it's as if the room's skin is being shed, and the salt-filled air and dramatic natural soundtrack of the crashing waves come in on a light, soothing breeze. It's easy to forget about the food when you're so gripped by the natural spectacle, so take your cue from the scene outside and just relax – the restaurant has one of the best wine selections (available by the glass) in the city, and generally this is simply one of our favourite places to celebrate anything – thanks to Jacques this will no doubt become an even more difficult-to-book event.

Food 7, Service 6/7, Atmosphere 8

Savoy Cabbage *(top)*

101 Hout Street, City Centre
Tel: 021 424 2626
www.savoycabbage.co.za
Open: noon–2pm Mon–Fri;
7–10.30pm Mon–Sat
International/Eclectic   R280

A pseudo-bohemian kitchen carved out of a brick warehouse, this is where quality-sensitive diners head for their fix of upmarket *paysanne* food, a refined seasonal menu of extremely well-crafted comfort foods, from home-smoked salmon and beer-braised beef short rib, to the finest crème brûlée you'll taste outside France, and a much written-about butterscotch pannacotta. A trendsetter that doesn't try to be trendy, Savoy Cabbage ranks amongst the first local restaurants to have launched Cape Town into the international culinary limelight, having racked up strong praise (notably for the sublime tomato tart, available only in summer) when it launched way back in 1998. On a sidestreet location that's sadly missed by all but the most diligent gourmands, this is an awesome, unusual L-shaped double-volume space that fuses nouveau and contemporary styling with industrial architecture (exposed air ducts and iron girders), achieving a surprisingly romantic, atypical, and slightly fantastical ambience. Sit upstairs, near the bar, for a bird's eye perspective on the flying cabbage leaf light fittings, or stay down below if you'd prefer to keep an eye on Chef Peter Pankhurst's hard-working team in the open, bistro-style kitchen.

Food 9, Service 8, Atmosphere 7

Sidewalk Café *(bottom)*

33 Derry Street,
Vredehoek, City Bowl
Tel: 021 461 2839
Open: 8am–10pm Mon–Sat;
9am–2pm Sun
Café/Eclectic   R175

A deliciously kooky eclectic mishmash crammed into a corner venue in the wind-blasted but view-blessed residential neighbourhood of Vredehoek, this is perhaps Cape Town's most intuitively wonderful eatery – not only because it's totally off the tourist track (yet minutes from the well-worn rut), but what comes out of that postage-stamp kitchen is simply scrumptious. There are a handful of tables on the eponymous sidewalk, all at a slight angle as if to fall onto the street – superb beneath the stars, or behind a pair of shades on a sunny day – but for delicious aromas to stimulate your appetite, it's worth waiting for a table inside. If so, park yourself on a high stool at the window counter and spend time bantering with the hostess – too charming to be considered batty, but certainly no ordinary dame – who'll tell you the cheesecake is produced by the cheesecake fairy, and probably means it. There's easy slippage between breakfast, lunch, afternoon cocktails, and a night of rollicking good fun and delicious feasting; Patagonian calamari is recommended, as is lentil moussaka, or go with the flow and let your flirting waiter make up your mind.

Food 8, Service 8, Atmosphere 9

Signal   *(left)*
Cape Grace, West Quay,
Victoria & Alfred Waterfront
Tel: 021 410 7100
www.capegrace.com
Open: daily, 6.30–11am, noon–3pm,
and 6.30–10pm
Cape/International   **R380**

A focal point of this sophisticated all-day 5-star waterfront hotel venue is the massive mural depicting Cape Town's harbour some 350 years ago – a perfect choice, given the multiplicity of cultures and diverse influences that have washed up on these shores, and continue to inspire the menu here. As a result it's a fairly eclectic menu, such as smoked crocodile niçoise or ostrich prepared with the spices that Cape Malay chef Malika van Reenen would have grown up with. On the one hand she's developed dishes that are original and experimental, whilst on the other, she takes great pride in showing off the Cape's culinary heritage – from the French Huguenots, British and Dutch settlers, to the Asian traders and Malay communities. Similarly, the décor works to reflect these multiple layers: aged yellowwood furniture and quaint culinary antiques find a home alongside (a bit of a yawn) Ghost chairs and heavy crystal chandeliers.

Food 8, Service 8, Atmosphere 7

Sloppy Sam   *(right)*
51A Somerset Road,
Green Point
Tel: 021 419 2921
www.sloppysam.co.za
Open: 6.30–10pm Mon–Sat,

**Mediterranean/Middle-Eastern
R165**

An ebullient gentleman who loves flying and food in equal measure, Hooman Saffarian is the kind of restaurateur whose disposition alone will lure you back time and again, even if just to bask in his vast personality, never mind the tasty, homegrown delights that roll out of his kitchen. Hooman, who left Iran in 1979, doesn't like to label his cuisine, and while there's some Persian influence, such as using saffron basting, he's taken much inspiration from the Greeks. In fact the name 'Sloppy Sam' goes way back to the mid-1930s, when it was a Greek dive down the drag in Sea Point; Hooman's slightly ramshackle and deli-like version is on the fringe of the gay quarter. Rustic and down-to-earth, it's a wonderful hodge-podge of tins, carpets, boxes, pottery, paintings, sacks of fruit and vegetables, large glass jars of sundried limes, lampstands, copper coffee urns, imported pomegranate juice, and piles of packaged food. Hooman's calamari and kebabs are renowned, but it's the lamb shank that he's is most proud of, and claims to have converted a few vegetarians ('our lambs are all vegetarians', he'll quip).

Food 8, Service 7, Atmosphere 9

Tank   *(bottom)*
72 Waterkant Street,
De Waterkant, Green Point
Tel: 021 419 0007
www.the-tank.co.za
Open: daily, noon–11.30pm/2am
Japanese/Sushi   **R250**

eat...

Naturally the 22,000 litre fish tank (apparently the largest saltwater tank of its kind in the southern hemisphere) takes pride of place, dividing the neon-blue backlit bar from the strikingly bare restaurant interior, where a team of precision-motivated chefs engineer some of the city's most exceptional sushi. In summer, you should sit in the cobbled courtyard, exchanging glances with plenty of pretty, young Cape Town specimens. The hipster waiters tend to use their good looks and charm to distract you from their muddled cluelessness, but still manage, with cheerful sociability, to talk you through some brilliant-sounding sushi creations, and the results, when they finally arrive, are memorable. Be prepared to wait for your 'crazy boy' and 'spider' rolls, and ask about more adventurous gamefish, such as swordfish and dorado, or the octopus sashimi. Use the extra time to linger over at least one of Tank's famous cocktails – a blue-hued 'Tanked', with Tanqueray, lime and litchi juice,

should take the edge off, followed by a sake-fuelled cucumber and mint martini.

Food 8, Service 6/7, Atmosphere 6/7

Terroir *(left)*
Kleine Zalze Wine Estate, Techno Park
Tel: 021 880 8167
www.kleinezalze.com
Open: 12.30–2.30pm,
6.45–9.30pm Mon–Sat
International   **R380**

Portable chalkboards listing seven starters and seven mains are carried around as required; in the background, a narrow strip of window reveals a huge team of chefs cooking up a storm. If the weather's good, book a table on the shady terrace outside; whereas inside, behind the foldaway glass doors, the décor is modern country: charcoal-coloured accents against off-white walls.

Lively waiters defer to you as 'the lady' and 'the gentleman', and provide a very personal understanding of the food on offer. Michael Broughton is a younger, more laid-back chef (shorts in summer) than you'd expect given the awards he has drummed up over the years. His approach is simple and unassuming; very seasonal, very local (only the langoustines are imported – from neighbouring Mozambique), yet coaxing rich and satisfying flavours onto the plate. Scallops, dusted with curry and Parmesan, are unforgettable, as is the trout *tartare*, so beautifully presented it looks like a work of art – even after you've licked the ginger and lime foam off the plate. Beef fillet with Bordelaise sauce competes well against braised Karoo lamb, and don't pass on desserts. To drink, choose from the vintages under 'INTEREST-ING WINES.' Pity about the locale, in a security estate.

Food 9, Service 8/9, Atmosphere 8

Wakame *(right)*
cnr Beach Road and Surrey Place, Mouille Point
Tel: 021 433 2377
www.wakame.co.za
Open: daily, noon–3pm & 6–10.30pm Mon–Thurs; noon–3.30pm & 6–11pm (10pm Sun)
Pacific Rim/Asian Fusion   R250

This sleek venue positively radiates with the city's glam set, here not so much for the modest-to-good Sino-fusion food, as for the views of Table Bay and distant Robben Island – not to mention the spectacle as sunset transforms the scene into something akin to visual opera. And then, since the show simply must go on, the glittering lights of passing ships like stars reflected off the water. It's one of the simple pleasures of living in Cape Town, which is why so many of the locals are really here for cocktails on the lounge-style wooden deck (or at the sexy upstairs bar, Wafu; see Drink), served up with a touch of sushi. It's a local take on modern Oriental design, with loads of cherry wood surfaces and enormous tanks in which colourful, bewildered fish provide a counterpoint to the restrained yet smart styling. Although some think Wakame relies too heavily on its reputation, you'll understand at least part of the fuss if you order the tea-smoked tuna – served on wasabi mash, it competes admirably with the same fish crusted with sesame.

Food 7, Service 7, Atmosphere 8

....

Willoughby & Co   *(right)*
Shop 6132, Lower Level, Victoria Wharf, V&A Waterfront, Tel: 021 418 6115/6
Open: daily, 11.30am–10.30pm
Sushi & seafood   **R225**

Serving up the best sushi in town, this is just about the only Waterfront restaurant that's likely to show up on any Capetonian's regular list of essential dining experiences, even if it can feel a bit more like a pitstop that an opportunity to settle in for any length of time. Located inside the mall, with all the neon lighting and non-stop flow of passersby (almost every single one of them begrudging the fact that you're enjoying the best sushi in town while they attend to more mundane matters), this is certainly a first-rate prospect if you've been shopping at the Waterfront, or are simply a sushi addict keen to add your vote. Don't ignore the more elaborate offerings on the menu (all the seafood is super fresh, and there's even a fresh fish counter if you feel like preparing something yourself),

and do make sure your server – good-looking, but perhaps a bit distracted by the demanding mob of diners – gives you an unabbreviated run-down of what's interesting and likely to have escaped your attention.

Food 8, Service 6/7, Atmosphere 5

drink...

Dipsomaniacs be warned. The reasons for imbibing here are overwhelming, with a city so visually arresting even teetotallers will want to toast their good fortune. You can do so from the top of Table Mountain, looking down upon the city spread beneath you, or choose to gaze up at its imposing hulk, surrounded by shimmering waters in Table Bay; lie about on manicured lawns, a well-stocked cooler box keeping you as vibey as the live jazz drifting through the Cape's most gracious garden, or shout 'salut' from an inner-city rooftop. Perhaps because of our turbulent roller-coaster history, the city has nurtured a drinking culture, as a cruise along the bars lining the lower end of Long Street and Camps Bay's sunset strip reveals. It's a culture that can veer towards excessive consumption, but goes hand in hand with relaxed socializing – aside from the places covered in this chapter you'll find numerous drinking spots dotted around the city and its suburbs, where locals pop in for what is ingeniously called a 'quickie' (knowing full well that the outing is unlikely to be brief).

Truth is, drinking may be in our genes. Grapes have been growing at the Cape since the Europeans first arrived, and the need to refuel passing ships with fresh supplies of liquor was for many years a priority. What took the European palate by surprise was just how good the wine wrung from grapes grown here was, with early fans including Napoleon Bonaparte, Otto von Bismarck, Louis XVI of France, Frederick the Great of Prussia and Jane Austen.

You needn't be an oenophile to spend a pleasant morning cruising from one spectacular wine estate to the next in pursuit of your favourite vintage. It's an adventure best undertaken with a knowledgeable guide (See Culture) as you can usually only sample (assuming you have as much difficulty spitting as we do) the offerings from around four estates before your palate, amongst other things, is more or less blown.

Our wines are delightful, but despite growing international appreciation (Obama's choice of libation on the night of his election was for instance a Graham Beck Brut NV), beer is in fact what rules the market: we like to think that the global success of our national beermaker, today one of the world's biggest breweries, was not without a great deal of participation from South Africans, who consume their lager with serious dedication. Together with such lowbrow (but delicious) concoctions as 'brandy and coke', it's an essential component of any *braai* and sports gathering. But, like most things, all beers are not created equal, and you'd be well advised to stick to the Windhoek range or better still, check out the cult that's brewing around quality crafted premium beers (such as those served at & Union; see page 136).

drink...

Whatever your tipple, there's a great deal of choice when it comes to where you want to drink it – from tavern-like dives like the Vasco da Gama in Greenpoint (Tel 021 425 2157), until not that long ago a male only-enclave, where the smell of lager has saturated the floorboards, to toney new places, where players with models on their knee and money to burn try to impress anyone who'll look by ordering bottle after bottle of imported bubbly. And then some seriously gorgeous spaces – like Planet, Raya Lounge and The Bar Lounge – where you'll love the look as much as what you have in hand. Aside from the drinking holes lining Long Street and Camp's Bay's beachfront, there's usually a happy gathering in the city's Pink Quarter, as the Cape Quarter in De Waterkant is affectionately known. Although you'll get a good sense that these venues are primarily for men who like men, the scene is extremely straight-friendly and Capetonians are by and large very open-minded and accepting these days, so no need to shy away from even the campest bars or cafés.

Finally, it's worth knowing that – although many South Africans take drinks with them to beaches and parks – drinking in public is strictly speaking, illegal. In fact, you can expect bouncers to get edgy when you step out of their premises with beverage in hand, a misdemeanour for with the establishment may be fined. And, if you're out having a good time and no longer feel fit to drive, call a cab or, if you're in a hire car, call Smart Guyz (Tel 0861 762 786, www.smartguyz.co.za): they provide a chauffer to you back to your hotel safely and efficiently – in your own vehicle.

& Union Beer Salon /Charcuterie *(left)*

110 Bree Street, City Centre
Tel: 021 422 2770
www.andunion.com
Open: 7am–11pm Mon–Sat

In a small excavated warehouse beneath the recently restored St Stephen's Church, & Union is indeed a place of worship. & Union beers are naturally brewed – for up to 16 weeks – without any of the post-carbonation processing that so sullies the commercial beer market. Aside from a limited range of heritage lagers, and luxury beers and ales, they serve a bottle-fermented cider and a small hand-picked wine list, as well as the best charcuterie in the city. You should also try the juicy artisan sausages – one is made with unsweetened Belgian chocolate and chilli springbok, while there's also a springbok sausage with apricot and cashew nuts. With its chic rough hewn exposed brick walls and umbrella-shaded outdoor benches, this beer salon also represents the first step in Cape Town's move towards a more mature beer-drinking culture, one where imbibing a fine brew is more important than getting drunk. There's live music (singer-songwriter stuff) three times per week, and there's a good chance you'll see members of major South African bands doing pared down, acoustic performances.

Airstream Trailer Park Rooftop Bar *(middle)*

The Grand Daddy,
38 Long Street, City Centre
Tel: 021 424 7247
www.daddylonglegs.co.za
Open: 8.30am–8.30pm Mon–Wed and Fri, 8.30am–10.30pm Thurs, 2–8.30pm Sat, 2–10.30pm Sun

Get an alternative look at the city's

drink...

downtown business district from the rooftop of Cape Town's longest-serving hotel – it may only be a few floors up, but surrounded by concrete office blocks and glass towers is as close to experiencing Cape Town as some kind of toned down Gotham as you're ever going to find. And you get to scope out the Airstream Trailer Park, the collection of vintage steel-skin caravans that's been converted into a hotel for the adventurous and budget-minded. Also up here is the city's one and only rooftop cinema, the Pink Flamingo (see Culture) – during screenings on Thursdays and Sundays, the bar stays open later. Fridays often sees the occasional music mini-event held up here; particularly entertaining is local cult figure, Dave Ferguson, who does magical things with his harmonica, and is a regular fixture (typically between 6 and 8pm). The rooftop bar is decidedly more novelty-geared than an exercise in class: service at the bar – which is

simply too tiny to cope with demand – can be sluggish and standoffish, and the cocktails aren't perfect ('though the on-tap frozen daiquiris are a quick fix against the heat of summer).

Alba *(right)*
above Hildebrand Restaurant, Pierhead, V&A Waterfront
Tel: 021 425 3385
www.albalounge.co.za
Open: daily, noon–1am

Melt-in-your-mouth chocolate hues and sleek, contemporary design on the harbour's edge make this the ideal space for the upmarket glamour crowd, yet it's relaxed and friendly enough to attract families with children. The main attraction at this classy yet well-cushioned cocktail lounge is the awesome view onto the Waterfront's harbour. As the sun descends and the harbour lights come up, the scene becomes even

137

more alluring, slightly festive even, and the plush sofas and armchairs are just the place to relish it. As you might expect from a family-owned Italian joint, Alba is essentially a pre-dinner venue for the downstairs Hildebrand Restaurant, owned and run by Aldo and Linda Girolo. They're recently added a restaurant up here, though, with light meals – so-called 'ladies portions' – are now served. But that shouldn't distract from the well-designed list of cocktails and shooters. Expect an atmosphere of elegant, classical refinement – although not much by way of innovation.

aMadoda! Braai *(top)*
Strand Street, Woodstock
Tel: 021 447 2133
Open: 4–11pm Thurs and Sun, 4pm–4/6am Fri and Sat

After the Europeanized, sanitized safety of the Waterfront or the Cape Quarter an evening here is as much exhilarating cultural experience – an eye-opener, really – as it is a chance to tuck into barbequed meat and quaff beers by the bucketful. The regular clientele wouldn't even consider buying anything as anti-social as a single serving of beer, and because this is a 'shebeen' (traditionally an illicit liquor store typically prevalent in black townships), spirits are sold in bottles rather than tots – prepare for a night of mayhem. Things kick off rather late (don't expect a crowd before 9 or 10pm), and by the time the buzz gets going, the entire neighbourhood (dodgy, but kept secure by hired guards) is packed to overflowing with BMWs, SUVs and a suave, predominantly black crowd

that's dressed up and ready for serious action. Nobody minds that the space is right next to the railways tracks, décor is cheap and garish, or that the music blasting away (either out of the jukebox or from an out-of-control DJ) causes spontaneous dancing in just about every nook and cranny. Welcome to the real Cape Town.

Asoka *(bottom)*
68 Kloof Street
Tamboerskloof, City Bowl
Tel: 021 422 0909
www.asokabar.co.za
Open: daily, 5pm–2am

Feng shui apparently defines the layout of this sophisticated bar, located in a pretty Victorian house amongst the tawdry neon of busy Kloof Street. With bamboo pillars and plush seating nooks, the Oriental-style Asoka has always – since it was known as Café Dharma in the 1990s – lured a sexy, trendy, mature (no under-23s door policy) crowd; the kind that will lead you to conclude that Capetonians are an instinctively elegant species. On Tuesdays, when Restless Natives provide live, extremely cool jazz, the mix can be slightly alternative (some of Cape Town's hipper hippies join in), whilst Fridays sees younger pups come out to play; Saturday is traditionally an 'older' night. Respected house DJs play Wednesday through Saturday, with a little dancing on the tiny impromptu dancefloor right beneath the oldest olive tree in Cape Town, festooned in fairy lights. Cocktails here are among the best in the city (try the porn star martini), with a no-tricks approach to preparing drinks with the freshest ingredients – you come here to be taken care of, not to watch bartenders showing off their flaring skills. There's a good champagne and wine list, and if you're hungry, there's a selection of Asian fusion tapas, including mini Moroccan lamb burgers.

▨ The Bar Lounge *(top)* at The Opal Lounge
30 Kloof Street, Gardens, City Bowl
Tel: 021 422 4747
Open: daily, noon–late

If you haven't yet dined within the sumptuous Opal Lounge (see Eat), then do at least make it here for a drink, and spend an hour or so lounging around in the comfortable, very plush sofas. Like the stone for which it's named, it's a precious, sensuous space that feels not unlike stepping onto a movie set – surreal and decadent, and worth dressing up for. Primarily a place for restaurant guests to enjoy a pre-dinner drink, it also offers a wonderful sense of intimacy, and you won't find just any Tom, Dick, or Harry sauntering in here; it's also extraordinarily unknown to locals. The cocktail list includes a handful of interesting alternatives to the norm; the wine menu is encouraging. And, if you want to puff on a cigar or cigarette, the adjacent African-Colonial theme lounge is another very beautiful space in which to do so. Unquestionably, the prettiest bar in town – with no need for views, other than of the handsome staff.

▨ Bascule Whisky *(left)* Wine & Cocktail Bar,
Cape Grace Hotel, West Quay, Victoria & Alfred Waterfront
Tel: 021 410 7082
www.capegrace.com
Open: daily, 7.30am–late

Stepping into the Bascule is rather like chancing upon a spacious below-deck cabin that's been transformed into a handsome bar, stocked with a gratifyingly large assortment of whiskys (over 400 at last count, including a 50-year-old Glenfiddich which sells at R18,000 per tot). One of the most sociable and refined drinking spots in the city, the Bascule is right at the edge of Cape Town's international yacht marina, and you can easily spend all day soaking up the good vibes on the waterside terrace. Enquire after one of the regular whisky tasting events, in which you're taken on an enlightening journey through the history and experience of (primarily) Scottish single malts. Some are paired with food (discovering that Laphroaig goes with gorgonzola, for example), and the sommeliers are brilliant – a fantastic way to kick start one of the most memorable nights you'll have in Cape Town. You can also sign up for membership of the city's most exclusive whisky club, making this forever a bar that you'll feel at home in.

▨ Beaulah Bar *(right)*
30 Somerset Road, cnr Somerset Road and Cobern Street, Green Point
Tel: 021 421 6798
www.beaulahbar.co.za
Open: 5pm–2am (4am Fri–Sat) Tues–Sat

Beaulah is local gay slang for 'beauti-

drink...

ful', and it's an ideal that most people standing around this friendly little bar try to live up to. Although boys and men are welcome, it's traditionally a favourite hangout for ladies who like ladies; like all of Green Point's gay establishments, though, the crowd tends to be extremely mixed, across the age, colour and gender spectrum. Be warned that although it may start off quiet, with plenty of space for everyone, it inevitably fills to capacity, so establish a rapport with the bartender as early as possible. During the week it mostly functions as an after-work meeting spot with the focus entirely on drinking, but at weekends there's commercial dance music until the wee hours, making the smallish dance floor a proposition for anyone not keen on the sweat, mayhem and lasers at neighbouring Bronx/Navigaytion (see Party).

....

Belthazar *(top)*
Shop 153, Victoria Wharf,
Victoria & Alfred Waterfront
Tel: 021 421 3753
www.belthazar.co.za
Open: daily, noon–11pm

Styling itself as the home of the biggest wine-by-the-glass selection on the planet, offering around 250 individual vintages – all from the Cape and stored in high-tech anti-oxidation equipment – Belthazar is a way to tour the Winelands without leaving the Waterfront. (It's also a very decent steakhouse with a good seafood selection, too.) The wine menu is an epic list of different vintages, but an elaborate and impressively detailed chart, rating each wine

according to its individual character as well as recording its score in the highly-regarded John Platter's South African Wine Guide, makes navigation slightly easier. It's a very useful way to taste a wide selection of new wines, and the menu pairs them with suitable dishes (and if your memory's rusty, you can check the list on their website, later). If you're feeling more adventurous, or a small group, order a bottle – there are some 600 listed on the menu, starting with some very good daily-drinking bottles, and finishing off with some impressive rarities. Done up, as is the norm among steakhouses in South Africa, in brass and dark wood, décor is not as memorable as the wines.

....

Boo Radley's *(bottom)*
62 Hout Street, City Centre
Tel: 021 424 3040
www.booradleys.co.za
Open: 11am–2am Mon–Fri,
5pm–2am Sat

Boo Radleys is both a relaxed bistro, good for pre- or post-show dinners, since The New Space theatre is just upstairs (where Clint Eastwood sourced the all-boy band to produce much of the soundtrack for *Invictus*), and a very sociable place to grab a properly mixed cocktail and/or good glass of wine. Black and white checkerboard floor tiles, leather banquettes, lots of polished wood and marble, and a deep space with high ceilings and big glass walls looking onto the little side street (just off Long) on which it's situated, means that this is one of the most immaculate-looking drinking venues in the inner city, well-preserved by the type of crowd that hangs here – a little urbane, slightly sophisticated (but not in the least pretentious), and always celebratory (even if it's just to toast the end of the day at the office). Owner Jay Haupt is a stickler for genuine cocktails, and he prides himself on specializing in the classics, preferring to use only authentic ingredients. Music is a serious mix of wispy and gracious jazz and blues, and occasionally includes local one-man cult figure, Dave Ferguson.

....

Café Caprice *(top)*
37 Victoria Road,
Camps Bay Atlantic Seaboard
Tel: 021 438 8315
www.cafecaprice.co.za
Open: daily, 9am–late

For a couple of seasons now, this has, for reasons unknown, been the most popular sundowner hangout in Camps Bay, meaning it gets extremely packed with the see-and-be-seen crowd, often overflowing onto the sidewalk (which is directly across the road from the city's equally popular beach). It's quite a small venue, with two efficient bars facing one another from either end; there are a handful of loungey seating areas (you'll need to book these or ask your concierge to make special arrangements if you want to sit here in summer), and a few tables (preferably for diners) out on the sidewalk. Befriend one of the beefy barmen by leaving a large tip or secure a waitress as soon as you arrive and make sure to hold her attention – or be prepared to wait a while for your drinks. What makes Caprice work are the views of the setting sun, framed here by col-

umns and arches that are backlit in a golden glow once it starts to get dark. The effect is pure glam, even if the crowd gets raucous and uncouth and there are no restrictions on what you wear – many punters come straight off the beach and just don't leave until way after midnight.

....

Cape to Cuba *(bottom)*
Main Road, Kalk Bay
Tel: 021 788 6396
www.capetocuba.co.za
Open: daily, 9am–late

This is one of the most fabulous seaside bars in the Cape Peninsula, memorable as much for the detailed Bohemian atmosphere as it is for the unassuming location right besides the railway tracks, with views across the lines towards the low-key commotion of Kalk Bay's quaint little fishing harbour. While you're left with little doubt that you're visiting a small coastal village, there's plenty of Latin spirit and a long list of cocktails – the best mojitos and fruity frozen daiquiris – and an assortment of differently-styled areas for you to try out. Although the island-style bar is groovy, it's really the restaurant alongside that's particularly beautiful with so much Catholic and antique bric-a-brac that it's like wandering through an overstocked Mexican décor shop – it's not the most reliable place for food, though, so stick to the drinks and maybe order a few snacky starters to stave off a hunger, then dine elsewhere in Kalk Bay (Kalky's or Harbour house – sea Eat).

....

Cape to Cuba *(top)*
(Cigar Bar & Che Bar),
Long Street, City Centre,
Tel: 021 424 2330
www.capetocuba.co.za
Open: 9am–4am Mon–Sat

Although Cape to Cuba poses as a Latin-themed restaurant, every Capetonian knows that (like the sister Kalk Bay outlet) the food here is simply an elaborate front for Long Street's long-awaited cocktail revolution. During the day you might want to ask to be seated on the balcony overlooking the heady throng on the street below, but at night you must check out the intimate and sophisticated bar that's hidden round the back. Head all the way up the stairs and then ask for the Cigar Bar; as you're led there, you'll pass through an attractive space done out in all kinds of Catholic kitsch – a serious counter-point to the clubby leather sofas and smartly dressed barman in the back room, essentially a mix between a library lounge and a discreet, slightly secret gathering spot for informed locals. Do not leave before trying a chocolate tequila or just about any offbeat-sounding concoction the barman chooses to suggest. Downstairs, the diminutive sidewalk Che Bar has a retro-spunky Andy Warhol-goes-to-Havana atmosphere, somewhere between beach bar and all-white den of iniquity. The beret-wearing barmen aren't revolutionaries of the political kind but, like their smartly dressed colleagues upstairs, tend to mix cocktails that'll inspire an instant regime change.

Caveau Wine Bar & Deli *(bottom)*
Heritage Square,
92 Bree Street, City Centre
Tel: 021 422 1367
www.caveau.co.za
Open: 7am–10.30pm Mon–Sat

Like many of Cape Town's best ideas, Caveau – a very European wine bar carved out Bree Street's chichi Heritage Square – started as a direct reaction to the overwhelming lack of decent after-work venues. Today Caveau has become a real Cape Town institution, appropriately occupying part of the same Georgian property where the country's oldest living wine-producing grapevine grows. The wine bar offers a daily-changing chalked-up tapas menu and you know they're serious about their everything-fresh policy since the moment an item sells out, it gets a line through it. However, the priority here is wine. There are over 400 different wines on the list, and 80 by the glass; the accessible menu spells out what's available, listing them according to your potential mood, so there are wines to wake up your palate, 'food wines', wines for winding down at the end of the day. There's also a 'discoveries' list, featuring lesser-known, non-commercial wines. Riding on Caveau's huge success, the entrepreneurial owners have since opened the excellent Headquarters steakhouse (see Eat) as well as another Caveau in Newlands (The Mill), which is also open for Sunday brunch.

Daddy Cool Bar *(left)*
First Floor, The Grand Daddy
Hotel, 38 Long Street, City Centre
Tel: 021 424 7247
www.granddaddy.co.za
Open: 4–11pm Mon–Thurs; 4pm–1am
Fri; 6pm–1am Sat

Interior designer Tracy Lynch mixed
updated classicism with some fun riffs
from the dubious postmodern stylings
of gangster rappers – so expect to
see gigantic gold Rolex watches and
dollar signs as part of the tongue-in-
cheek décor, alongside one-of-a-kind
gold prints by artist Brand Botes. Classic armchairs are refurbished in white
leather, and there's more white used
to accent elements within the original
Victorian-era room design. Chandeliers are jangly mother of pearl discs,
and everywhere there's a golden-hued
chimera which is designed to dazzle
once you've settled in for a night of
fun, perhaps accompanied by live
music by smaller-name local bands
(Wednesdays and Thursdays). Things
get more fired up at weekends thanks
to a DJ-induced party atmosphere.
The crowd tends to be pretty trendy,
and naughty enough to have stolen
one or two pieces of art from the walls
of the entranceway, which – just to
put you in the mood – features plasma
TVs in gold frames that comprise the
city's only digital art gallery. More interesting, however, is the aquarium in
the men's bathroom, meaning you look
though the watery collection of tropi-
cal fish while using the urinal.

Jo'burg *(middle)*
218 Long Street, City Centre
Tel: 021 422 0142
www.joburgbar.com
Open: daily, noon–4am Mon–Sat;
6pm–4am Sun

It's testament to the Capetonian pro-

clivity for irony that they not only accept and support this bar – named for the city up north which most of them claim to loathe – but do so with such huge enthusiasm. Attendance here has more of a cult-quality or edge of fanaticism than one would typically associate with a night out in search of a drink. More multicultural and racially diverse that any other bar on Long Street, Jo'burg is festooned with images of Apartheid-era Johannesburg and above the seating booths hang Deco installations and other eye-catching pieces of decorative art; things get loud in here and more than a little chaotic. Just like the city after it is named, Jo'burg is a bit scruffy, with a fair amount of sleaze, and a raucous, near-maniacal throng inside that often spills out onto the street. Alongside Jo'burg is Pretoria, where there's a DJ-powered dancefloor, and a restaurant at the back known as the Jo'burg Country Club (you'll want to avoid the food there). And above it all, a party venue known as L/B's Lounge.

....

Julep *(right)*
Vredenburg Lane, City Centre
Tel: 021 423 4276
Open: 5pm–2am Mon–Sat

Expertly-mixed cocktails are the primary highlight at this cozy, sociable little hangout that's hidden away from the mainstream, but nevertheless manages to pull in a seriously hip and lively crowd, many of whom already appear to know each other. It's a bit like arriving in someone's private lounge party, or an up-to-date version of a chilled party scene straight from a Blake Edwards movie. The bar itself is tiny but extremely efficient, and staff come to you before you start to feel ignored. Things start out pretty tame – a casual vibe for after-work relaxing – but start to pick up and liven up considerably

149

as the night evolves. DJ sets are a bit like having a few friends over to try out their latest records, and you can't help feeling that this is the bar where you wish everyone really did know your name.

Leopard Room Bar *(top)*
The Twelve Apostles Hotel and Spa, Victoria Road, midway between Camps Bay and Llandudno, Atlantic Seaboard
Tel: 021 437 9000
Open: daily, 8am–8pm (summer), 9am–8pm (winter)

With it's kooky, somewhat old-fashioned décor, the lounge-style Leopard Room doesn't at first glance fit the bill – done out in a decadent contemporary colonial mishmash of busy fabrics, leather armchairs, and plantain leaf-design wallpaper, the room can't decide if it wants to be cosy or cluttered. And for followers of a more contemporary design aesthetic, it's difficult to get beyond the obsession with leopard iconography. But if you ignore all of this and keep your eyes focused seaward you will enjoy one of the most spectacular sunsets, without the riff-raff that typifies Camps Bay. The bar opens on to an elevated terrace – small, so arrive early – and from which you can spot seals, dolphins and whales (the latter more seasonal), until finally the sun touches the horizon and the sky transforms into fantastic, dizzying shades of amber, gold, and sometimes a startling red – pity it's 24 hours before the next show. Back inside the bar, though, staff will continue to supply you with drinks, whether you're flopped down in one of those over-elaborately-patterned sofas, or propped up at the clubby all-wood counter.

Martini Bar *(bottom)*
Cellars-Hohenort Hotel, 93 Brommersvlei Road, Constantia
Tel: 021 794 2137
www.cellars-hohenort.com/martini
Open: daily, 11am–late

As you might imagine, the bar in the Cellars-Hohenort Hotel, known to some as the 'Constantia Mount Nelson', is stylish and sophisticated, with elegant seating in a large, pale space, and catering only for a more grown up crowd. However, unlike the rooms, Martini Bar has a lively modern edge, without looking or feeling cold, or plastic, or limited to straight lines and cold hard edges. Circular patterns, in fact, are used extensively, so in part you feel like you're hanging amid the coloured balls that float around the inside of a lava lamp – polka dots, chic stripes, and some flower-bespeckled sofas, armchairs, cushions and barstools, making this at least look like a truly fun place to drink. But the real reason your head may start to spin is the drinks menu featuring Cape Town's longest list of martinis – the hardest part of your day may be choosing from among 52 different types, not to mention the additional option of 228 cocktails and some

exceptional wines, too. At this rate, you'll be shaken and stirred.

Mersey Bar *(left)*
6 Watson Street, City Centre
Tel: 084 443 3392 or 079 495 6143
Open: 10am–5pm Mon, 10am–late
Tues–Fri, 5pm–late Sat

Open only to over-23s, Mersey is a slick little place in an unexpected location – in the city centre but away from Long Street, where most other drinking establishments are found. Occupying two floors of bar, lounge and restaurant space, Mersey is, as the name alludes, an extension of a professional recording studio, and ends up being a hang out for musicians and DJs to engage with Jack Daniels after finally laying down those final layers on their latest albums. As a result this is the best place in Cape Town to find out what's hip and happening for the night or the week ahead. It's also a treat to look at, with seating areas featuring decadent sofas and slick, chic, modern armchairs beneath the chandeliers and tall windows. Svelte hideskin rugs on original wooden floors, and a couple of black and white silhouette canvases of Jimi Hedrix and Jim Morrison against purple-taupe walls, provide the kind of environment you can imagine a host of classic rock stars hanging out in if they were around today.

....

Neighbourhood *(middle)*
163 Long Street, City Centre
Tel: 021 424 7260
www.goodinthehood.co.za
Open: 4pm–late Mon–Thurs,
2pm–late Fri–Sat

An assemblage of good ideas and strong, well-executed design, this is a stand-out drinking establishment on bustling Long Street. Five friends – including two sets of brothers – set about creating an environment that

drink

looks at least as trendy and well-mannered as the crowd that hangs out here. This place feels a lot like home, comfortable and inviting and – something that's often lacking along this strip – carefully designed and well looked after. It's no wonder locals love coming here to play board games and pool, and just 'blom' (colloquial slang for hang out). As you order a signature Neighbourhoodlum cocktail, or an ale from the considerable beer menu, check out the handcrafted woodwork, the bar counter with fragments of old watches set in resin, reupholstered vintage furniture, and displays of personal collectibles – matchboxes, postcards, and impressive photographs. There's a covered terrace where you can catch a bit of Long Street's vibe, and even a chichi library lounge with pale olive green walls. It won't take long to settle in with the regular crowd – especially since there's a prolonged happy hour

commencing early.

Planet Champagne *(right)* & Cocktail Bar

Mount Nelson Hotel,
76 Orange Street, Gardens, City Bowl
Tel: 021 483 1737
www.mountnelson.co.za
Open: daily, 5pm (3pm Fri)–late

You don't need to be a resident at Cape Town's most celebrated hotel to enjoy one of its hippest, sexiest, and most beautiful bars. The Mount Nelson (see Sleep) may be a bastion of cool colonial-era sophistication, but this schmoozy bar has a contemporary sparkle in her eye. From the hotel's main lounge, you enter an intimate, sumptuous space, a hip-but-classic re-working of a 110-year-old room with leather floor, gigantic drapes, and lots of plush, decadent fabrics to comple-

ment the elegant refurbishment that makes this feel utterly chic. The bar's name is reflected by the intricate mobile sculpture of the solar system that hangs at the centre of the main room, but it's easy to also imagine that it's a reference to discovering your status in the stellar system. Whether you're star-struck (plenty of celebs have been spotted here), or choose to find a seat outdoor beneath the stars, you can't help feeling that this is one Planet you want to be on all through the night.

Polana *(left)*
Kalk Bay Harbour, Kalk Bay
Tel: 021 788 7162
www.harbourhouse.co.za
Open: 6–10pm Mon–Fri; noon–10pm Sat–Sun (lounge remains open till late, and until very late on Fri)

At one end of Kalk Bay Harbour's concrete pier, beneath much-celebrated Harbour House (see Eat), Polana is another eatery whose dramatic position makes you feel as though you could reach out and touch the waves (certainly, on a rough day, it's not unlikely that the spray will reach you). Making it clear that you're here for drinks and wish to sit in the lounge, assume the position in one of the leather sofas, clearly designed for lazing, and scope the wine list before the ocean views mesmerise you completely. With bara-za-style seating, and massive sliding windows framing the ocean that lies just beyond, this is a place to drift into a reverie of meditative calm, soothed by an endless flow of cooling cocktails, well-priced South African wines, and – of course – the roar and crash of waves tumbling against the rocks onto which the lounge is built. As night unfolds, candles are lit in white table lanterns, creating a romantic counterpoint to the sparkle of stars reflected off the sea.

Raya Lounge *(middle)*
Kitima, Kronendal Estate, 140 Main Road, Hout Bay, False Bay Tel: 021 790 8004 www.kitima.co.za
Open: 5.30pm–2am Mon–Sat; noon–5pm Sun

In case you're wondering where to find Cape Town's most expertly crafted cocktails, then you owe it to yourself to make the drive out to Hout Bay to discover one of Cape Town's loveliest restaurants, Kitima, which is in turn blessed with its most studiously-run bar. Mixologist Karl Lamar is not only a stickler for detail, but he takes his cocktails very seriously and not only designs his own – many of which have an Asian influence (since Kitima serves Asian food) – but is also working on a book of cocktail recipes. He mixes a mean Thai martini, infused with chilli, and creates some scintillating and exotic concoctions (enquire after the Tiger Milk and Thai Trip). You can watch Karl working up a storm behind the restaurant's bar counter or take in the decadence of the Raya Lounge, set a little back from the restaurant proper, and decked out with pink velvet-covered antique-style furniture. Partially set in a canopied garden, with soft lighting and service by on-the-ball waiters, this is a romantic spot that becomes rather fun. In fact, things at the bar have been known to get quite carried away, prompting one rule in the menu to spell out, explicitly: "No bare chests."

Rick's Café Américain *(right)*
2 Park Road, Gardens, City Bowl
Tel: 021 424 1100
www.rickscafe.co.za
Open: 11.30am–2am Mon–Sat

In a century-old Victorian house on a little road laden with small eateries, this is a laid-back venue with many nooks and crannies, each with a slightly different atmosphere to meet your mood. There's some attempt to capture the feel of Casablanca – a film most of the clientele will never have seen – although it's most definitely a slightly hipped up version of the world inhabited by Rick Blaine and Ilsa Lund. Relax on the roadside terrace – a great place to check out passing pedestrians heading to and from nearby Kloof Street. Or head upstairs into the cosy, intimate, and cushioned loft – perhaps the most romantic of Rick's spaces, which opens on to a breezy terrace that works best on a summery day. Food here includes obvious allusions to Moroccan fare, but is perhaps a bit too global to be taken seriously; the tapas selection includes excellent chilli poppers, however. Incidentally, this is one of the few places in Cape Town that serves non-alcoholic beers, and they have a premium South African beer, Jack Black, available on tap.

Sapphire Cocktail Lounge *(top)*
The Promenade
Victoria Road, Camps Bay,
Atlantic Seaboard
Tel: 021 438 1758
www.sapphirecocktailbar.com
Open: daily, 10am–4am

Until late-2009, this was Baraza, one of the longest-running of Camps Bay's sunset strip venues, and an essential part of any Sunday's inevitable come-down vibe at the end of a disgustingly good weekend. Not too much has changed since the name inexplicably transformed into yet another reference to the impossibly blue scene that's vis-ible from its large bay windows, framing Camps Bay's exquisite sunsets. It's a small bar with big views, dressed in a cool organic beach-house style, with three-dimensional stars and disco balls dangling from the ceiling and good, vibrant tunes courtesy of the usually talented, low-key DJs. One serious problem here – besides the fact that it's often packed to capacity – is the poor service; in a place purporting to be a specialist cocktail lounge, you'd expect them to get the mixed drinks right all of the time – often they don't. Also, be sure to double check your bill; some of the waiters seem to think you'll be so overwhelmed by the setting that you won't notice being overcharged.

St Yves Beach Club *(bottom)*
Level 2, Promenade,
Victoria Road, Camps Bay,
Atlantic Seaboard
Tel: 021 438 0935
www.styves.co.za
Open: 3pm–late Tues–Sun

Easy on the eye and, all things considered, a very glam space to unfurl yourself on one of the outdoor gazebo-style lounge platforms on the terrace attached to this vast club. There are big bar areas and the dancefloor is sizeable, too, but the biggest attraction here is probably the daytime view over Camps Bay beach. It would take a massive crowd to fill this space and Capetonians – being that they like to be seen – don't generally hangout in places that aren't crowded to capacity. So, it's a great, handsome arena in which to sip cocktail, slowly, and drape yourself over a comfy sofa, but it's hardly likely to become a watchword in hardcore

partying, although DJ Shaun Duvet (of Bang Bang Club fame) has started to introduced Sunday afternoon dance sessions which finally injected some life into this place towards the end of an otherwise slow summer season. In its favour, St Yves (a preposterous name for a Cape Town club) starts with a line-up of stunning ladies at the door and equally cute barmen to mix your drink – all mixed up with pretty damn good service service (a request for a summery non-alcoholic drink was rewarded with a glass of freshly-blended watermelon juice). And if it weren't for the trip up the stairs and the obviousness of the shopping centre location, this might really feel like it were right on the beach, rather than looking down on it. Dressing up (at night at least) is mandatory and men must be over 25 to get in (women over 21, though)

Wafu *(top)*
1st Floor, cnr Beach Road and Surrey Place, Mouille Point
Tel: 021 433 2377
www.wakame.co.za
Open: daily, noon–11.30pm

Wafu, an elegant open-to-the-elements terrace bar that works as an upstairs extension to the popular Wakame (see Eat), offers the same great views of Table Bay, which starts across the road, as well as close up views of some of Cape Town's best-looking socialites. Be prepared to rub shoulders with Cape Town's prettiest and most unhinged tribes, all working the moment to the max and taking advantage of the comfortable outdoor lounge-style seating (shaded by umbrellas during the day). Beyond the prolonged summer

season, Wafu remains a formidable after-work drinks venue, although, if it's cold, you'll probably be relegated to the somewhat hard-edged interior, with a chic upmarket café atmosphere and seated on orange polypropylene Jo chairs designed for quicker dining than downstairs (although the menu is the same). Sushi from Wakame's extensive Pacific Rim menu vies with fine Asian tapas to prolong an evening's drinking. Wafu benefits from staff who take their job very seriously, meaning that service is generally slick and no-nonsense, which is something the Camps Bay restaurants and bars can't promise.

The Waiting Room *(bottom)*
above Royale Eatery,
273 Long Street, City Centre
Tel: 021 422 4536
Open: 6pm–2am Mon–Sat

A narrow near-vertical stairway behind an ancient doorway leads to this cosy bar, with its warm, home-away-from-home ambience. Having gained approval from the buff doorman (who'll sell tickets if there's a performance planned for the night), head up as determinedly as your legs will allow – the old wooden steps are just wide enough for a single person, and their use is on a first come, first serve basis. High heels are not recommended. Once up there, though, you'll be happy to have made the trip. There's a warren of spaces here, including a terrace overlooking the heaving part of Long Street from which you've just ascended, and myriad lounges, some of them tucked away (don't miss the back terrace). Mondays and Tuesdays sees a line up of small, excellent solo artists and bands; Saturdays there's a funky DJ session known as The Boogie, and various other DJs of all genre persuasions take the decks on alternate nights. The atmosphere might remind you a bit of an arty Bohemian hangout from your student days; there's a hint of grunge, but it's been cultivated with real warmth (and someone's grandmother's hand-me-down furniture and lampshades).

mostly huge stocks of wine, in boxes and on shelves. And when you need to stretch your legs or simply want a breather, there's a doorway with direct access to the adjacent SMAC (Stellenbosch Modern and Contemporary) art gallery, which on occasion houses extraordinary exhibitions.

....

Wijnhuis *(right)*
First Floor, Dorpsmeent Centre, cnr. Church and Andringa streets, Stellenbosch
Tel: 021 887 5844
www.wijnhuis.co.za
Open: daily, 8am–11pm

A fantastic idea – a large lounge-bar specialising in wine in the middle of the biggest and most popular winelands region in the country. Wijnhuis, which translated simply means 'Winehouse', naturally has an epic winelist, representing a huge array of vintages and blends from over 60 individual estates; this being a university town, education happens on all levels, and you could develop considerable oeno-expertise in a single sitting here. Rather cosily built into a large loft-style setting on the first floor of a building that's right in the hub of Stellenbosch's bustling central bar and restaurant quarter, Wijnhuis comprises a cheerful warren of spaces, from a sky-light bedecked conservatory-style dining area that feels almost open-air, to a more intimate and tucked away section, and of course a large lounge-style tasting lounge with a pub-style bar, TVs showing important sports games, and décor comprising

snack…

Perhaps it's the heat, ensuring there's usually as much skin as fashion sense on show, but for most Capetonians, snacking is preferable to eating. As such, what differentiates the eateries that follow from most of the restaurants reviewed in 'Eat' is their informality, along with the surrounding clientele, which will be predominantly, if not exclusively, local. What's on your plate may still astound you, but it's mostly about enjoying a truly local atmosphere than about what's on the menu.

A culinary meander through the city's smaller eateries – a mix of cafés, bakeries, bistros or snack bars – provides real insight into the work ethic of what Jo'burgers like to call 'Slaapstad' (rhyming with 'Kaapstad', Afrikaans for Cape Town, and literally translated as 'sleeptown'). Whether you chance upon mobile freelancers perched on their laptops, or models slouching over smoothies as they text their agents, or the stress-free specimens who call themselves 'in the arts', or unemployed-and-not-looking, there are plenty of delightful places where you'll witness Capetonians going about their 'daily grind'.

Early mornings, when the 9-to-5ers join the caffeine queue, is the best time of the day to view the extraordinary variety of Capetonians as they kick off the day – from the cool media types to the clean-cut execs, the oversized-sunglass models to the long-haired hippy posses, almost all the city's tribes have representatives gathered behind the glass-topped counter of a Vida e Caffè. After the morning rush you'll see a continuous drip-drip of hungry or caffeine-starved faces throughout the day, with a quick rush over lunchtime – at least in the inner city, where office workers determine the pace. If you're a bit of a caffeine afficionado, base yourself at an ultra-serious barista-minded spot, like Origin, Truth, or the classy

Table 13

little newcomer, Espressolab (Tel: 021 447 0845, www.espressolabmicroroasters. com), the latter hidden away at The Old Biscuit Mill in Woodstock. Of course, if you think a caffeine shot is just foreplay, better base yourself at a fashionable and sexy café like Loading Bay, or a rustic-chic retreat such as Birds, both establishments that offer an experience – and a menu – that avoids clichés.

What makes the coffee shops and cafés so sociable, too, is that it really doesn't take much to transform a quick stop-off for coffee into an all-morning (and later) affair. Fuelled by the arrival of fellow caffeine addicts, Capetonians will happily recharge their cups and a quick snack stop might soon evolve into a round of drinks, lunch, and the inevitable quest for early evening sundowners. This is particularly true at places like idiosyncratic Manna Epicure, an all-white haven of exquisitely fresh flavours (including the most fragrant cocktails) and The Sidewalk Café (see Eat) where you can commence with 'The Monday to Friday Really Cheap Breakfast' or a slice of their magic cheesecake, and end up with an early-evening snack platter of capers, red peppers, rye bread, feta, and cold meats to accompany your chilled glass of wine. It's the kind of experience that makes you wish you never had to book for a formal restaurant again, and the city is well-stocked with such places – just look for a crowd schmoozing on the terrace of any good-looking space along Long Street, in Green Point or De Waterkant.

Wherever you choose to refuel during the week, we know where you need to be on a Saturday morning: the weekly Neighbourgoods Food Market at Woodstock's Old Biscuit Mill complex. It's the sassiest, liveliest weekly gathering of gourmands and round-the-clock socialisers, and the edibles on offer just tremendous in scope – see you there!

163

Andiamo *(left)*
Cape Quarter,
72 Waterkant Street,
De Waterkant, Green Point
Tel: 021 421 3687/8
www.andiamo.co.za
Open: daily, 9am–11pm

Throughout the day locals drop by this excellent deli-cum-Italian restaurant to fill their baskets, gossip over coffee, or create a mix 'n' match salad from food bar and sit out on the cobblestone courtyard – a faux European piazza centred around a fountain and pepper tree. Reliable, and known for its generous portions and simple plating of straightforward, instantly recognisable dishes (no fine dining aspirations here), Andiamo ('let's go') is a cut above the regular pizza and pasta joints, although you still need to make a special request for al dente pasta. The deli stocks over 2,000 local and imported products, and it's a great place to put together a sandwich, combining freshly baked breads with Italian meats and crisp fresh salad ingredients. Sitting down pushes the price of anything selected from the deli counters. Waiters are big, beefy, brawny South Africans who probably knew nothing about Italian food before they started working here; they're a little less than friendly but know how to deliver a well-extracted espresso.

Beefcakes Burger Bar *(right)*
Sovereign Quay,
40 Somerset Road, Green Point
Tel: 021 425 9019
www.beefcakes.co.za
Open: daily, 11am (5.30 Sun)–11pm

There's entertainment a-plenty in this Miami-styled diner, both on the extremely camp (even homoerotic) menu and occasionally on the stage; the live drag act can be a pretty provocative accompaniment to a Buffy the Hamburger Slayer burger, especially in a room full of whooping and cheering gay men. And with a pink piano, pink flamingo wall art, and a bevy of spectacularly fit waiters wearing tight pink aprons, there's no mistaking that this is a flamboyantly gay restaurant – the beefy burgers aren't meant to be butch at all, and desserts are listed under the heading 'Happy Endings'. While neither the Greek God nor the Beach Boy burgers are likely to be as satisfying as they sound, there's enough eye-candy doing the rounds to make a session here an amusing prelude to a night of dancing at nearby Bronx or Crew, or more drinks in the Smoke and Mirrors bar downstairs.

Biesmiellah *(bottom)*
2 Uper Wale Street,
Bo-Kaap, City Bowl
Tel: 021 423 0850
Open: 11am–10pm (11pm Fri/Sat)
Closed Sundays.

A Cape Town institution, this authentic and downhome preserve of the Bo-Kaap community is where you can sample true-to-its-roots Cape Malay cooking, served up in a bare-bones environment by members of the multi-generational Osman family. Don't come here expecting a view, much by way of service, or anything resembling décor. It's a pretty empty shell filled with aromatic fragrances wafting up from the kitchen, and perhaps a chance to listen in on the kind of garrulous (and sometimes seriously coarse) banter that can flare up between members of this community. On the menu are chilli bites (or *daltjies*) and *samosas*, both snack-style finger treats that you must try, but the tamarind-spiked lamb stew known as *denningvleis* is what will make the adventure into this dishevelled cobblestone corner of Cape Town truly unforgettable. Another treat, while you're here – and since this Muslim establishment doesn't serve alcohol – is the Indian-style rosewater milkshake known as *falooda*. For a similar experience, coupled with extraordinary views (and a more tourist-centred atmosphere), try the Noon Gun Tea Room and Restaurant, see page 188.

Birds Boutique Café *(top)*
127 Bree Street, City Center
Tel: 021 426 2534
Open: 7am–6pm Mon–Fri; 8am–2pm Sat

This unusual café is in many ways emblematic of the style-revolution that's taken place in the city. When Mathilde and Heike Stegmann arrived from Namibia and started their sparse and countrified café, they did so in a part of the inner-city that was pretty dangerous, hardly fit for a fundamentalist-organic café done out in white. That was six years ago; today the area around their 1780s townhouse has clearly responded to the call for change and is brimming with great venues and vibe. Spare, simple, unfettered, Birds has nothing but a few tables, a wooden bakery counter,

and cushioned double-level old crates for seating; light fittings are porcelain swans nose-diving towards the tables. It's an experiential café with an ongoing smell from the kitchen of baking bread, and Mathilde's famous chicken pie. There are no machines, so no aural distraction from the non-stop birdsong soundtrack – the idea is that you should have a chance to breathe, sit, and relax. And you will, with delicious wild boar pies, wild fig juice, pancakes, organic wines, herbal tea straight from Mathilde's garden and vegetables from their biodynamic township supplier.

The Café *(bottom)*
(aka The Showroom Café)
Ground Floor, The Grand Daddy,
Long Street, City Centre
Tel: 021 424 7247
Open: daily, 6.30am–10pm;
7am–9pm Sun

From the imagination of Bruce Robertson, one of Cape Town's most recognisable and – following the successive closure of a small string of culinary ventures in 2009 – notoriously unreliable, celebrity chefs, this sidewalk café proves that there's something to be said for small and simple enterprises. Here Bruce has gone for a contemporary chic look, tying in with the semi-bling, budget 'luxury' atmosphere and feel of the historic inner city hotel in which it's located. Beneath big copper-surface orbs, small tables with designer plastic chairs share space with a row of banquets in green crocodile leather and Phillipe Starke ghost chairs; between the glass doors that open onto the side road that feeds Long Street, a

variety of South African wines occupy the glass shelves. Or sit at the counters where large hatch-like windows open up onto the hustle and bustle of Long Street. Aside from a basic, healthy buffet on the 'central market' at breakfast and lunchtimes, the Showroom Cafe offers sandwiches and wraps throughout the day, and heartier a la carte offerings that include whole roast duck, prime cut sirloin, catch of the day, ostrich burger, and even oysters. It's a café, and not a showcase for Bruce's legendary show-off cuisine; prices are extremely good, which probably explains the many locals who join guests from the hotel.

Caffe Neo *(top)*
South Seas, 129 Beach Road, Mouille Point
Tel: 021 433 0849
Open: daily, 7am–7pm

Virtually across the road from Mouille Point's squat red-and-white candy-striped lighthouse, with great sea views, this funky little family-run spot has diverse fans. A long timber table dominates the indoor space – here the mobile office brigade use the free (but sometimes unreliable) Wi-Fi, sipping their lattes whilst scanning the room over the top of their laptops. Waiters, in jeans and branded T-shirts, place orders on your behalf, summoning up breakfasts, crisp salads, sandwiches, *mezze* platters, *keftedes*, *pasticcio*, and other Aegean specialties (it's Greek-owned, after all) chalked up on the wall. Around you, the look is a semi-cluttered jumble of breezy contemporary design and off-set with

the intensely personal: a central pillar with shelves features books and family photographs. Outside, on the wooden deck, things are breezier, with chrome and plastic designer chairs and views over the parking lot to Mouille Point's grass-covered promenade and the ocean beyond. This is the ideal spot to touch base with Cape Town's laidback approach to a busy day, prompting that much-asked question: 'Does anyone in this city actually work?'

Cheyne's *(bottom)*
108 St Stephen's Church, Bree Street, City Centre
Tel: 021 422 3358
www.cheynemorrisby.com
Open: 8am–4pm Tues–Sat

Having worked as a private chef for the likes of Eric Clapton and Kate Moss, Cheyne Morrisby has opened a tiny, casual bistro-style restaurant of his own. It's in one of the converted bunker-style spaces beneath the stone hull of beautiful St Stephen's Church, increasingly at the epicentre of Bree Street's ongoing revival. A simple space – not much larger than a generous-sized dining room, dominated by a Miele-powered kitchen – there's not much to disguise the original architecture of this street-level catacomb, with seating inside for just 16 people. Artworks on the walls are for sale, two communal-style dining tables, a pile of culinary-inspired books; a freestanding fan works hard to keep things relatively cool belie the simplicity of the place. Cheyne's does delicious breakfasts and serves up elegant variants of straightforward comfort lunches – these vary

each day and are listed on the chalk-board attached to the front doors; a couple of selected wines are served by the glass. At night, Cheyne's transforms into a private dining venue where all bets are off and you get to negotiate the rules and the menu – advance arrangements essential.

Depasco *(top)*
8 Kloof Street,
Gardens, City Bowl
Tel: 021 424 7070
www.depasco.co.za
Open: daily, 6.30am–5.30pm,
7.30–3pm Sat–Sun

New Yorkers would probably take one glance and recognize this as an obvious spin from a style they do so well – a massive space surrounded on two sides by humungous glass windows looking onto Cape Town's most intense traffic intersection and, beyond that, the Long Street Baths. Inside, the ceiling feels miles above your head, and you truly feel you have room to breathe, idle through the newspaper (or a fashion magazine, of which there's a small stock), and sip great coffee. It's a totally non-denominational, everything-goes type of place – smart, pared down, and light-filled, with the mirror mosaic-covered pillars adding a hint of dazzle. Order from the counter and take your number to your table, ensuring you have proximity to a good view of the action; your food (hearty breakfasts, well-stuffed sandwiches, salads, and a few bistro-style meals) arrives swiftly and you needn't get up to replenish your stock. Despite its very prominent position, Depasco is very much part of a neighbourhood scene,

discovered by those who happen upon it whilst hoofing it through the city.

Eastern Food Bazaar *(bottom)*
The Wellington, 96 Longmarket Street, City Centre
Tel: 021 461 2458
www.easternfoodbazaar.co.za
Open: daily, 11am–9.30pm (10pm Fri–Sat, 9pm Sun)

The heady scent of aromatic spices mingles with a bustle of seemingly ravenous people to create an environment you simply must investigate. This is very much a community hang-out, and – for visitors to the city – a place to experience a local way of life that's neither upmarket nor sophisticated, but right on the money when it comes to all-round appeal. Comprising various foodstalls, the location is in the former Welling Fruit Grower' Market – the building itself dates to 1934, forming a narrow wedge of real estate linking Longmarket and Darling streets – which offers character and an authentic sense if history. In a place that some might label 'fast food', you might expect plastic chairs, but instead they've put in wood and granite (although you eat with plastic utensils), and in fact, they've gone to extraordinary lengths to create a welcoming ambience, with ornate detailing amidst a space of warm, earthy hues. Cobbled stones underfoot, wooden pillars, decorative screens and crafted artefacts, with Moghul paintings on the walls, and chandeliers above. Decide what to eat – mostly Indian, but with other ethnic cuisines on offer, too – and then order and pay at the central terminal and use your receipt to pick up your meal. It's thoroughly no-frills, but the food is delicious, authentic and, truly, dirt cheap.

....

Empire Cafe *(left)*
11 York Road, Muizenburg
Tel: 021 788 1250
www.empirecafe.co.za
Open: daily, 7am (8am Sun)–4pm
(9pm Wed–Sat)

Empire was named for the eponymous Empire Theatre, long an old run-down relic of another era, but now it's the two-storey café that's become synonymous with the step-back-in-time atmosphere of this old Victorian holiday town that is increasingly the home to Cape Town's most laid-back hippies. For some, it's the sudden sense of having time traveled back to the Fifties that makes Muizenberg – and Empire – such a memorable outing, but we rather appreciate the opportunity to gel with (or simply observe) the wetsuited, dripping wet surfers that makes this Muizenburg favorite such a delight. Sit upstairs, and you can keep an eye on the water, watching the surfers with whom you've just had coffee with catch a few waves. Food's good, too, thanks to an owner –chef who's committed to making delicious wholesome meals – no soppy health-food labels here, it's all about the taste. That, and a vibe that's typical of this city community.

....

The Foodbarn Deli *(right)*
Noordhoek Farm Village, Village Lane, Noordhoek, Southern Peninsula
Tel: 021 789 1390

www.thefoodbarn.co.za
Open: daily, 8am–5pm

It's firstly a bakery; the bakers arrive at 3am, and set about preparing 18 different sorts of breads, as well as croissants and pastries, using stone ground fibre-rich flour from the nearby Eureka Mills. By the time you arrive, as early as 8am, the place will be full of pleasantly intoxicating aromas, making it almost impossible to walk out empty handed. In fact, do yourself a favour, and sit down – the traditional European country deli atmosphere is quite unique for Cape Town, and there's quite a bit more to take in here than at the slightly refined (even sterile) places that you'll find in the city. This takes as its cue, a real, no- nonsense farm stall, only with the advantage of having The Foodbarn's chef, Franck Dangereux (see Eat) at the helm. Breakfasts, light lunches, cold cuts, biscuits and cakes – the selection is dizzying but without hesitation, select one of the incredible, super-heavy 200 gram pies which, like everything Franck touches, is delicious.

....

Frieda's on Bree *(bottom)*
15 Bree Street, City Centre
Tel: 021 421 2404
www.friedasonbree.co.za
Open: 6am–4pm Mon–Fri

Cool and funky, this café – a long warehouse-style space decorated with vintage vinyl-topped tables, sofas from the Fifties covered with bits of cloth and cushions your grandmother might have knitted, and a motley assortment of disused old school bric-a-brac – is

another worth visiting, even if you're not peckish. It's a great combination of contemporary and old-fashioned flair: A scrap metal model airplane hangs above the deli-like counter, and the small, open-plan kitchen churns out a selection of groovy breakfast plates and a few select lunch items: scrumptious smoked salmon salad; Frieda's special burgers, warm chicken salad, and a vegetarian stir fry with noodles. They make the fluffiest eggs in town, served on the darkest rye. Although in the throb of the city, it's thoroughly laid-back, with piles of magazines, ill-fitting sculptures and collectibles, and a general spirit of friendliness and warm welcomes. Nothing fancy, no pretences, such a good way to fill a gap.

....

Fyndraai   *(top)*
Solms Delta Wine Estate,
Deta Road, off the R45,
Franschhoek Valley, Winelands
Tel: 021 874 3937
www.solms-delta.co.za
Open: daily, 11am–8pm (4pm
Sun–Mon)

Way before European colonists arrived at the Cape – and, in fact even before Nguni and Bantu tribes arrived from more northerly parts of Africa – the indigenous Khoi might have eaten pigskin or porcupine skin as a starter. At this innovative restaurant housed in a 276-year-old Cape Dutch building on a 321-year-old wine farm (which you can investigate at the on-site museum before partaking of one of the most enjoyable wine-tasting sessions available in the Winelands), such extreme culinary traditions are tempered by

modern. Having worked within the French traditional (under, amongst other, Harald Bresselschmidt at Aubergine; see Eat), Chef Shaun Schoeman has developed a menu of dishes inspired by older local traditions, including Afrikaner *boerekos* and Cape Malay (slave) food. The menu is seasonal, with herbs such as sorrel and wild rosemary from the farm's own garden. What you do want to try is the springbok *wildspastei* (wild pie with Klein Karoo springbok leg), and the curried smoked snoek and salmon fishcakes – usually served with a thick mango chutney (blatjang). Sit outside on the terrace looking across the gardens and at soaring, magnificent mountains; or – better still – go for the excellent-value picnic menu available in summer. The restaurant is a 15-minute walk from the house where Nelson Mandela lived during his final two years of imprisonment at what was then known as the Victor Verster Prison.

....

Giovanni's   *(bottom)*
Deli World
103 Main Road, Green Point
Tel: 021 434 6893
Open: daily, 7.30am–9pm

The Esposito brothers have been running this traditional Italian deli — known to many as Little Italy in Cape Town – for over two decades, and you get a sense of the neighbourhood buzz without even setting foot inside. It's so much part of the fabric of Green Point's street life – and now almost impossibly close to the new football stadium – that you'd swear many of those regulars perched on the roadside terrace are permanent fixtures. There's always a crowd here, and even if you just stop by for a powerful espresso or a freshly-made sandwich of imported Parma, pesto, and serious cheese, you'll probably end up wanting to hang around for hours caught in the grip of conversational gossip. Besides the tantalisingly stocked shelves, there are pre-cooked meals that you can take away with you, and more than enough fantastic ingredients to fill up that picnic basket – including wine.

High Tea at the Nellie *(top)*
Mount Nelson, 76 Orange Street, Gardens, City Bowl
Tel: 021 483 1000
www.mountnelson.co.za
Tea served: daily, 2.30–5.30pm

In some senses this is the most formal of our snack suggestions; though there's no dress code, it is with a distinct sense of living the high life that you sink into a sofa at Cape Town's most celebrated colonial-era hotel (see Stay), and sip tea to the tinkling of a pianist. For an unexpected buzz, order the Gunpowder Temple of Heaven – a super-strong tea concoction that'll put hairs on your chest – and do a couple of laps around the buffet table before deciding what to pile onto your plate (don't miss the extraordinary cheese-cake). The real pleasure in some ways is the crowd that gathers here; a surreal sampling of every possible type, from local socialites to world travellers, grannies treating grandchildren to romantic trysts, all gathered amongst the antique chairs and sofas to enjoy the attentions of a swift waiter and the chance to self-time their brew chosen from amongst the exclusive and often

exotic blends produced by Nigiro (the tea label from local coffee brand, Origin; see page 190). It goes without saying that it's essential to book.

Jardine Bakery *(bottom)*
185 Bree Street, cnr Bloem and Bree streets, City Centre
Tel: 021 424 5644
www.jardineonbree.
Open: 8am–5pm (2pm Sat) Mon–Fri

You'll spot the queue forming in front of the sidewalk hatch; breads are fresh and the sandwiches the perfect antidote for a midday hunger lust. Casual, slightly scruffy chalk boards list daily specials with offbeat-sounding fillings, clearly best left to the imagination of a culinary wizard like owner George Jardine (one of the country's most formidable chefs, now concentrating on his new restaurant on Jordan wine estate; see Eat). Pies are the in-between meal of choice – if available, the Portobello mushroom and emmental filling is spectacular. Even if the pie of the day sounds somewhat leftfield, it's probably worth ordering, because it may never be produced again (when last did you have macaroni cheese stuffed inside a pastry shell?). The only problem here is putting up with occasionally diabolical service; given how dauntingly popular it remains, perhaps the bad attitude prevents it from becoming a 'hang-out' for scenesters, just as the limited availability of space to sit-down literally prevents hangers-on from hanging around.

Kassia & Figg   *(left)*
22 Dalebrook Place, Main Road,
Kalk Bay, Southern Peninsula
Tel: 021 788 3337
www.vanielje.com/kf/
Open: 9am–5.30pm Weds–Sun

Bathed in soothing shades of purple
and green – colours inspired by a
picture of a granadilla cake on a ce-
ladon-coloured plate – this is the kind
of deli, inundated with irresistible-
looking cakes, tarts, bakes and treats,
that fills one with joy. Until three years
ago, Kassie Watrobski had been running Jonkershuis, a restaurant on the
Groot Constantia Estate for over two
decades. To fill the gap, Kassie and her
daughter Inge started this fabulous eatery in an historic building across from
Kalk Bay's Dalebrook tidal pool, making it a superb spot for a low-key meal
made with the freshest ingredients
using organic and free-range produce
wherever possible. Each day, mother
and daughter dream up a selection
of dishes for the day, basing their impromptu menu on anything from the
weather to their mood – or perhaps
what you're in the mood for. Between
the layers of fresh-coloured paint are
walls of exposed brick and a couple of
paintings by important artists stashed
among the decorative paraphernalia
and pretty bits and pieces — a vibrant
space you can enjoy for hours at a
time.

L'Aperitivo   *(top)*
70 Loop Street, City Centre
Tel: 082 898 7079
Open: 9am–10.30pm (11pm Thurs–
Sat). Closed Sundays.

It's astonishing that in such a sociable
city, the aperitif culture is only now taking hold – and it's taken a modern-day
settler to really bring the concept into
its own: Swiss-born owner, Steff Rau,
brings a wonderfully relaxed approach
to life in this wine and cocktail bar, offering fresh food and excellent coffee.
Here, in a corner shop right next to the
João Ferreira Gallery and directly below The Bang Bang Club (see Party),
he's gathered a few of his favourite
things, including top-drawer cocktails
(mixed by his Bolognese partner, An-
drea), select wines and beers (from &
Union) and a daily-changing menu of
fresh, bistro-style food (Steff has done
a stint in a Michelin three-star). With
its bright red walls and stone floors,
upbeat soundtrack, and huge windows
framing the busy street, this spot really
does conjure up a corner of Europe. It's
just as much a sensible spot to pause
during a shopping safari or inner-city
sightseeing expedition, although once
you've made yourself comfortable
here, you may not want to move on for
a while. As tradition dictates, snacks
are dispensed to L'Aperitivo drinkers
between 5 and 7 in the evening; expect
quality artisanal cheeses and charcuterie to accompany your Negroni, Japanese Slipper or glass of Chardonnay
– and they make the best damn gin and
tonic in town.

La Petite Tarte   *(right)*
Shop A11, Cape Quarter,
Dixon Street, De Waterkant
Tel: 021 425 9077
Open: 8am–8pm (5pm in winter)
Mon–Sat; 10am–2pm Sun

The French model who established

L'Aperitivo Menu

Starters:
- Mixed Salad "L'Aperitivo" R35
- Greek Salad R45
- Thai Prawn Salad R60
- Parma Ham & Sweet Melon R40
- Smoked Salmon Trout Salad R60

Mains:
- Marinated & Roasted Chicken Breast
  with potatoes and Greek Salad R75
- Tagliata di Manzo with roasted potatoes

this neighbourhood favourite — a comforting nook carved into the side of the original Cape Quarter building in De Waterkant — may have sold up, but it remains one of the loveliest spots in the city to take a breather, either under the shade of the sidewalk trees, or wedged into a cushioned booth inside. It's a pretty place detailed with old-fashioned French tea tins and a few vintage-style crockery items, jars of fruit preserve, a single chandelier above it all, and Edith Piaf singing gently in the background. And the place smells as good as the food coming out of that tiny, single oven tastes. If you just want to fill a small gap, the oversized croissants are just the thing; perfectly crispy and fluffy and light. But check out the selection of interesting quiches displayed alongside the cakes and cupcakes and – of course – the eponymous tartlets. But most are here

for the traditional Parissiene *croque monsieurs* (there's even a tomato-only version for vegetarians) and don't miss the violet cupcakes topped with crystallised violet, made with essence of violet imported from France. Wine is incidentally also available.

Lazari *(left)*
Cape Quarter Extension,
cnr Jarvis and Napier streets,
De Waterkant
Tel: 021 419 9555
Open: daily, 8am–10pm

From the immense amount of staring, glancing and unadulterated flirting that goes on here, it is soon clear that – despite the legendary eggs Benedict, Thai wraps and much-touted cupcakes – food is not the main reason for coming. Done out in a hip, contemporary

take on Pop Art, it's the vibe and the presence of the fabulous owner, Chris Lazari, that makes this place sparkle. Buzzy, on-the-ball waiters tear around the place – which includes two outdoor sections if fresh air is more important to you than goggling fellow diners – delivering food along with a pleasant disposition. If you prefer a more intimate, laid-back atmosphere, the original Lazari is across the city in a tiny, tucked away venue in Vredehoek (cnr Upper Maynard Street and Vredehoek Avenue, Tel: 021 461 9865), where it's only open during the day, and is supported by a very loyal crowd who love its unpretentious good-value meals and warm service. Unlike the Cape Quarter venue, it's a seriously compact space – but that doesn't mean service isn't slow over lunchtime when every single little table is besieged by fans, so it's not a place for a hasty meal.

Liquorice & Lime *(right)*
162 Kloof Street, Gardens, City Bowl
Tel: 021 423 6921
www.liquoriceandlime.co.za
Open: daily, 7am–5pm
(4pm Sat/Sun)

Tiny, tranquil, and with an astonishing view of Table Mountain, this is located at the top-end of Kloof Street, right next door to the over-the-top, rambunctious Bombay Bicycle Club (incidentally, an interesting choice for a late night drink, once the dinner crowd has subsided, Tel: 021 423 6805). A green and black colour scheme, chequered flooring, soft banquets, a solitary, slow-turning ceiling fan, and vintage wall lights all signal the owner's obsession with Deco while simple, stylish meals will stave off a hunger, subdue a hangover, or tide you over between meals.

snack....

With just a handful of tables, a Sade (or similar) soundtrack, piles of magazines, and a small, curious selection of artisanal food products, this is a gentle escape from the world outside; all-day breakfasts, flame-grilled burgers (patties are made right here) and homemade pies are all good. While waiting for your meal (note that no alcohol is served), browse the shelves for tasty take-home treats from the Cook Sisters – the cranberry and peanut brittle is a winner.

Loading Bay Café *(left)*
30 Hudson Street,
De Waterkant
Tel: 021 425 6321
www.loadingbay.co.za
Open: 7am–6pm (10.30 Thurs)
Mon–Fri; 8am–4pm Sat

Dangling above this light-filled indoor-outdoor post-industrial rehabilitated warehouse space, the large black and yellow half-spherical light fittings are almost as striking as the long-eyelashed owner, a handsome 20-something entrepreneur. Selling beautiful imported clothing, excellent coffee, and the best breakfasts, perfect afternoon fillers, and early evening platters and Lebanese mezze. Thursdays' nights are a bit of fun, when burgers are served along with truffle salted fries. There's a good range of hand-crafted produce, from coffee to beer, and plans to bring a low-key farmer's market of sorts to the derelict space across the road.

Lola's *(right)*
228 Long Street, City Centre
Tel: 021 423 0885
Open: daily, 7.30am–midnight

If you want to feel part and parcel of inner city Cape Town, head for the loud, funky music blasting through this shaggy Bohemian café, situated in the heart of the backpacker quarter on bustling Long Street. A melange of retro-kitsch styling and haphazard thrown-together anti-glamour, it is one of the spots along this stretch to gather for hangover-quelling breakfasts, pre-evening drinks, and filling vegetarian meals that range from overly cheesy macaroni, to mushroom-topped lasagne that may be served a degree too cold. Still, it's the vibe you come for, and a seat on the sidewalk (hold on tightly to your bags) guarantees an endless succession of passing eye-candy and a chance to ogle Long Street's special brand of inner city bravado. Inside, the café is done up in bold retro colours, large fried egg-shaped daisies painted onto the walls and ceiling, and comfortable plastic chairs. A hatch behind the espresso counter allows you to peek into the tiny, slightly dishevelled kitchen, and there's a full bar service; beer specials are sometimes listed on the A-frame chalk board outside. (No

burgers in town, Jon-Paul Bolus is already a small-time hero, having dreamt up De Waterkant's ultimate daytime schmoozing venue, and been named South Africa's best-dressed man by GQ magazine. Street-cred and good looks aside, he has a take-charge approach to reinvigorating the inner city and his enthusiasm is evident in the way Loading Bay looks and feels like a million bucks, luring citywise regulars to this edge of Green Point's cobblestone precinct. Stop by for a light meal, always prepared from fresh, organic, personally-sourced ingredients; the selection is a clever mix of wholesome

point asking after Lola, incidentally; apparently the place was named for a former owner of the building.)

■ Manna Epicure *(left)*
151 Kloof Street,
Tamboerskloof, City Bowl
Tel: 021 426 2413
Open: 9am–6pm (4pm Sun) Tues–Sun

An all-white space with ever-changing décor elements (including the most interesting flower arrangements in town), Manna offers the healthiest, quirkiest, freshest selection of flavours on Kloof Street, along with a mature trendy crowd. Grab a table inside by getting here early (no bookings taken) or you'll have to sit on the balcony and, sunglasses in position, watch the scene on Kloof's busy sidewalk. Classic jazz and melodies from the Twenties spill out of white speakers, while the menu offers a selection of tantalising summer salads such as watermelon with watercress, feta, toasted pumpkin seeds and pecan nuts, or honey and mint *tabouleh* with

baby spinach, pear, goats cheese and roasted macadamia nuts. Breakfasts are served throughout the day, and they do a wonderful open omelette with roasted aubergine, gorgonzola, and fresh pear julienne. Tapas are a speciality here and their own freshly-baked breads are served together with delicious spreads. The line up of main dishes is short and divided into taste categories – sour, sweet, bitter, spicy and savoury, so there's literally something to satisfy all tastes. There's a small list of personally chosen wines, a few good choices available by the glass. Service waivers between pretty sprightly, and atrociously slow – you're paying for the innovative tastes, and the sometimes superb people-watching.

■ Man'oushe *(middle)*
Andringa Street, Stellenbosch, Winelands
Tel: 021 886 7545
Open: 7.30am–11.30pm Mon–Sat

Savvy young graduates who've re-

mained behind to work in this historic, increasingly hip little university town come here to lounge together at tables clustered onto the sidewalk, and goggle at the tourists who wander the streets in search of wine, Cape Dutch architecture, and a sensible place to eat. This is it, so pass between the olive trees flanking the entrance and flop into the sink-deep sofas before scanning the menu's healthy selection of Lebanese specialities; we recommend the mezze platter — *hummus*, *baba ganoush*, creamed cheese with chilli, and baby pies filled with spinach and spicy beef, served with large flat Lebanese breads topped with *zaatar* (wild thyme) – ideal for sharing. While so many other Stellenbosch cafés are trying terribly hard to be cool, this place gets it right without the least bit of effort thanks to the Beirut-born owner who ensures that the food is authentic and the selection of flavoured *shisha* tobaccos, an essential accompaniment to coffee, always fresh. It's the only genuinely 'ethnic' restaurant in Stellenbosch that manages to be totally unpretentious,

with chandeliers emitting a gentle light above the stone, rug-covered floors and pale white hookah smoke.

....

■ **Melissa's** *(right)*
94 Kloof Street,
Tamboerskloof, City Bowl
Tel: 021 424 5540
www.melissas.co.za
Open: daily, 7.30am (8am Sat/Sun) –8pm

One of Cape Town's healthiest fuel stops, Melissa's is driven by its philosophy of fresh, organic, wholesome, simple produce and the atmosphere – relaxed and chic rustic – underscores this. There are piles of magazines to keep you occupied or seat yourself at the mountain-facing window seats, great for loners and voyeurs. Breakfast and lunch sees a gorgeous buffet but don't forget to look at a menu that undersells the deliciousness of what's on offer. Even if you only stop by for an espresso, there's every chance you'll be browsing the metal racks and scanning the fridges

artisanal take-home ingredients for your next soiree (this is the best place to shop for a gift if you've been invited for dinner); they sell everything from preserves and baked goods to oven-baked crisps, pressed elderberry juice and the most delicious apple pie and carrot cakes in town. Be warned: service is slightly haphazard. Note that Melissa has spread her wing to several other locations (there's even a branch in Stellenbosch) and quality is fully on a par at all, but we like this, her original outlet, best.

....

Mila the Cake Shop (left)
87 Dorp Street,
Stellenbosch, Winelands
Tel: 021 886 8807
www.milacakeshop.co.za
Open: 7am–5pm Mon–Sat. Closed for 2 week over Christmas/New Year.

A range of decadently sweet and flamboyantly-topped treats awaits you inside Louise Veldhuizen's diminutive little shop on Dorp Street, Stellenbosch's original main road, still lined with heritage buildings and oak trees. You can sit beneath one bedecked with wire-and-silk pink butterflies, watching the flutter of students and tourists ambling past the whitewashed Cape Dutch gables, or station yourself inside, where the display of cakes and tarts and other sweet extravagances is sure to tempt. It's a bit of a torture chamber for anyone contemplating a diet, and simply a menace if you're an icing fetishist – her cupcakes are works of astonishing beauty, almost too gorgeous to eat. Coffee is the excellent Cape-based Origin (see page 190), and there are savoury options – a sandwich of the day, amazing *waterblommetjie* quiche (made with the lightest of pastries and garnished with ostrich carpaccio), and cheese or meat platters that'll go well with a glass or two of wine, of which a handful are listed on the board.

Miss K Food Café (middle)

Shop 1, Winston Place,
65 Main Road, Green Point
Tel: 021 439 9559 www.missk.co.za
Open: daily, 8am–4.30pm (1pm Sun)

There's something a little Alice in Wonderland about this upbeat, brightly-styled neighbourhood café, with its oversized teacups, piles of enormous pistachio meringues – like impossibly massive dollops of tinted cream – and bouncy waitresses dressed in blue. It's just great to be in a place that looks this fresh – never mind the scrumptious aromas and soulful strains of jazz. Diminutive kitchen genie Kirsten Zschokke spent a decade in Europe and the US working for demanding celebrities and insanely wealthy clients before returning to her native land to establish a 'casual, simple, fresh' little eatery on Green Point's Main Road. Not only does Kirsten churn out deliciously decadent sweets and cakes, but there are healthy options too, including freshly squeezed fruit juices, and great buffet breakfasts. Punters love the 'Hangover Eggs' (glorified beans on toast), the fabulous tomato and goats cheese tart, and superb *croque monsieurs*. During the week it's mainly mealtimes that are busy, but the buzziest crowd happens on weekends when you should grab an outside seat under an umbrella and watch the city's prettiest bits traipsing by.

Neighbourgoods Market (right)

Old Biscuit Mill,
373–375 Albert Road, Woodstock
Tel: 021 448 1438
www.neighbourgoodsmarket.co.za
Open: 9am–2pm Sat

Cape Town's most popular food market is where the loveliest-of-lovely Capetonians feast on nibbles from the city's most delicious-looking food stalls, operated by farmers, butchers,

snack...

mongers, bakers, grocers and local celebrity chefs taking time out from their restaurant kitchens. So, grab a platter of freshly shucked West Coast oysters (served with sparkling wine), steak rolls prepared by one or two of the city's top chefs, smoothies blended from all kinds of restorative berries, homebaked pies, unusual pizzas and ravishing assortments of dips, tapenades, and pestos, with lots of delicious breads that were whipped out the oven at the crack of dawn... And you're not even a third of the way through. Part of the revitalisation of grungy Woodstock, the market was started in 2006 by entrepreneurs Justin Rhodes and Cameron Munro; they've signed up over 100 top-end traders to keep us flocking to this imaginatively reinvented Victorian warehouse (the disused Old Biscuit Mill) adjacent are some fantastic shops (see Shop). You can eat while you browse, or there are plenty of large communal tables with the day's papers and large bowls of flowers.

■ **Noon Gun Tea** *(left)*
■ **Room & Restaurant**
273 Longmarket Street, Signal Hill,
Bo-Kaap, City Bowl
Tel: 021 424 0529
www.noonguntearoom.co.za
Open: 10am–10pm Mon–Sat

The road that passes up through the cobbled roads of the Bo-Kaap Malay community to this undistinguished family-run restaurant on the slopes of Signal Hill is steep enough to be a little disconcerting. But so worth it: step inside the simply converted dining room, and it's all about the views – the entire Table Mountain and Devil's Peak, the city spilling down its slopes towards the Foreshore and harbour, plus all of Table Bay with Bloubergstrand stretching beyond. The simple menu includes such traditional Cape Malay dishes as *denningvleis*, and Malay *bredie* (stew) made with vegetables and lamb. Be sure to order a *falooda*, a milk drink with rose water that comes out looking like a strawberry milkshake, and one of the Malay desserts, such as

milktart or a super-sticky and ultra-sweet *koeksister* – which may help you sweet talk a smile from the otherwise dour service. There's also no alcohol, this being a Malay-run establishment. Try to get here before noon so you can appreciate the extraordinary boom of the eponymous cannon fire that happens every day at midday, or walk up to the cannon for unprecedented views of the harbour.

Nzolo Brand Café *(right)*
48 Church Street, City Centre
Tel: 021 426 1857
Open: 8am–5pm (9.30pm Wed–Fri; 3pm Sat). Closed Sundays.

Afro-hip by design, friendly, terribly laid-back (service can be downright horizontal) and – above all – extremely colourful. Portraits of Barack Obama vie with typical African hand-painted adverts for hair salons, a pink-and-yellow ceiling and chandeliers made from recycled plastic bottles, while the whole, tiny space is presided over by a large red cock – *nzolo*, or rooster in Congolese. The place (once called Afro Café) made its name by creating beautiful packaging for the tin-canned African tea products (Afro Tea) that you still buy here. Besides ultra-strong coffee and home-baked cakes (the butternut cheesecake served on weekends is amazing), fare includes light meals such as *boere* burger (stuffed with South African farmer's sausage), salads with unusual names like bah-bah (lamb) served with traditional *vetkoek* (literally 'fat cake'). More grown-up sounding dishes – (pumpkin stew or Tanzanian fish curry, perhaps) – and evening meals are listed on chalkboards. Nzolo is usefully located just around the corner from Green-market Square, always a hub of tourist life but one we heartily encourage you to explore; outside, there are more tables and a string of flea market style tables selling everything from second-hand books to beaded sculptures.

Olympia Café & Deli   *(left)*
134 Main Road, Kalk Bay,
Southern Peninsula
Tel: 021 788 6396
Open: daily, 7am–9pm (3pm Sun)

In an old Victorian building facing the harbour area, this is a thoroughly laid-back and typically hippy Kalk Bay institution, the type of place where local surfers and long-haired poets congregate, along with ladies of the upturned nose brigade on one-off shopping expeditions from the southern suburbs – all here to share the eccentric vibe and brilliant food. Interiors are rustic and old-fashioned; regardless, claim a table as quickly as you're able, because it gets seriously busy in here. It's a grubby, groovy, laid-back; a thrown-together sort of place which wears its lack of pretence (and sometimes service) conspicuously: a notice on the wall menu includes a reminder that there'll be "NO SMOKING, SPLIT BILLS, SELF-DISCIPLINE, BULLSHIT", and while they don't serve mineral water, their

tap water is free. A compact menu will include such fare as lamb liver with balsamic jus, seared (real) tuna niçoise, pickled fish, and large and memorable salads (the roast apricot, goats cheese and strawberries is out of this world).

Origin   *(middle)*
28 Hudson St, De Waterkant
Tel: 021 421 1000
www.originroasting.co.za
Open: 7am–5pm Mon–Fri;
8am–3pm Sat

It's possible to get high on the aroma alone as you step inside this industrial coffee nirvana, with its wooden troughs and sacks laden with brown beans. Tucked into a reimagined tobacco warehouse just around the corner from the Cape Quarter, this is probably Cape Town's most serious coffee stop – you can tell the baristas all know their stuff (and drink it, too). Neatly coiffured, they appear forever hard at work, dusting and polishing

their equipment, making up coffee bean parcels, and extracting fresh brews for a mix of just-off-the-beach bunnies and serious-minded business-folk. In a glass-walled sanctuary at the back of the ground-floor coffee shop is Nigiro Tea House (www.nigiro.co.za) something like a large, sublime fish tank where the combustible energy of Origin (which is Nigiro backwards, get it?) is left at the door in favour of a totally different fragrant atmosphere somewhat reminiscent of a Japanese tea garden, with the occasional Japanese tea ceremony held here within the brick warehouse. Food is served upstairs, in the open courtyard.

....

Rcaffé *(right)*
138 Long Street, City Centre
Tel: 021 424 1124
Open: 6.30am–5pm (1pm Sat)
Mon–Sat

Eggs Benedict at four in the afternoon? No problem. This sociable inner-city refuelling station specializes in all-day breakfasts and regularly posts omelettes and French toast specials on its chalkboards (look for them near the entrance, they're easy to miss if you're the sort who's easily distracted by a good-looking clientele). The sandwiches are genius (as are the baked goods and confectionary – healthy muffins, filled croissants, candied Florentines, and dark chocolate and almond roll) while the buzz is as strong as the coffee, although when it's empty some say this is slightly too cavernous a rendezvous spot on Cape Town's busiest street. There's ever-present lounge music but it doesn't really help to dull the roar of traffic that constantly sweeps up Long Street and forms part of the ongoing passing parade of pedestrians, office workers out for a smoke, and curious onlookers who can't help staring back at you through the vast picture window frontage. Like a chill-out lounge without sofas, this is a rock-solid place to recuperate before part two of a seri-

191

ous shopping spree – Long Street's Camden-style boutiques are moment's away, as are Heritage and Greenmarket squares.

Rhubarb Room *(left)*
142 Buitengracht Service Street, Bo-Kaap, City Bowl
Tel: 021 424 2004
www.rhubarbroom.co.za
Open: 9am–5pm (2pm Sat) Mon–Sat

Like being inside a daintily-gift-wrapped present, this is possibly one of the quietest, quaintest, slightly-hidden-from-public-view spaces, located on the edge of the city centre. There are bits and bobs of decorative detail throughout: it's basically a store packed with artisanal homeware items, soft, handmade toys, luxury soaps, and summery dresses and unique, slightly offbeat ladies' T-shirts – at times it's difficult to establish what's for sale and what's part of the homely, casual décor. There's a tiny chalked-up menu

of croissants, quiches, salads and a selection of healthy, moist muffins, meringues, and rich chocolate cupcakes on display in belljars. Jars of tea and a few old-school bottled sodas – ginger beer, and colourless cream soda. They claim there is 'a taste of Provence' but you're here to relax, not worry over the authenticity of the menu. Recline in the sofa or sip tea at one of three tables, or on the terrace, and watch life flow by at a gentle ebb.

River Café *(middle)*
Constantia Uitsig, Spaanschemat Road, Constantia, Winelands
Tel: 021 794 3010
www.constantia-uitsig.com
Open: daily, 8.30am–10pm

The least-hyped of three excellent eateries of the fabulous Constantia Uitsig estate (see Sleep and Eat), the River Café has always done fresh, seasonal, unpretentious fare, and is on course for greatness now that it's been taken un

derwing by Luke Dale-Roberts, hailed in 2009 at the country's top chef. He's appointed Scot Kirton to head up the kitchen here and together plan to transform this laidback and sociable gathering spot into the country's top bistro. It's a casual, country-style venue that's open all day (recently extended into evenings) and is extremely popular at lunch when well-to-do ladies pop in to share the latest gossip over selections from a daily-changing menu that includes asparagus and porcini, poached duck egg, and an excellent fish pie with smoked haddock and prawns. They've developed an organic garden and plan to introduce increasing quantities of their own produce, including meats and cheeses and salmon, whilst produce that's brought in is artisan-sourced and top-quality. There are also plans to build a smokehouse, with an organic, farmy sort of feeling.

Sandbar *(right)*
Victoria Road, Camps Bay

Tel: 021 438 8336
www.sandbar.co.za
Open: daily, 9.30am–late

A pretty, low-ceilinged box opening out onto the sidewalk with full-on views of the beach and Atlantic Ocean, this is a stalwart on the Camps Bay sunset strip. The ceiling is decorated with a web of white driftwood, strung with fairy lights that emulate a starlit sky. Mosaic tiles, green fabrics, and a wallpapered wall silhouetted with a green-tinged Camps Bay sunset is a strange juxtaposition to the authentic golden sunset that you will in all likelihood witness opposite, above the ocean. There's nothing at all impressive about the food, but this is one of Camps Bay's calmer time-pass venues, and a less-manic place to ease the transition between beachtime and cocktail hour, perhaps lining your stomach with a tapas platter or a large healthy salad, combining beef fillet and avocado or mango and smoked chicken. Or, if you simply

can't wait, there's a full wine list and stocked bar—as the Peroni branding (on the umbrellas and on the servers) attests.

***

Superette *(left)*
218 Albert Road, Woodstock, City Bowl
Tel: 021 802 5525
www.superette.co.za
Open: 8am–4pm (2pm Sat) Mon–Sat

As unpretentious haven of fun décor and delicious light meals, and part of a trend towards creating a seriously hip vibe on busy Albert Road in steadily-reviving Woodstock, this – an original corner store dating from 1902 – is the spunkiest addition to Cape Town's collection of irreverently cool daytime hangouts. The crowd is predictably of the university (mostly art school) graduate ilk, tending to hold long and meaningful conversations about profound and inane matters as they stare deeply into each other's eyes. The small kitchen (headed by a tattooed chef with dynamite credentials) opens into a small service area fronted by an old-fashioned bright yellow linoleum deli counter; place your orders here, selecting from the menu hastily scribbled onto the white tile wall, and then take a seat, or help yourself to drinks from the vintage fridge (stocked with drinks and beers). The fashionably grey space is dotted with clever, simple distractions – curious artworks, a set of shelves packed with artisanal food products, yellow flower pots, single bulb lights dangling from the ceiling, and a beautiful buffet table packed with tasty breakfast and lunch items. Enormous windows,allow diners to watch the scene outside, too.

***

Table Thirteen *(middle)*
Unit 78 Victoria Junction, Ebenezer Road, Green Point
Tel: 021 418 0739
Open: 8am–4pm (9pm Thurs; 2.30pm Sat) Mon–Sat

Rich coffee aromas fill this intimate

purple-accented dark-hued space attached to a beautiful homeware store (T&Co.; see Shop) in a currently undiscovered spot not far from De Waterkant. A motley collection of chairs, virtually none of them matching, are gathered around white marble-topped tables beneath an exposed industrial ceiling juxtaposed with flamboyant crystal chandeliers – a fine balance of baroque and bohemia. Feminine without being frilly, it reflects something of Laura's accidental restaurateur approach – she claims she tried hard to avoid the food business, but thanks to her mother, a culinary doyenne with two successful London eateries, cooking is in her blood. Which is good news for Capetonians. Slow-cooked and homestyle are the signatures here, with delicious comfort food served through the day (with one dinner session per week) – a small choice of just five or so exciting-sounding dishes, such as slow-roasted duck, or wild mushroom, gorgonzola and leek pie. Also likely to make you an instant returnee is the dessert buffet – don't miss the super-

chocolately espresso-and-macadamia-nut cake (which just happens to be wheat- and dairy-free).

....

Tokara DeliCatessen *(right)*
Helshoogte
Tel: 021 808 5950/1
www.tokara.co.za
Open: 9am–5pm Tues–Sun

A sublime setting on the beautiful Helshoogte mountain pass that links Stellenbosch and Franschhoek, Tokara is considered one of the region's finest wineries, and enjoyed a long-run of favour for the richly experimental dishes served up in its restaurant, with extraordinary views. But we think the best bet, more in touch with today's dining trends, is this all-day deli-style eatery facing the estate's vineyards and olive trees, beyond which lie the estate's exhilirating views. It's wholesome and healthy menu with a twist, dreamt up by a mother-and-daughter team who oversee a beautiful designer kitchen, captivating outdoor seating area and impeccable, ultra-contemporary indoor space, complete with underfloor heating and squishy Norman Mehl leather sofas to settle into. The design is crisp and clean-lined, signalling a revolution in the deli concept – no country barn this, rather a modern gallery with spectacular photographs of 'African delis' by local photographic genius Obie Oberholzer, along with a spectacular recycled plastic chandelier by Cape Town designer Heath Nash, and wall cabinets by James Madge. The deli produce – mostly organic, all-natural cheeses, hams, cakes, pastries and dairy – is worth the trip, too.

Truth. coffeecult *(left)*
1 Somerset Road, Green Point
Tel: 021 419 2945
www.truthcoffee.com
Open: 7am–6pm Mon–Fri, 8am–noon Sat

Despite the overt cheekiness of its branding – with plenty of hyperbolic allusions to coffee as religious experience – David Donde really is Cape Town's original coffee innovator: the entrepreneurial spirit who co-founded Origin, he also brought the international barista championships to South Africa and trained the two-consecutive-year winner. Conveniently located alongside the intersection of Cape Town's new walkway and bicycle route connecting the city with Green Point, this latest is a small, experimental project that aims to veer away from Vida and Origin's more clique-driven focus on lifestyle, with a modern, stripped down interior – part of the new Prestwich Memorial – featuring just a few prefab tables and chairs (specially designed by Cape Town's Biblioteq). The main focus is on the immaculately-packaged (all-white and glossy) coffee that David blends on-site, as well as his vintage, reconditioned Probat roasting machine, and brand new Jet-Stream espresso maker – apparently the world's most sophisticated coffee-extraction technology. To go with your cup of Donde's Chaos or the Resurrection Blend (strong enough, apparently, to resuscitate those who stupidly drank

the Kool Aid), there's a small selection of wraps, pita-style mini-burgers, and confectionary.

- -

Vida e Caffè *(right)*
Various locations throughout Cape Town, including Kloof Street, Camps Bay, V&A Waterfront, Green Point, and Stellenbosch
www.vidaecaffe.com
Opening times vary by store and by season

Most card-carrying Vida-loyalists will tell you that their branch of this high-octane coffee shop is the best in the country but we love Camps Bay (Victoria Road; Tel: 021 424 5829), predictably a huge draw with surfers and cyclists, and the original Vida, in Kloof Street (34 Kloof Street, Tel: 021 426 0627) – there's plentiful eye candy in both, with a motley collection of city-slicking vamps, media louts and undiscovered models. The Portuguese brand – which translates as 'coffee and life' – has only been a franchise operation in the past couple of years (the original owners now have their fingers in other pies, such as the beer emporium, ⋃ see Drink), but somehow manages to retain a sense of individuality in every outlet (featuring an all-male confident crew who bark out orders along with sassy flirtatious reparte). Food selection is limited by the croissants, pastries and muffins (the four-cheese Quattro is addictive) are perfect accompaniment to the rich coffee, served in eco-friend cups (made from potato skins and corn).

party...

Cape Town reached its clubbing heyday during the years leading up to the end of the last millennium. Full-on hard sweaty house dominated and you could find a major gathering headlined by a top-drawer international DJ just about every second weekend, with massive 'raves' taking over some of the largest available venues and converted warehouses. The following morning, the party continued in clubs that opened at dawn, catering to those of us who simply refused to go home or sleep. The question was not so much whether to go, as where.

Those were the days of Cape Town's drawn out love affair with ecstasy, and a bit of a longwinded comedown from what a few veterans still refer to, slightly tongue-in-cheek, as South Africa's very own prolonged 'Summer of Love'. We'd just abandoned Apartheid, and the sense of relief, combined with a sudden and furious connection with the outside world spawned a happy entanglement with dance music, DJ culture, dodgy nightclubs, and recreational chemicals. Many say that it was the all-consuming drug industry – escalated activity by underground cartels, and the prevalence of underaged teens in the clubs – that killed the party. On the other hand, Cape Town's club scene – although far tamer – has diversified, smartened up in some cases, and been subjected to increasing restraints from the law. Liquor sales now cease at legally-regimented times, and the only daytime dancing happens (mostly) outside the city limits at outdoor festivals and trance parties; the latter being the city's ultimate expression of hedonism.

A few hard-rocking dance clubs persist, but there's no denying a more mellowed energy and a tendency towards smaller dancefloors, meaning trance parties are just about the only space where you can dance yourself silly alongside literally thousands of other uninhibited revellers. Claiming to be no-holds-barred events, for true party animals the only problem these days is deciding which ones to attend – except for dedicated trance-heads, since they go to every party, existing in an acid-fuelled delirium. In terms of music quality and production values, the psytrance parties – with their mind-boggling LED screens, massive lighting rigs, and mind-blowing psychedelic décor – far outstrip anything that happens within the confines of even the best of the city's clubs these days. Certainly, the annual Rezonance Party thrown by collaborating psytrance organizers, Alien Safari and Vortex, is the single largest New Year's Eve event anywhere near the city.

If you've had your fill of trance, electro, house, and industrial drum 'n' bass, then it's time to consider one of our city's more unique musical offerings. Bucking trends and getting beyond the niche tendencies of the club world (which let's face it, can get pretty insular in a city the size of Cape Town), are a couple of bold anti-establishment parties which truly get our vote as the hippest gatherings in and around Cape Town. Definitely see if you can manage to be in town for one of the

party

kanology

quarterly Balkanology or Fiddle East events – they're mind-blowing, otherworldly multiple-genre parties that feel like a culmination of cleverly synthesized cultural moments whipped up by party-creator Ma'or Harris's desire to bring together different cultures in one big whopping ho-down. With narrative themes that help you decide what to wear and what accessories to bring, these are an amazing opportunity to combine a regular booty-shake with out and out fantasy. If for no other reason, check it out to experience the sensational sound of a DJ like To-by2Shoes, or the unique musical styling of the fabulous Kolo Novo Movie Band, or to see Ma'or himself spinning some unprecedented tunes straight out of the Balkans or Middle East.

Look out, too, for the sensational DJ collective, Fong Kong Bantu Sound System (www.myspace.com/fongkongbantu) which brings together some of the best-established underground DJs in the city. They perform at above-ground venues (like Zula Sound Bar), but also at community-centred venues and spaces off the beaten track (such as the All Nations Club, 281 Main Road, Salt River); well worth tracking down, if you're into alternatives; their sound surfs the genre wave from Afrobeats and Kwaito to Dub, Soul and Funk. Or, if you like your electronic beats silky smooth, clean, and even a touch experimental, line up at least one night in the company of Killer Robot, a DJ trilogy with regular appearances at Fiction, the city's foremost club purveyor of edgier urban dance music.

Cape Town is also considered Africa's gay capital – as much to do with tactical marketing as the agglomeration of fabulous spaces (natural and social) where those in pursuit of same-sex hedonism can hang out, hang free, hang loose, what-ever. The obvious places to head if it's a pink party you're after are Bronx/Navy-gaytion and Crew in Green Point, but queer parties happen from time to time at clubs around the city. Biggest of these – and beyond the scope of any one club - is the annual MCQP (Mother City Queer Project) party, a big camp themed fancy dress that attracts anyone and everyone who's up for a throbbingly fabu-ous bash. The straight hangers on and couldn't-care-less groupies are never far behind, either.

Naturally gregarious, Capetonians are a fickle, indecisive bunch, which can mean a night of cruising between venues, switching dancefloors, and vetoing DJs mid-set, or simply not pitching, having gotten caught up in the pre-party drinks session that's happened spontaneously at someone's home. As a result clubs open and shut with amazing frequency, with name changes or, bizarrely, same name but a complete turnaround in market position; do check before heading off what's hot and happening (though for the most part, we've opted to include those that have stood the test of time). Party-happy Cape Town is extremely well connected via Facebook, so you can keep your finger on the pulse by joining the pages of the venues and clubs that appeal to you, and follow their event line-up on the web.

Albert Hall *(right)*
206 Albert Road, Woodstock,
City Bowl
www.alberthall.co.za
Open: Whenever there's a show or party

A once downtrodden, derelict hovel has been transformed into one of Cape Town's most exciting venues: Albert Hall is one of the city's stand-out spaces for just about any kind of party or performance and has in no small way put Woodstock back on the map as a night-time destination, especially if you're into quirky, full-tilt events that pack out with the coolest crowd in town. The Hall celebrates the owner's love of antiques with smatterings of designer inventiveness. In a signature palette of black, white and red, everything echoes the obsession with left-of-centre nostalgia, from the antique Coca-Cola fridge in the entranceway to the vintage paintings and prints that decorate the walls alongside the long, narrow dancefloor-cum-auditorium. A small stage – more like a curtain – and speaker-bedecked raised area at one end of the hall is used by anyone from live artists, to DJs hosting underground parties, and top-rated comedy performers—this venue has no commit ment to any single event so there's a anything-goes, never-to-be-repeate approach. The downside can be atro ciously slow service at the bar, when i packs out (and there are two outdoo areas for the crowd to spill into, mean ing they let big numbers through th door) you may struggle to get near th counter.

Balkanology & *(right*
Fiddle East Parties
various venues around the City Bowl
Tel: 072 211 5563
www.balkanology.co.za
Parties happen every 3 months, more or less; join them on Facebook for regular updates.

omewhere between a gargantuan theatrical happening and a full-on concert, Balkanology – together with the smaller, but no less energetic, Fiddle Cast parties (sometimes at the aforementioned Albert Hall) – is the most hyperbolic and sensational one-night party to hit Cape Town since the fabulous annual MCQP events started in the 1990s. Taking as its cue Europe's vibrant underground Balkan party scene, Balkanology is a local collective from the imagination of Israeli-born Ma'or Harris (a self-styled, self-taught DJ who grew up on a farm and ended up in Cape Town studying sound engineering). Determined to stoke Cape Town's cultural scene, Ma'or gave it wings with his love of Balkan music (similar in feel to the sound of his homeland)

– not inherently 'cool', but the type of unhinged fun-inducing sound that stimulates uninhibited dancing a la Black Cat, White Cat – and brought DJs, artists, designers, musicians and actors together to create a kind of ritualized party happening. Wild extravaganzas brimming with atmosphere – not to mention farmyard animals, mountains of hay bales, re-enacted weddings, funerals and revolutions, belly dancers, tarot readers, performance artists, kick-ass bands, and unabashedly alternative tunes (think Serbian rave, traditional Hebrew party anthems, mad remixes of Gypsy electronica, and even Mediterranean melodies, jazzed-up folk rhythms and oompah bands) – offer the chance to party with Cape Town's hippest intelligentsia.

The Bang Bang Club *(left)*
70 Loop Street, City Centre
Tel: 021 426 2011
www.thebangbangclub.co.za
Open: 10pm–4am Wed–Sat

By contemporary club world standards, Bang Bang is a survivor, having proved its mettle by surviving threats of closure since before it even opened – and it's still pulling in the crowds. Once beyond the slightly combustible scene at the front door (where bouncers vary their tone from casual militancy to thuggishly imbecilic), the stairs lead you into a totally different world, accompanied by decorative designs and painted city-fantasy fake windows on the walls around the stairs. It's a world that's glamorous and – for a sweat-inducing club – surprisingly attractive. The interior shell of the heritage building is on display too, with original wooden ceiling beams and arched sash windows, but there's the post-industrial impact of exposed cooling ducts and an open mezzanine level where wood and leather booths help shield you from the pulsating state-of-the-art sound system that pumps ou beats downstairs. The wraparoun jungle-theme mural feels like a nod t the Seventies, although it's chandelie instead of mirror balls that conjure u unbridled fun. It's a provocative spac in which to strut your stuff to top loca and international DJs from a multiplic ity of genres; club owner Shaun Duve is Cape Town's best-loved house D but they fly in some big names, an even have a regular trance night (whe alternative décor is brought in).

Bronx/Navigaytion *(middle*
22 Somerset Road, cnr Somerset Rd and Napier St, Green Point
Tel: 021 419 9216
www.bronx.co.za,
www.navigaytion.co.za
Open: daily, 8pm–2am

Just about anything goes in this, Cap Town's longest-running gay bar, an al night sweaty mob of all persuasion. Since moving from its old base acros the street (where the new Cape Qua ter extension shopping complex no

tands), they've added plasma TVs (oddly, featuring unsexy animations), nd there's now a private men's only ar tucked in the back. What hasn't hanged, is the key location of the entral island bar, worked by brawny, sually bare-chested bartenders. While Bronx features some of the hammiest f commercial house tunes (from so-alled 'gay classics and remixes' on a Tuesday to anthems and vocal house n a Wednesday), it gets better as he week advances, with progressive racks on Thursday, disco on Friday, nd a mixed (hand)bag on Saturdays. t can all sound a little clumsy, trying to atisfy all tastes, but that doesn't stop he out and out madness from taking old as even the most uncoordinated unters dance and wobble in just about ny available space – although the bar ounter is strictly reserved for authen-ic go-go dancers. A stairway leads up o the more respectably club-like and ardcore Navigaytion, where the DJs nean serious business and the only ght is given off by pulsing lasers, eflected in the inevitable overhead nirror balls. If you're gay, or like to hang with a shamelessly cutting loose crowd, you daren't miss at least one night here.

....

Chrome *(right)*
6 Pepper Street, City Centre
Tel: 083 700 6078 / 9
www.chromect.com
Open: 9pm–4am Weds; 10pm–4am Fri/Sat

Somewhere at the end of that long, long queue, Chrome has been go-ing strong for years now, playing it safely within the realm of commercial house as well as hip-hop, R'n'B, and electro. Monumental drinks displays and a huge, industrially-proportioned dance arena are what make this place work and keep the crowd of (mostly) younger party animals queuing till late. If finding a bit of serenity amid the mayhem is important, pay for access to Platinum Privé, a dedicated VIP lounge which has a view of the main dance floor, while yet another VIP sec-tion caters to the champagne swilling high-rollers who need to have their

205

own DJ and dance floor, and don't like to get their own drinks. Although this is one venue in Cape Town where you might catch a classic house DJ, like Lisa Lashes, flown in for a special event, what makes Chrome a serious contender is that you might actually get a chance to witness the mayhem of a full-blown Kwaito party, exposing you to the sound of 'real' South African urban music culture, as preferred by sophisticated post-hip-hop groovers.

Club Chevelle (top)
84 Harrington Street, East City, City Centre
Tel: 021 461 8701 www.chevelle.co.za
Open: 10pm–4am Wed–Sat

Proclaiming itself the only real club in Cape Town is a bit of a stretch (particularly since Fiction and Bang Bang Club tend to be far more music-savvy), but the organizers do get in some wicked DJs and the crowd is an eye-pleasing mix of model types, dressed the part: Expect plenty of pretty blondes in push-up bras and short skirts, and boys in pointy shoes. It looks at least like they spent a lot of money on the décor, re-fashioning an old warehouse space into a multi-level labyrinth of well-groomed bars, lounges, VIP rooms, and one large well-equipped dancefloor, known as the Temple (which unfortunately doesn't open till very late). The look is sexy – a blend of industrial and Russian tearoom, with jet-black offset by flecks of gold and plush velvety fabrics making this feel very chichi and very svelte. Entertainment is eclectic, from trip-hop to commercial tracks; there's even a trance evening when the state-of-the-art sound equipment is truly put through its paces. Marketing hyperbole aside, the real drawback is that it's filled with snooty, poncey types who spend as much time queuing for the loos (and waiting, waiting, waiting for a drink) as they do pretending to enjoy themselves on the dancefloor.

Club Galaxy (bottom) /West End
College Road, Rylands,
Athlone, Southern Suburbs
Tel: 021 637 9132
www.superclubs.co.za
Open: 9pm–4am Thur; 5pm–4am Fri–Sat

Off the map in more ways than one, Galaxy (located in way off the tourist track Athlone) is Cape Town's oldest club, with three decades under its belt. Opened since 1993, sister club West End comes in second; no mean feat for a city that has seen so many groovy venues come and go. Galaxy is, predictably, completely commercial and mainstream, with all the theatrical lighting rigs, state-of-the-art sound technology and smoke machines you'd expect of an Old School superclub, but catering to a sassy, mixed crowd. West End, which is open from earlier in the evening, but only on Fridays and Saturday, is a live music venue (and no under 21s are allowed); chic, deep-red drapery, soft lighting and contemporary furniture sets the scene for that chance encounter with a beloved local or international artist – be they jazz or otherwise. In total there are enough bars here that you could spend the night ordering each round from a different location, and make hundreds of new friends as you do so.

Crew Bar _(top)_

30 Napier Street, Green Point
Tel: 021 418 0118 or 083 274 3579
www.crewbar.co.za
Open: daily, 7pm–2am

Yowzer! If there's one party venue that's threatening to usurp Bronx's long-standing position as Cape Town's number one gay club, then this is it. Just a short stumble down the road from Bronx, Crew functions on much the same formula, only it gets pumping much earlier these days, and scores major points for the quality of its bar staff (who are far friendlier and, since they avoid the roughneck sailor formula, a whole lot prettier than their beefier counterparts up the drag). Whereas Bronx tends to fill up with just about anyone who is capable of ordering a drink (although not always able to hold their liquor), Crew is defined by the overwhelming abundance of gorgeous men, be they twinks, muscle-bound hunks, or lithe models looking for a new spot to pose. To ensure that it's usually packed to capacity (which inevitably draws in even more fine young things), the managers keep the more recently launched, sleekly-styled upstairs lounge-bar, Madisons, closed until much later in the evening, meaning you'll spend a considerable portion of the night squeezed between a heaving mass of beautiful and brawny men. There's a dancefloor with rather commercial, sometimes downright cheesy house that gets the crowd into a fulltilt celebration just as soon as the first person dares to set foot on it.

Decodance _(bottom)_
Underground

The Old Biscuit Mill, 375 Albert (Lower Main) Road, Salt River
www.decodance.co.za
Open: 8.30pm–2am Wed; 8.30pm–4am Fri/Sat

Can you say cheese? Well, even if you're not a fan, it's worth knowing that Cape Town's quintessential Eighties' music venue really likes to turn Old School into cool. The vibe, crowd and music are eclectic and unified only by a desire to dance, flirt and drink to the accompaniment of familiar tunes that come straight from the Seventies Eighties and Nineties. The Cure finally collides with The Clash, and Michael Jackson is resuscitated for a much-applauded appearance alongside Duran Duran and Bonnie Tyler. There's quite a grungy sound, too, and some more rock-based music from those eras, so not always ideal if you're the type who prefers the smooth, even beats of the electronic age. The venue is a pretty cool place to hook up with free-spirited, open-minded individuals, since the whole idea here is to go against convention, not to mention the pretence and posing of most modern clubs. Even the location, at the seriously funky Old Biscuit Mill – where the Neighbourgoods Market (see Snack) is held each Saturday – has an alternative edge, and when you walk down the entrance stairway into the darkened, windowless cavern (so typical of Eighties clubs in South Africa), you'll feel as if you're stepped into a time-travel capsule.

Fez Club *(left)*
11 Mechau Street, City Centre
Tel: 0861 787 737
www.vaudeville.co.za
Open: 9pm–2am Tues–Sat

A fez-capped doorman greets you at the base of a stairway and then it's quickly up into an enormous Moroccan-themed lounge. Here, above the enormous Vaudeville supper theatre (see Culture), there's loads of room to dance and roam, or sit and chat – that's unless it's packed to capacity, in which case you'll be standing in that queue outside all night (have your concierge make special arrangements). Designed like an indoor *kasbah*, with billowing tented ceiling, Moroccan lights, mosaic bar counters, and cusped cornices, archways and columns, the Fez is actually a reinvention of its former self – a few years back this was the longest-running club in the city centre, and always a popular mid-week or Sunday night spot to schmooze or dance to mellower, slightly leftfield tunes. The crowd has definitely grown up – literally, since it's an older, more mature group that gathers here now – and most of the crowd has found its way here straight from the circus-style show that goes on downstairs (a natural progression, given Vaudeville's high-octane extravaganza formula).

Fiction DJ Bar & Lounge *(right)*

226 Long Street, City Centre
Tel: 021 424 5709 or 082 785 3760
www.fictionbar.com
Open: 10pm–4am Tues–Sat

Join the shiny, happy – and undeniably music-obsessed – people on Cape Town's hottest dance floor; this is one club which takes music seriously, providing the very best in experimental, underground and ground-breaking urban DJ-inventiveness. Wrapped around a thumping, postage stamp dance floor is a sexy montage panel depicting dozens of unearthly and otherworldy characters – all fictional B-grade movie heroes and villains, from Swamp Creature to Planet of the Apes. A disco ball spins overhead and on the walls, detailing from a lava projector or fine-tuned lazer beams dance like miniature universes. Elsewhere the fiction theme continues – with vintage movie posters as you ascend the Victorian stairs, a TV in one corner perpetually screening Manga cartoons, a South Park freeze frame on a dysfunctional television atop the bar fridge, a Pac Man ghost mosaic as you step out of the unisex bathroom, and a violent video arcade game next to the doors leading to the wraparound outside terrace overlooking Long Street. It has all the trappings of an interactive museum of

popular culture, but the real interaction is on the dance floor where you share space (squeezed in real tight, in fact) with a let-rip kind of crowd, getting off to music that is hypnotic and intoxicating.

![Hemisphere icon] **Hemisphere** *(left)*
31st Floor, ABSA Building,
2 Riebeeck Street, City Centre
Tel: 021 421 0581
www.hemisphere.org.za
Open: 10pm–late Thurs–Sat

If you want to dance with your head in the clouds, surrounded by a dressy, glamorous crowd, then this club, on the upper level of a downtown high-rise, will do you just fine. There's eye-candy aplenty – as well as plush, luxurious seating, Italian marble underfoot, handcrafted tiles and a fantastical space-age fibre optic chandelier above the glowing drinks displays behind the oval bar; but the best thing about this place is the view – the twinkle and glimmer of the cityscape at your feet is sublime; they even have drinks named for the experience – get high on a 31st Floor, followed by a Skyscraper. Aside from this, the music doesn't break any new ground. Thursdays sees a slightly younger crowd (anyone who's legal and properly dressed – no T-shirts, trainers, or sandals – can get in) and entertainment runs from hip-hop and R'n'B, to funk and house. But, on Friday and Saturday, you need to be over 23 (over 25 if you're a guy), and the sound is definitely commercial, often straight off the latest (if you're lucky) Top 40 list – when Justin Timberlake sings Sexy Back, here, though, the crowd takes him very seriously, so expect plenty of long legs in short skirts performing provocative movements. A strict door policy – enforced by a pair of toughs in black suits – means you need to make an effort when dressing.

House of Kink *(right)*
3 Park Road, Gardens, City Bowl
Tel: 021 424 0758 www.kink.co.za
Open: noon–6pm Mon; noon–2am Tues–Fri; 6pm–2am Sat

'Crazy shit happens here', is how owner Gia Pra-levis describes the eclectic mix of parties and events she organizes – exhibitions and post-exhibition parties; premieres of offbeat movies; student photography exhibits; an afternoon Mad Hatters Tea Party Market; tantric workshops (The Art of the Tongue); stand-up comedy; music video launches; swing bands; masquerade balls; James Bondage party; Studio 54 parties; and much more. What started out as an upmarket lingerie and sex shop has gone through a number of transformations, culminating in an off-kilter multi-sensory groove venue for drinking, dining, and partying. With any plans to be clandestine derailed by its instant popularity, this is one of the funkiest late night lounges in the city. House of Kink takes drama as its cue – it's not kinky because they sell lingerie and dildos, but because the vibe, the décor, and the experience are all designed to provoke a sensual response. And while things sound decidedly eccentric, one scan of the filthy cocktail list (laced with double entendres) reveals a total lack of pretence. It's a creative, classy mix of spectacle (yes, there might be a bit of burlesque, a video projection of photographic artworks and nudes, and an Edward Scissorhands garden), meant to encourage you to have fun. And, in the mix, too, there's non-commercial music – so expect to hear local DJ heroes (such as Adam Klein, one of Fiction's three Killer Robots) playing the sort of tunes that they want to play; on Saturday, you can listen to quality minimal and experimental, deep sounds.

Jade *(left)*

above Manos restaurant, 39 Main Road, entrance on Vesperdene Road, Green Point
Tel: 021 439 4108
www.jadelounge.co.za
Open: 8pm–2am Tues–Sat

Through a near-indiscernible hole in the wall on a side-street just off Green Point's Main Road, a stairway leads into an inviting space penetrated by a warm, golden glow, and a hot, pretty crowd. This is an unusually handsome venue bedecked, inevitably, by all kinds of fabulous people. They tend to be a little older in here, and there's a gentle sophistication at work, with everyone working to look and feel their best. Décor is slightly glitz-glam – drape yourself over one of the antique-style armchairs, pose seductively against the Oriental patterned wallpaper, and click your high heels across the chequer-board floors. There's no rule saying you should do any of this, but everything here's been designed to make you look like a million bucks as you strut your stuff amidst a pleasant, friendly crowd – that gets very large at weekends. The cushy lounges are arranged between the two bars, the handbag-sized dance-floor, and a partially enclosed terrace – all good spaces to watch the night unfold. DJs devote themselves almost exclusively to tunes of the commercial pop variety, with a bit of urban rhythm thrown in for good measure.

Karma Lounge *(right)*

Penthouse Suites, The Promenade, Victoria Road, Camps Bay
Tel: 021 438 7773
www.karmalounge.co.za
Open: 9pm (7pm Sun)–2am Wed–Sun

The hangout for celebrities (James Blunt, Jared Leto, Edward Furlong and Don Cheadle have all partied here recently) and models, it also works well for anyone wanting to dress like celebrities and models, move like them, and – ultimately – get wasted just like them. Once the sunset scene at Caprice (see Drink) has faded, and you're feeling decidedly friskier and in the mood for a classy jam on the dancefloor, this is the obvious next stop. Dom and Kristal flows all summer long, lubricating a crowd of elegant and scantily clad high-heelers and high-rollers that fill the large, well-dressed, straight-lined space. Lighting is subdued; the design elegant and well-meaning, as is the attitude at the door. On Sundays, you can expect to find a much, much younger crowd (Monday morning lectures being strictly optional); music is hard, pumping electro, and the dancefloor buzzes (on these nights the queue at the door can be preposterous, with six doorman to keep things under control). If you don't want to fight the crowds, you'd best pre-reserve a table, and then be sure to turn up and be prepared to pay for the privilege of instant entry, a place to sit, and guaranteed service. If you really want to see what's what, cough up the dough and make your way to the SKYY Bar, which is a slinky, white-design VIP section – if ever there were a team of rowdy party animals with deistic complexes, this is where you'll find them posing, strutting and getting down. Drinkswise, they stick to the basic cocktails, serve only premium brand spirits, including top-of-the-range tequilas (they sell more Patron than Jose here).

MCQP *(left)*
(Mother City Queer Project),
Cape Town
www.mcqp.co.za
Party happens one night in
mid-December

Steadily approaching it's 20th anniversary, MCQP is the biggest costume ball on the continent, with many die-hard fans and party animals ascending on the Mother City from all over the world just to be here. It's a gigantic celebration of queer identity and also a chance for anyone and everyone to get together for a night of unhinged fun, be it in spandex, sequined leather, or nothing more than a tassled cowboy hat. With at least three dancefloors,

some dynamite DJs (in multiple genres – from cheesy commercial house to harder electro and even some experimental sets ranging from minimal to tech house), and a crowd of seemingly possessed party bunnies, this is a huge event where inhibitions get tossed to the wind for one extraordinary night of dress-up fun. To prepare for the mayhem, a sprawling venue is dolled up for the event, and there are bars, food outlets, and all kinds of interesting people to bump, er, heads with. You're meant to team up with a group of friends, co-ordinate your outfits and prove that you've gone in the spirit of the theme's brief – be it disguising yourselves as a posse of Size Queens or coming as a bunch of Extra-Large Cucumbers, all

ets are off when it comes to choosing your costume for the night – just remember that you'll need to move in it, and dancing is essential, too. Dressing down, revealing as much flesh and as much bulge as you can muster is considered fine form, so feel free to unleash your inner exhibitionist.

....

Outdoor Trance Parties
various venues, typically within a 30–150km radius of downtown Cape Town

Alien Safari:
www.aliensafari.net
Vortex:
www.intothevortex.co.za

Origin:
http://originfestival.com

Prepare for an unapologetically hedonistic marathon music event, often in the most beautiful natural surrounds. With relentless, pounding beats churned out by the indisputable future-trend-setters of the local musicscape, the psytrance scene serves as a kind of tribal gathering for anyone who needs to let off steam, get wasted, dance like no-one is watching, dress up, dress down, undress, drink, trip, or simply observe the whole spectacular performance unfold before them like a phantasmagoria of psychaedelic excess. Depending on the size of the party, which varies according to who's

party...

organized the event (the best are listed above), there may be multiple dancefloors (the main stage is always dedicated to full-on psytrance where the music is fast, furious and trippy), firedancers, stiltwalkers, costumed clowns, and all kinds of shenanigans. There are usually non-stop bars (unless the cops show up) and the music doesn't let up until the final set has been played. If you're planning to attend the entire party, arrive early to find the best possible spot to pitch your tent; take as much food and drink and whatever as you think you'll need. If you're going for a shorter period, decide carefully what kind of party you prefer – nights tend to be harder and (no pun intended) darker, often with a more intense and unrelenting sound; the sunrise set is always brilliant and uplifting and likely to make you want to stay for the rest of the day. If you want a flawless set, look out for a line-up featuring the always-excellent veteran DJ Bruce – but for something extra-special, the most interesting local producer-DJ working in Cape Town today is Adam Metcalfe (aka "Headroom"), so look out for his sets, usually on a Sunday afternoon, although he tends to perform more internationally than locally these days. Whatever your poison, you're likely to find it here, somewhere, although you need to know that despite the overwhelmingly 'everything goes' atmosphere and strong neo-hippie sentiment, you do need to be discreet.

Live Music

The space between club and live music venue tends to be very fluid, with the transition between audience and participation an easy one, and many of the acts performing here encourage you to get involved, dance and mingle. A few of our favourite drinking venues, including & Union, The Waiting Room and Asoka (see Drink), are very pleasant spots where you can catch live shows, and during the busiest part of summer (December and January) you can usually catch Goldfish – South Africa's most successful electronic export (they've mixed the covermount disc for DJ Magazine, and played Ibiza, Miami, Moscow, Barcelona and more) – live at La Med (Tel: 021 438 5600, www. lamed.co.za), which is a lovely spot from which to witness a sunset, but is otherwise a bit of a meat market and heaving with a very young crowd. Or simply keep watch for a more appealing Goldfish performance by checking out www.goldfishlive.com – if you can don't miss their Sunday performance at the Kirstenbosch Summer Sunset Concerts.

Always up for an outdoor event, Cape Town these days plays host to all sorts of live music festivals, from the recently-resuscitated three-day Synergy Live (www.synergylive.co.za) to the Fynbos Music Festival (on the outskirts of Malmesbury), not to mention live bands worked in to otherwise DJ-driven music events such as the annual New Year's Eve Rezonance party (a three-day trance festival). And there are events farther afield, such as Up the Creek, a music festival lasting

a weekend in February on the banks of the Breede River near the town of Swellendam (www.upthecreek. co.za). But the best dedicated live music events have got to be Rocking the Daisies (for rock and other danceable rhythms) and The Cape Town International Jazz Festival, worth booking your dates around if you're a jazz fan. For a celebration of local music, specifically, try the Music van de Caab (The Cape Music Project) which happens over Sunday at Solms Delta wine estate in the Franschhoek Valley (Tel: 021 874 3937, www.solms-deta.co.za); there, on Saturday evenings, commencing at

the end of October, there's a sunset concert comprising local bands belting out some of the regional heritage sounds such as *vastrap*, *goema* and *boeremusiek*, not to mention alternative jazz and sounds that don't quite fit traditional genres at all; there's also an outdoor buffet of Cape food from Fyndraai restaurant (see Snack). If you're staying urban, there's Jazz at the Rainbow Room in the basement of Mandela Rhodes Place. Tickets to many of the top events are available through web tickets (www.webtickets. co.za)

The Assembly *(top)*
61 Harrington Street,
East City, City Centre
Tel: 021 465 7286
www.theassembly.co.za
Open: 11pm–4am Mon–Thurs;
11pm–close Fri–Sat

With the best sound and technical equipment of any live music club in the country, The Assembly is at the cutting edge of a pretty fierce and lively South African music scene; besides working hard to nurture new talent, they've pretty much catered for every single big band in the country, from Prime Circle, aKing, Fokofpolisiekar, Springbok Nude Girls, and Freshly Ground. Cutting edge South African bands and DJs are the staple here, and the crowd waivers between serious-minded fans to groovers looking for any excuse to party. The line-up can range from internationally-established live electronic innovators such as Goldfish, to world music events, and rock 'n' roll bands which are the real driving force of the club. The venue takes up to 850 people (previously 1,500, until noise restrictions kicked in), meaning it's a relatively intimate (if very large) space that just about always feels like a huge party. Friday nights have become Discothèque parties with a varied line-up of electronic DJs (playing anything from minimal and electro, to drum and bass, and trance). The space changes according to the requirements of whoever or whatever is playing, and there a few distractions for the pre-event warm up hours (football, video games) and loungey seating areas scattered through the vast revamped-industrial space. Tap into their website or join the Facebook group for regular (and pretty incessant) updates on forthcoming events; tickets are available at www.webtickets.co.za/assembly.

Cape Town *(bottom)*
International Jazz Festival,
Cape Town International Convention Centre, Heerengracht, Foreshore
Tel: 021 422 5651/3
www.capetownjazzfest.com
Usually the first weekend in April

Considered amongst the five best music festivals on the planet (ahead of Switzerland's Montreaux Festival and the North Sea Jazz Festival in the Netherlands), this is one event that lives up to its billing as 'Africa's Grandest Gathering' – the line-up of key international jazz musicians is small but stellar, and the commitment to sharing the schedule equally between African artists and performers from the rest of the world creates a magical cultural balance. Performances happen in and around the Cape Town International Convention Centre, where there are several indoor performance stages as well as outdoor arenas (the largest space caters to 3,500 spectators) where the atmosphere is more geared towards partying. Since its inception in 2000, the festival has virtually doubled in size, attracting over 33,000 spectator and revellers in 2009. You can purchase either a day ticket, or for a few extra rand, get entry for both days. There's also a free concert, enabling the community to check out a sampling of acts, usually in Greenmarket Square on the Thursday before the main festival kicks off.

The Hidden Cellar *(left)*
above De Akker, Dorp Street
Stellenbosch, Winelands
Tel: 021 883 3512

Tucked into the loft space above De Akker Stellenbosch's oldest licensed pub, where generations of students have gathered for beer, mellow vibes and long-winded conversations – The Hidden Cellar is a legend in its own right. The creaky wooden boards have seen some of the country's top musicians break into the limelight under the watchful gaze of students who tread the fine tightrope of being both artfully intellectual and finger-on-the-pulse cool. There's a full bar, a little stage, and now even a sound system to match the quality of the performances. There's a good chance that the bands playing here will be Afrikaans, but that shouldn't prevent you from having a good time; the locals love to wax lyrical about the ins and outs of the scene and will gladly share their knowledge,

opinions and, often, a personal introduction to the 'star' on stage.

Kirstenbosch *(middle)*
Summer Sunset Concerts
Constansia
Tel: 021 799 8782/3
www.oldmutual.co.za/music
Open: Every Sunday 5.30–6.30pm between late November and early April

Rather than letting the Sunday blues get to them, Capetonians inevitably wind down their weekends with another party – truly, in this town, the week can wait. And the most appealing place to bid the weekend goodbye is at this series of concerts, lined up throughout the main summer season and celebrating not only some excellent bands-of-today, but also paying tribute to the setting sun and the great outdoors. The staging is ingenious, in fact, occupying a naturally inclined lawn at Kirstenbosch Gardens (see Cul-

ture), this open-air auditorium ensures fresh air, and a majestic backdrop that's as thrilling (or more so) as the gigs on stage. You can arrive as early in the day as you want with a picnic basket and as much wine as you require (there are no bins in Kirstenbosch, so you're responsible for taking away your own litter), although you can also purchase eats and drinks at one of the venues at the Gardens. The series of increasingly hip concerts includes such great local outfits as Freshly Ground, Goldfish, Fokofpolsiekar (translates as Fuck Off Police Car), and Dirty Skirts, all major bands that range in genre from danceable electronica (Goldfish) to intelligent rock (there's poetry in the lyrics of Dirty Skirts).

 Mercury   *(right)*
Live Lounge
43 De Villiers Street,
Zonnebloem, City Bowl
Tel: 021 465 2106

www.mercuryl.co.za
Open: 8pm–4am Mon, Wed–Sat

Some would call it a dive (like so many great rock venues), but this slightly frayed-around-the-edges venue is still considered one of the serious performance spaces for live acts in South Africa, and extremely popular, especially if you're into rock, a genre that has shown a surprising growth in popularity in recent years. Students flood in here for the drinks specials (especially on the provocatively titled Manic Mondays) but the crowd varies depending on who's playing, or what the buzz on the ground has been. During the week, the smaller downstairs venue may host outfits still getting their first taste of the limelight. At weekends, you're likely to find more established local names bringing down the house, and there's a very serious drum 'n' bass night on the first Saturday of the month – it's called Homegrown and is the country's most successful event of its kind. Thrown into the mix during the week, are cool cat DJs who prefer Old School and retro vinyl tracks to the electronic stuff that's the mainstay of most of the city's clubs today.

Rocking the Daisies *(top)*

Cloof Wine Estate, Darling
Tel: 021 481 1832
www.rockingthedaisies.com
Festival happens for three days in October

The hippest live music festival in the Western Cape, Rocking the Daisies is a three-day musical celebration which for most involves setting up camp and diving head first into an all-day party that brings together the country's top (primarily) rock bands performing back-to-back on the main stage. The line-up (kicking off mid-morning) might include a few solo small-time cult figures, followed by a succession of bands that range from up-and-coming to chart-topping; you will get the full spectrum of South Africa's coolest and most respected music entertainers, although there's not much by way of 'black music'. The crowd tends to be a very pleasant (and sociable) mix from youngsters to veterans. Beside the live music, there's an electronic tent for dance music junkies that gets absolutely thumping with a committed crowd of hardcore clubbers who can't take too much 'real' music on the main stage; mixing it up with anything from reimagined disco and psychaedelic soul to hard-as-nails electro and genre-bending hypnotic beats that range from minimal to dubstep and everywhere in between, the party here typically goes on till about 3am. And, for a more relaxed time between bouncing up and down on the dance floor, there's a multi-genre performance festival going on as well, with everything from dance entertainments to stand-up comedy. If the idea of pitching a tent puts you off, either organize accommodation in the nearby town of Darling well in advance, or book a space in the mobile tented hotel, Kreef Hotel (literally Crayfish Hotel, www.kreefhotel.co.za) where you'll be assured of a better night's sleep than most (if sleeping is at all on your agenda); ask for the 'Caviar' option, which includes stretchers, a bedside 'wardrobe', a light, and even room service. Food stalls cater for essentials, and there's a market where you can shop for all kinds of arbitrary paraphernalia.

Zula Sound Bar & Restaurant *(bottom)*

196 Long Street, City Centre
Tel: 021 424 2442 www.zulabar.co.za
Opening times vary, but daily till late

Zula is an incredibly relaxed and welcoming space, where anyone is admitted and there's no concern about what you look like, what you're wearing or who you know. The crowd is studenty, but really gets down and appreciates whatever's been staged for them, whether it's an evening of rock, ska, funky African rhythms, experimental jazz, or even performance poetry with a bit of bite; some of the country's top bands (including Freshly Ground, Bed on Bricks, and 340ml) have performed here, although most of those bands have now moved on to much bigger performance spaces Zula remains inti-

mate and low-key. When things get too packed inside, head for the Victorian-era terrace overlooking the bustle of Long Street; you'll still be able to hear the band but won't necessarily sweat quite so much. The crowd is generally of the ultra-mellow variety, making it feel like you've walked into a room full of future-hippies, but there will be a fair number of anti-establishment trend-setters here too. Monday evenings is a stand-up comedy night, and Tuesday kicks off with an acoustic session before the main act. Zula is also a venue for occasional performances by the DJ collective, Fong Kong Bantu Sound System, definitely worth experiencing at least once.

Adult Entertainment

During the Apartheid era adult clubs with erotic dancing and a non-mainstream sexual agenda were banned under a tight censorial authority. This does not mean that there wasn't plenty of hanky-panky going on underneath the proverbial table – just that social suppression and moral high-mindedness made adult venues extremely underground (another term for 'dangerous'). With democracy came a swift opening of the floodgates as the 'smut' and 'filth' the moral guardians so feared finally poured onto the market. The dust has now settled, and there are a selection of clubs and venues to cater for specific tastes and interests, and while some South Africans may still harbour deeply entrenched anxieties about these places, it doesn't necessarily prevent them from checking them out while others frequent them with dedicated regularity.

Fetish Clubs

Bar Code
18 Cobern Street,
Green Point Green Point,
Tel: 021 421 5305
www.leatherbar.co.za
Open: 10pm–2am Sun–Thurs,
10pm–4am Fri–Sat
(reduced hours in winter)

Frisky gay men looking for grown-up action will undoubtedly find it in Cape Town's one and only venue with a men-only fetish vibe. This is Cape Town's version of a serious Tom of Finland hangout, complete with hanky code and 'naked pork' parties on a regular basis (Mondays, Thursday and Saturdays). If you're into leather, uniforms, jeans, or nothing but tight-fitting underwear, this men only 'leather, uniform and jeans' fetish bar will scrub you up the right way; there's a tight dress code (explained with pictures on the website), pertaining mostly to what you may not wear (you're welcome to disrobe on the way in). There are dark rooms, slings, cruising areas, and on-going hardcore video screenings. If you're looking for a more casual place to build up the courage before hitting Bar Code, start with drinks at the Amsterdam Action Bar (Tel: 083 626 4615, www.amsterdambar.co.za), a few doors down. Proclaiming itself the 'friendliest gay bar' in the city, with absolutely no rules and no pretences, it's ideal if you prefer to come as you are rather than dressing up (or down) to fit in. It's also a likely hangout for leather, rubber or hairy-chest fetishists, and if you have any predilections of the studded belt variety, this is probably where you'll find a mate to drag along to Bar Code.

Strip Clubs

House of Rasputin
56 New Market Street,
City Centre
Tel: 021 461 2262
www.rasputin.co.za
Open: 7pm(1pm Fri)–4am
Mon–Thurs & Sat

A good-looking club with a svelte interior of leather, wood, curtained table booths, pretty chandeliers and even prettier dancers – the space is designed to look as decadent as the experience. Most of the ladies are either South African, or from Russia and Eastern Europe (which explains the exotic-sounding name), and the décor is meant to feel a bit fantastical, too, luring you into a sense of a more opulent era. You can either keep an eye on the main stage or order a private dance, in which case the curtains around your table will be drawn.

Mavericks
68 Barrack Street, City Centre
Tel: 021 461 9988
www.mavericks.co.za
Open: 7pm–4am Mon–Thu;
1pm–4am, 7pm–4am Sat

Compared to Rasputin's overt emphasis on imported sensuality, this strip club is like tried and tested commercial pop music. Running since 2001, Mavericks is the most popular place in the city to eyeball pole-dancers, have svelte ladies dance on your table or on your lap, and even settle in for an informal chat, or conversation. Leather armchairs on the ground level mean you can relax comfortably while watching events on two dance floors. Then, there are two VIP lounges, with plush velvety drapes, private booths and an overt sense of exclusivity, with the Platinum lounge going for opulence with its cage-style stage, and more private rooms for lap dancing. There's a properly stocked bar, and women are welcome, too.

Teazers
7 Raglan Road, Belville
Tel: 021 948 7924
www.teazers.co.za
Open: 7pm–late Tues and Sat;
12.30pm–late Wed–Fri

Part of a Johannesburg-based chain, this venue apparently used to only get full when South Africa won a rugby match and the drunken, celebrating *manne* (men) got together for some celebratory (or consolation) fun. Things have been tempered with time and experience and Teazers now pulls a regular crowd of punters who like its unpretentious atmosphere: this is one strip club that isn't pretending to be something it's not. No under 21s are admitted, there's a reasonable dress code, and a reasonable display of erotic dance talents in the main arena and the private lapdance rooms.

culture…

You'd be forgiven for assuming that a city at the southernmost tip of Africa might be thin on culture, but you'd be wrong. While its reputation is predominantly built on its beguiling natural beauty, one can't discount the many historic monuments and cultural diversions that vie for the visitor's attention.

That said, there's no escaping the sheer dominance of Mother Nature. You will be captivated by the city's most alluring landmark, Table Mountain, as much by default – since it dominates the cityscape no matter which way you look at it – as by sheer compulsion. Once the preserve of leopard and lion, the flat-topped chunk of rock is part of a chain of craggy mountain peaks that stretches inland and south into the peninsula, a spinal ridge that culminates in Cape Point, that dramatic thrust of sharp, rocky headland on which the Old Lighthouse (1860) perches, the cliffs below ever-pounded by the Atlantic (www.capepoint.co.za). It's a journey no visitor should miss, as much to explore the Cape Point Nature Reserve as for the delightful drive along coast-hugging roads, with plenty of pit stops along the way, including Walking with Baboons near Kommetjie, or swimming with the jackass penguins at Boulders, just outside the naval village of Simons Town.

Though things are slowly changing, visitors to Cape Town and the Winelands are often struck, this being Africa, by how predominantly white everyone is. The reason for this is partly geographic – the vast majority of black Capetonians

live some distance from the city centre, far from the playgrounds of the Atlantic Seaboard. Few white South Africans make the effort to explore the black suburbs (known colloquially as 'townships'), which is a shame, because life here may not have the gilt-edge opulence of Cape Town's mainstream experiences, but it is far from lacking a pulse. The best way to explore this is with visionary outfit Coffeebeans Routes who offer arguably the most authentic way to see how the other half lives, breathes, and parties – taking you on what Time magazine called 'a cultural treasure hunt'. It may also be your only chance to catch Cape Town's uniquely local music, Goema, named for the Goema drum, originally made by slaves from wine barrels. Likened by some to the Samba in Brazil, the Goema beat and rhythm derives from the cultural integration of Indonesian and Angolan slaves, Portuguese sailors, Dutch colonists, migrants from other parts of Africa and the indigenous, including Xhosa-speaking people from the Eastern Cape.

Annexed by the Dutch in 1652, Cape Town's early culture was in fact dominated by slaves – most of whom came from other parts of Africa and Indian Ocean countries – who outnumbered Europeans by a vast number. These imports had significant influence, not only on music and cuisine, but on the developing language – the earliest written Afrikaans, later to become a symbol of Apartheid oppression, was scribed in Bo-Kaap, and the Cape Malay influence is symbolically represented in the Afrikaans Language Monument, a phallic sculpture that will interest modernists, located just outside Paarl in the Winelands.

December 1838 saw the emancipation of around 38,000 slaves, but social and geographic segregation remained, finally gearing up in the 1960s, when a series of forced removals in the East side of the city displaced 60,000 Capetonians of mixed race and black descent. District Six – considered the creative hub of Cape Town at the time; now an open wasteland at the edge of the city centre – was to become concrete symbol of Apartheid's great evil and the experiences of the people who once lived there are captured in the District Six Museum in the East City. While the museum is edifying, to get a real sense of what was lost, visit the only pocket that escaped Apartheid's bulldozers – the Cape Malay quarter of Bo-Kaap, sprawling up the lower slopes of Signal Hill. Here, rows of houses – many of these painted in bright, eye-catching colours – stand side-by-side with numerous mosques, including some of the oldest Muslim houses of prayer in the country.

Certainly your experiences amid the city's living history will leave you with a sharper understanding of the city's unique dynamic than a visit to over-hyped Robben Island. A place of incarceration and suffering for many South Africans – of which Nelson Mandela was merely the most famous – this World Heritage Site has sadly become a bit of an embarrassment, with a conveyor-belt attitude to mass tourism, poorly maintained infrastructure and ongoing allegations of corruption (despite huge numbers of visitors, the Island struggles to make a profit). If, however, you simply cannot resist (and the moment spent at Mandela's cell – now whitewashed – cannot fail to move), book your place early (it's a real cattle market, usually sold out days, sometimes weeks, in advance; Tel: 021 409 5100, www.robben-island.org.za).

A more vivid account of the city's history is provided by Garth Angus on his Footsteps to Freedom Walking Trail (Tel: 021 465 2032 or 083 452 1112, www.footstepstofreedom.co.za), a tour covering one square mile. Alternatively, set your own pace, starting with the Castle of Good Hope, the oldest building in Southern Africa, then strolling down Adderley Street, the city's oldest thoroughfare, to Church Square — an open space near Parliament where eleven black granite blocks memorialize the shameful legacy of slavery. It was in this square, under the branches of the Slave Tree (removed in 1916), that slaves were auctioned, after which their new master or mistress could attend a service in the adjacent church. Diagonally opposite Church Square, the Slave Lodge (Tel: 021 460 8242, www.iziko.org.za/slavelodge) is today a cultural history museum, sometimes housing excellent temporary exhibitions. It also marks the edge of the city's oasis, the Company's Gardens – what started out as the vegetable patch to supply the Dutch East India Company ships in the 17th century is today Cape Town's very own Central Park, a gorgeous green lung where many of the city's museums are situated, of which the National Gallery, home to the country's premier art collection, should not be missed.

In fact Cape Town has always been a magnet for artists – the light is believed to be especially good, and our natural surrounds a balm for the creative spirit. As such the city – and even outlying towns and villages – has some fabulous galleries showcasing the very best in contemporary South African art. Best among these are the Michael Stevenson Gallery (www.michaelstevenson.com), the Everard Read Gallery (www.everard-read-capetown.co.za), Goodman Gallery (www.goodmangallerycape.com), Erdmann Contemporary (www.erdmanncontemporary.co.za), Joào Ferreira Gallery (www.joaoferreiragallery.com), Blank Projects (www.blankprojects.com), YoungBlackman (www.youngblackman69.com), and the award-winning Whatiftheworld / Gallery in Woodstock (www.whatiftheworld.com).

Inevitably, many of the city's public artworks make direct reference to Apartheid, often providing provocative commentary: from the top end of St George's Mall, take a stroll up Victoria Street and look for the two benches outside the High Court Civil Annex. One is branded "NON-WHITES ONLY" and the other "WHITES ONLY" – both form part of an artwork entitled 'Race Classification Board', referring to the institution that classified South African society into different race groups based on skin colour and hair texture, dividing not just communities but families in the process.

But thankfully Cape Town is slowly shedding the claustrophobia of its dark history, with cutting-edge commentary and world-class performances, from the YouTube phenomena Die Antwoord (The Answer; www.dieantwoord.com), the self-styled 'zef' (redneck), funny, audacious rap rave crew that took the YouTube world by storm early 2010, to the opening of The Fugard, theatrical home to the acclaimed award-winning production company Isango Portobello. Then there's the ever-delightful and amusing Pieter Dirk Uys, aka Evita Bezuidenhout, the continent's most famous drag artist. Uys' famous Evita se Perron Theatre/Restaurant is in Darling, a small town not too far from the city (www.evita.co.za); if you are here during September, make every effort to attend his Voorkamerfest, in which the inhabitants of Darling open their living rooms to local and international performers who enthrall small audiences in a sell-out weekend of music, drama and comedy (www.voorkamerfest-darling.co.za). Finally, if it's a younger shape-shifting South African diva you want to see, make a point of tracking down Odidi Mfenyana, sometimes to be seen in one-off performances at queer-friendly spaces such as Beefcakes and Lazari (see Snack). To find out where the camp Odidi is strutting her stuff next (she occasionally takes shows such as 'House of the Holy Afro' abroad), you can call her (Tel: 072 342 0513) or follow her Facebook profile.

If history, art and theatre leave you cold, there is, of course, the fabulous culture surrounding wine … Offering huge variety in flavours, jaw-dropping views and superb dining opportunities (see Eat), the Winelands also offers perhaps the city's most fabulous architecture – from gracious Cape Dutch gabling to contemporary glass boxes, winetasting is a feast in every sense.

231

Bo-Kaap *(left)*
lower slopes of Signal Hill,
City Bowl
Museum Tel: 021 481 3939
www.iziko.org.za/bokaap
Museum Open: 10am–5pm Mon–Sat

With its deeply mottled cobblestone streets and vividly coloured houses, Bo-Kaap (literally 'Above Cape') is historically where Cape Town's former slaves settled following their emancipation by the British. Once known as the Malay Quarter (though it is thought that only 25% came from Indonesia, Bali and other southeast Asian islands), this was also where a number of political exiles, Muslim pioneers and holy saints established the earliest mosques in the Cape – the oldest of these is the Auwal Masjid, built in 1795. It's believed that this

mosque is where Afrikaans was first taught, and it's a little known fact that Afrikaans – frequently referred to as a form of 'kitchen Dutch', used to communicate with the slaves – was first written in Arabic script here. Auwal is one of 13 mosques squeezed between the rows of Georgian and Cape Dutch houses, so the chances of hearing the call to prayer during a visit here are fairly good, and on Fridays you may even witness some of the local men praying outside one of the mosques, on the street. Although there's a dedicated Bo-Kaap Museum, you need hardly step inside to appreciate this special community – the neighbourhood, bustling with life and energy, is sufficiently intriguing. In recent years, along with slow gentrification that's begun to creep in, there are also a number of 'outsiders' and foreigners who have moved in, establishing this as a desirable neighbourhood with excellent proximity to the city centre. For a unique insight into the Bo-Kaap area, you could sign up for a Cape Malay Cooking Safari (Tel: 021 790 2592, www.andulela.com), an experiential tour of the Malay Quarter which culminates in an interactive cooking lesson where you spend time in the home of a local family, assist with the preparation of a meal, and then sit down with them to enjoy the fruits of your labours. It's fun, totally engaging, and a cut above the average tourist experience.

▓ Boulders *(bottom)*
▓ Penguin Colony
Boulders Beach, Kleintuin Road,
off the M4, Simons Town,
Southern Peninsula
Tel: 021 786 2329
www.tmnp.co.za
Open: 7am–7.30pm daily (Dec–Jan), 8am–6.30pm daily (Feb–Mar), 8am–5pm daily (Apr–Sept), 8am–6.30pm daily (Oct–Nov)

Among the quirkiest of Cape Town's 'cultural' experiences, you'll hear these inimitable little fellows before you see them, their delightful donkey-like braying having spawned their alternative moniker – jackass penguins. Authorities have built boardwalks amid the dunes at the edge of Foxy Beach, so visitors can walk among the knee-high birds without disturbing them. The penguins, many of their rituals very human-like, are surprisingly entertaining – it's not unlike watching a kind of delightful, tuxedoed soap opera. The penguins have been expanding their numbers here since 1985, having

grown from just two breeding pairs to over 3,000 birds, and while human intervention has helped preserve the integrity of the environment, this remains a natural habitat for these creatures. It's possible to swim at nearby Boulders or Seaforth beaches, with the good chance of the penguins joining you in the False Bay waters, mercifully a little warmer than the sea at Clifton or Camps Bay.

....

Castle of Good Hope *(left)*
cnr Strand and
Buitenkant streets,
City Centre
Tel: 021 787 1249
www.castleofgoodhope.co.za
Open: daily, 9am–4pm

Moat? Check. Spooky dungeons? Check. Five defensive bastions? Check. But if you're looking for a European-style castle, you will be disappointed. The only royals who've spent any

meaningful amount of time here have been Cetshwayo, the last king of an independent Zulu nation, who was imprisoned here, and then again, during the 2002 MCQP costume ball (see Party), when thousands of the city's campest queens assembled here for one of the city's most memorable parties. For many years the administrative headquarters of the Cape colony and the epicentre of its social and military existence, it was never attacked, so there are no signs of cannon fire or damage, other than through neglect. Built between 1666 and 1679 (the entrance – built of small yellow bricks known as *ijselstene* – is a unique Cape Town example of 17th-century classical Dutch architecture), the Castle's defensive outer perimeter was clearly designed to last and served as lookouts points for potential invaders – hard to believe but the pentagonal construction was once right on the seafront, a barrier against the ocean before the

existing Foreshore area was claimed from the sea during the 1930s. The Castle is today rather poorly managed and maintained, but there are guided tours everyday (11am, noon and 2pm) except Sunday if you really want to learn about the structure and its history, as well as visit the dungeons and torture chambers – but come simply to get yet another perspective on the city, with spectacular views of Table Mountain and much of the city that spills down her slopes. Get as high up as you can – as you circumambulate the upper bastions, you'll spot the 1905 façade of the old City Hall, the domelike bulk of the Good Hope Centre, and the soaring edifice that constitutes the seat of contemporary Cape Town's local government. Incidentally, between the Castle and City Hall, the open area (used as the major Fan Park during the FIFA World Cup in June/July 2010) is the Grand Parade, one of the city's important historical squares,

where Nelson Mandela greeted his jubilant countrymen a few hours after his release.

....

Coffeebeans Routes *(right)*
70 Wale Street, City Centre
Tel: 021 424 3572
www.coffeebeansroutes.com
Tours happen according to varying schedules

There are around 400 tour operators in Cape Town, so no shortage of experts and pseudos eager to show you around the city. But if you prefer to dig deeper and get under the skin a bit, Coffeebeans is the way to go. What started as a slightly clandestine operation taking visitors into unknown territory, this small, savvy organization has quickly evolved into one that's earned accolades from visitors from around the world for its unique and inventive tours that explore diverse and exciting

aspects of our local culture; like other tour companies, they do versions of the highly recommended Township Tour, but have elevated this to the Township Futures tour which reveals how people living in some of the city's poorest areas (what might be called slums elsewhere) are working to carve out a positive future for themselves and their communities. Their journeys aim to take you into untouristy places where you'll meet locals – they're great levellers, in fact, that work on the premise that while it's easy to get into a restaurant, it's another story altogether visiting a family from a totally different walk of life, meeting them in their home and literally breaking bread with them. Most popular are the Cape Town Jazz Safari and the Storytelling Route, both of which are enchantingly interactive, as is the Soccer Route (where you get to play football with some local lads) and the Rootz Reggae Route in which you discover the broad spectrum of reggae-related musical influences; not only that, but you get to bop for a while alongside members of the Marcus Garvey Rastafarian community at the Friday night Reggae Dance Hall in Philippi, just outside Cape Town. And there's a new tour covering the Cape's scientific innovations, proving that the city is more than just a pretty face.

◼ The Company's Gardens & the Parliament of South Africa *(left)*

Government Avenue and Queen Victoria Street, Gardens, City Bowl
Gardens Tel: 021 400 2521
Parliament Tel: 021 403 2266
www.parliament.gov.za
Gardens are open 7am–7pm (summer) and 7am–6pm (winter)
Parliament tours: 10am and noon Mon–Fri, by advance booking only

Foraging squirrels, office workers playing hooky, lovers curled up in each other's arms, tourists aghast at the homeless sleeping off a fearful hangover, fountains, sculpted memorials, fish

...onds, an aviary, and a mix of wonder-
...ully jungly, overgrown foliage, tailored
...awns, ancient trees and styled flower
...eds – the Company's Gardens are the
...emains of the original fresh produce
...arden planted here in the 1650s by
...he Dutch East India Company when
...his was a victualling station for pass-
...ng ships. At the 'city' end of the gar-
...ens are the darkened stone walls of
...t George's Cathedral (www.stgeorg-
...scathedral.com); the foundation stone
...still visible as you enter the gardens
...om the top of Adderley Street) was
...aid by the Duke of Cornwall and York
...who went on to become King George
...) in 1901, this was more recently
...he home turf of the country's most
...elightful cleric, Archbishop Emeritus
...esmond Tutu. At the 'upper' end of
...he gardens stands the city's planetari-
...m and natural history museum, which
...adly remains Victorian in conception
...nd execution. Fringing the Gardens
...long their eastern border are the Par-
...amentary buildings, visible through
...hick metal railing, along with De

Tuynhuys (literally 'the garden house',
where the official gardener once had
his hut, but is now a palatial house
where the State President entertains
formal guests), and the South African
National Gallery, a repository of some
of the country's greatest artworks. Access to Parliament – with a chance to
witness this astonishing democracy in
action (or inaction, if the sometimes-
sleeping MPs are anything to go by)
– is by free, pre-arranged tour (Tel: 021
403 3341); entry (bring your passport)
is on the far side of the buildings, on
Plein Street.

District Six Museum *(right)*
25A Buitenkant Street,
City Centre
Tel: 021 466 7200
www.districtsix.co.za
Open: 9am–2pm Mon; 9am–4pm
Tues–Sat; Sun by appointment only

One of the most heartbreaking and
shameful events in Cape Town's living

memory is the whole-scale destruction of the once vibrant creative-hub known as District Six. Declared a "Whites Only" neighbourhood in 1966, bulldozers moved in and displaced around 60,000 people – almost one-tenth of the city's population – mostly coloured people (Cape Muslims), but also other non-whites considered undesirable by the racist regime were instantly ghettoized and relocated to the distant, near-uninhabitable plains at the far outer reaches of the city, known appropriately as the Cape Flats (where, today, communal strife, gangsterism, and poverty persist). In deference to this shameful act, no one was prepared to build on the land (other than the government-funded Cape Technikon) and it remains to this day a vast virtually untouched barren wasteland. This museum, near the outskirts of District Six, not only memorializes the eradication of this community, but also celebrates the people who once lived

there. Always a multicultural and inter-denominational area, District Six was home to Portuguese, Dutch, English and French settlers, and the population included descendants from slaves who were brought here from the Caribbean, Mozambique, Malaysia, Madagascar and Indonesia; there were also many Jews from Lithuania and Latvia, and Xhosas from the Eastern Cape. The museum deals critically and intensively with District Six as a microcosm of the programme of social engineering that was going on throughout the country – this was just one of 42 areas where people were 'relocated'. It's an interactive museum, using photographs, documents and oral history, where people come and tell their stories, providing very personal insight and first-hand understanding of how Apartheid afflicted ordinary people.

....

Franschhoek   *(left)*
Motor Museum

L'Ormarins Wine Estate,
Groot Drakenstein Road (R45),
Franschhoek, Winelands
Tel: 021 874 9000 www.fmm.co.za
Open: 10am–4pm Tues–Fri; 10am–
3pm Sat–Sun

With well over 220 vehicles, ranging
from the pre-fin de siècle Beeston mo-
torized tricycle, and culminating with a
Ferrari Enzo, a supercar built in 2003,
this is the private vintage car collection of billionaire Johann Rupert and,
for anyone interested in the triumphs
of modern man over the last 100 years
or so, an eye-opening and exciting way
to spend at least an hour. Guided tours
happen during the week, but at weekends you can explore the museum on
your own, which means you lose out
on the storytelling, but get to spend as
long as you like ogling the technology.
There are all manner of notable, exotic, and even bizarre vehicles spanning
the antique, veteran, vintage and post-
vintage periods: One of the more in-

triguing specimens is an indigenous car
known as the Protea Protea, manufactured in 1957 – only 20 were produced
and although it could reach 136kmph,
turned out to be financially unviable.
Only 80 cars can be displayed at any
given time and the exhibition, which
occupies four massive de-humidified
halls, is rotated periodically.

Groot Constantia *(right)*
Homestead and Wine Museum
Groot Constantia Estate,
Groot Constantia Road, Constantia
Tel: 021 794 5128
www.grootconstantia.co.za
Open: daily, 10am–5pm

It may be a touch touristy, but this really is the mother of all South African
wine estates, where Simon van der Stel
(then governor of the Cape) planted our
first vines, establishing the oldest wine
industry outside Europe and the Mediterranean. Van der Stel had named the

Stel had named the enormous estate (groot means large) after his daughter Constancia, and some of the wines produced here have gone on to strike accord with several illustrious Europeans, including Napoleon, who took a fancy to the 'Vin de Constance' during his exile years. Over the centuries, of course, the estate was parcelled off and pieces of it have gone on to become wine farms in their own right, each with their own Cape Dutch homestead. Besides partaking of the fare at either of the two restaurants, picnicking on the manicured lawns, or strolling the oak-lined avenues, you can take a walk through the original manor house, packed with Cape Dutch furniture, tour the antique wine cellar, and studiously follow the estate's history in the small wine museum, where there's considerable focus on the role played by slaves in the agricultural output of early wine-farming here at the Cape. N.B. The wines you can taste are very good, but winelovers should not miss an opportunity to sample the wines at nearby Klein Constantia which are generally superior (this is also where Vin de Constance is made) as well as those at Eagles Nest, also in Constantia.

....

Irma Stern Museum *(top)*
Cecil Road, Rosebank,
Southern Suburbs
Tel: 021 685 5686
www.irmastern.co.za
Open: 10am–5pm Tues–Sat

This intimate little art gallery allows visitors to share in the passion of the artist whose works are collected here in the home where she lived for four decades. Irma Stern (1894–1966) achieved international recognition during her lifetime but was initially maligned in her own country, with one early critic panning her work as part of a 'cult of ugliness'. Today she's revered as a major South African artist and the museum was established posthumously under the auspices of the University of Cape Town in 1971. The curators have maintained several rooms just as Stern would have kept them (upstairs rooms are used for temporary exhibitions-for-sale by contemporary artists) and everywhere you look there is evidence of her desire to create, comment, and respond to the world around her. A relentless artist who typically completed each work in a single sitting, under the influence of nicotine and caffeine, she worked in a variety of media – not only on canvas, but also through sculpture and ceramics – and her work covers a gamut of themes, from portraits of African tribal women to landscapes. The museum also shows off her fascinating collection of artefacts – from tribal masks to Buddhist art, Coptic weavings, and other religious art. And, in her studio, apparently untouched since her death, are Stern's palettes, paint-box and brushes, as well the personal displays she chose to surround herself with in her working environment.

....

Kirstenbosch *(bottom)*
National Botanical Garden
Rhodes Drive, Newlands, 13km from the city centre, Southern Suburbs
Tel: 021 799 8899
www.sanbi.org
Open: daily, 8am–7pm (6pm Apr–Aug)

Considered one of the seven most magnificent gardens on earth, Kirstenbosch is draped against more than 500 hectares of Table Mountain's eastern slopes – an extraordinarily green wonderland designed to blend imperceptibly with the fynbos-clad mountain. With the noted exception of the almond hedge (planted by Jan van Riebeeck in 1660 to indicate the 'border' of his colony and protect his animal stock from the indigenous Khoi people), some magnificent oaks, and the Moreton Bay fig and camphor trees planted by Cecil John Rhodes, everything you encounter is indigenous. It'd be impossible to get to grips with even a fraction of the 9,000 or so species that grow here (many of them endemic, i.e. growing nowhere else on earth) but there are guided tours and audio guides that will at least give you an introduction to the Cape Floral Kingdom, the world's smallest and richest. You can seek out the fragrance garden, elevated for easier access to the scents; a pelargonium *kopje* (hill); a protea garden; a sculpture garden; and a section with plants used for *muti* (medicine) by *sangomas* (traditional African healers). Or you can join in with the locals who come to laze on the lawns, their children exploring the burbling brooks, and simply luxuriate in the setting – the perfect antidote to a rough night on the town. There are a couple restaurants, and probably the funkiest time to visit is during the weekly Summer Sunset Concerts (see Party, Live Music) that draw massive audiences to the green lawns every Sunday evening.

....

Rhodes Memorial   *(left)*

Groote Schuur Estate, above UCT on the slopes of Devil's Peak, Rondebosch, Southern Suburbs
Restaurant Tel: 021 689 9151/2
www.rhodesmemorial.co.za

Built in 1912, the view from this mock Athenian temple shows a Cape Town that doesn't usually make it onto the visitor's itinerary, stretching beyond the airport and the Cape Flats to the

distant Helderberg and Hottentots Holland Mountains. Prime minister of the Cape Colony between 1890 and 1896, Rhodes was not only a hardcore imperialist (British 'Cape to Cairo' was his dream) but Cape Town's most powerful homosexual, having made a tremendous impact on the city and the continent. The monument, built from public contributions, acknowledges his triumphs on behalf the British Empire (making no mention of the suffering caused by his rapacious mining concerns). Designed by Sir Francis Macey and Sir Herbert Baker, the monument, with its doric columns and a stairway of 49 steps (one for each year of Rhodes's life), is flanked – in imitation of the Avenue of Sphinxes in Karnak – by eight cast lions modelled on those surrounding Nelson's Column on Trafalgar Square. At the base of the steps is an equestrian statue with a rearing horse saddled by 'Energy', a rider who appears to be shielding his eyes from the glare of the sun – symbol of Rhodes's boundless determination perhaps; above, overlooking all, is the bust of Rhodes, with an inscription composed by Rudyard Kipling, a dear friend. His home, Groote Schuur, was a short horse ride away and the stately mansion is now the official Cape Town residence of the President; Groote Schuur also gave its name to the country's most famous hospital, also nearby, where Christiaan Barnard performed the world's first heart transplant. Finish up, or start, your visit to the Memorial with a light, dependable meal at the tearoom-style restaurant (which enjoys similarly astonishing views), and then set off on a hiking excursion along one of the paths that start here and lead up or around Table Mountain.

....

Rupert Museum *(right)*
Stellentia Avenue, Stellenbosch, Winelands
Tel: 021 888 3344
www.rupertmuseum.org
Open: 9.30am–1pm, 2–4pm Mon–Fri; 10am–1pm Sat

An enviable collection of around 350

pieces, this is the country's finest anthology of South African art produced from 1940 to 1970. The personal collection of Anton and Huberte Rupert, it showcases many their favourite artists, including Irma Stern (see earlier), Maggie Laubser, Jean Welz, and the sculptor Anton van Wouw. It's a straightforward gallery, with clean, pared down exhibition areas in big barnlike wings and few frills – nothing is allowed to detract from what's on display. Some think it's a tad bland, and there's certainly nothing to excite the contemporary art lover but there's clearly been a conscious decision by the owners (who have money to burn) to avoid any hype; simple notes on wall panels provide artist background, but for most of your exploration, you're on your own to simply figure out which artists you like and immerse yourself in artworks, some of which will move you in inexplicable ways.

South African National Gallery *(top)*

Government Avenue, Company's Gardens, Gardens, City Bowl
Tel: 021 467 4660
www.iziko.org.za/sang
Open: 10am–5pm Tues–Sun

Although there are over 8,000 artworks within its collection – including examples of South Africa's specialized indigenous crafts – this small gallery is physically limited and able to display only a small portion at any given time. Funded with a single bequest in 1872, the government-owned gallery has had to tread carefully due to financial restraints, but is still the finest repository of South African art. While the collection of Dutch and English oil paintings in the Sir Abe Bailey Collection – with English country hunting scenes and dark landscapes in the Italian-French tradition – may strike you as irrelevant, recent acquisitions have focused on contemporary South African art, including work that went unnoticed or was renounced during the Apartheid era, often because of its subject matter or because of the colour of the skin of the artists. Look out for works by such internationally renowned names such as William Kentridge, David Goldblatt, Gerard Sekoto, Jane Alexander, Willie Bester, Jackson Hlungwane, Jacob Hendrik Pierneef (known for his landscapes), Irma Stern, and numerous others. The gallery hosts regular cutting edge exhibitions that combine national and international artists, often with formidable guest curators from the upper echelons of the contemporary South African art scene – as the Dada South? and Picasso in Africa exhibitions attest to.

Taal Monument *(bottom)*

Paarl Mountain,
just outside Paarl, Winelands
Tel: 021 872 3441
www.taalmonument.co.za
Open: daily, 8am–8pm (5pm May–Aug)

A source of controversy and admiration, the Afrikaans Language Monument, overlooking South Africa's third-oldest town, appears to suggest some eternal skyward thrusting, signalling perhaps the immense aspirations of the cultural movement it symbolizes or perhaps a religious ambition, linking this world with heaven. Though

Afrikaans is a hybrid language drawing on Dutch, English, French, Malay, German and multiple indigenous languages, it has been stigmitized as the language of the oppressor, and strongly associated with Apartheid policies, especially those designed to establish Afrikaans as the dominant mode of education (which triggered the Soweto riots in 1976, widely thought to have been the beginning of the end of Apartheid). Nevertheless, it's easily forgotten that Afrikaans is also spoken widely by non-White communities, and is the official language of the Cape Coloureds (as the local mixed race group is referred to), who form the majority of the city's population. The precise symbolism of this 1975 monument – designed by Jan van Wijk in 1975 – is pretty convoluted (and explained on-site), but in essence the futuristic-looking structure pays homage to all of Afrikanerdom's cultural roots (with the main 57-metre column representing Afrikaans itself). There's not all that much to see or do here, but the views are spectacular. Full moon picnic events are held from December through March,

when all the lights are switched off and the glowing disc in the heavens above becomes part of a thoroughly surreal spectacle.

Table Mountain *(left)*
Tafelberg Road, Higgovale, City Bowl
Tel: 021 424 8181
www.tmnp.co.za
Aerial Cable Car Open: 8.30am–7.30/8.30pm (season and weather dependent)

A diva with multiple personalities, her sorcery affects the weather, swinging the mood of a city that can be wet and miserable one instant; sunny the next. And when her tablecloth of thick white clouds flows down her 250 million-year-old table top like a living boa, it signals the arrival of the infamous Southeaster, and the entire city groans. To some, the mountain is an ancient custodian, Umlindiwengizimu – the watcher of the south – placed here by the creator, Qamata, to watch over the entire continent. Rising from the shoreline, Cape Town's ancient inhabitants

– the Khoekhoen and San – called it Hoerikwaggo, the 'mountain in the sea', and it is acknowledged as one of the world's oldest mountains, having withstood six million years of erosion. Rising to just over 1km above sea level, its iconic table top dominates the landscape, and is visible from at least 150km out to sea. Climb aboard the aerial cable car – operating since 1929, it was upgraded 70 years later to enable 65 passengers travelling in a revolving glass bottomed gondola to reaches the summit in roughly five minutes – for an invigorating journey with epic views all the way, before arriving in what feels like another universe, a flat-topped mountain wilderness. The vistas of the city and the Atlantic Ocean spreading out far beneath your feet are matchless, while closer to your feet you'll spot furry dassies (or rock hyraxes – surprisingly, they're related to elephants) and agama lizards ducking amongst the rocks. If you're feeling more energetic – or keen to view the mountain's floral kingdom (with over 1,470 species to call its own; more than are found in the entire United Kingdom), it is a relatively easy climb up, with a few hundred trails on, up, or around, to choose from (see Play), making it the world's most hiked mountain.

....

Walking with Baboons *(right)* Baboon Matters, 3 Cruiser Close, Sun Valley, Southern Peninsula Tel: 021 785 7493 or 084 413 9482 www.baboonmatters.org.za Walks are conducted twice daily Monday through Saturday, and once a day on Sunday

Spending time amidst the baboons, appreciating them in their own environment without fear, is not unlike the famed gorilla interactions in the rainforests of Rwanda, and is perhaps the most invigorating wildlife experience in Cape Town. Surviving against great odds in an environment that's been heavily encroached upon by human development, the Chacma baboons of the Cape Peninsula have had to adapt to changing conditions at lightning speed, and today there are around 350 baboons squashed into the Peninsula's wilderness areas. These remaining primates get plenty of bad press, given that they have come to see humans as a source of easy food, and are remarkably adept at accessing vehicles, bins, handbags and homes in the suburbs of the southern peninsula. There are many advocates for the forced removal – even eradication – of these hapless creatures, but Jenni Trethowan is avowedly not one of them. With the launch of Baboon Matters, she has facilitated a rare opportunity for humans to get to know these fascinating creatures, so similar to us, yet completely primal. This is not a zoo or a sanctuary, but a visit that takes place in the wilderness at the edge of an urban environment. For most of the time, which flies by, you'll see these animals fighting, swimming, mating, playing, grooming, minding their young, and performing high-wire acts as if you're not present. However, they're not oblivious, and some take a keen interest in observing the observer, displaying a very human curiosity and may even touch you (you could suddenly find an adolescent male examining your toes!)

Entertainment

Artscape
DF Malan Street,
Foreshore, City Bowl
Tel: 021 410 9800
www.artscape.co.za

The brutal Apartheid-era architecture of the city's main theatre complex conceals some of it's best-equipped spaces (there's considerable competition from the 5,000-seater Grand Arena at the Grand West Casino, but that's hardly a space for any sort of genuine cultural endeavour), which in turn makes this the obvious destination for international quality musicals (most of Lloyd Webber's blockbusters have been staged here) as well as a of number of large scale homegrown productions. Besides it's main 1,500-seat Opera space (completely refurbished in 2009), the building shelters a decent mid-sized theatre where most local dramas and smaller musicals are staged, as well as the tucked-away Arena Theatre, often showcasing the country's best cutting-edge, experimental performances.

The Baxter Theatre
Main Road,
Rondebosch, Southern Suburbs
Tel: 021 685 7880
www.baxter.co.za

Part of the campus of the University of Cape Town (UCT), this ostensibly anti-apartheid theatre was designed in the Seventies by renowned Cape Town architect, Jack Barnett; opened in 1977, it's considered an iconic architectural landmark, a facebrick block informed by the Arts and Craft Movement and inspired by the early-Twentieth Century National Romantic Movement in Scandinavia. Cascading down three floors, the main entrance staircase deposits you in a vast foyer while high above are the theatre's distinctive orange fibreglass dome-lights. The Baxter strives to stage a dynamic and far-reaching programme, from Shakespeare to classical music to serious political theatre. The main theatre seats 666 people, and there's a large concert hall and smaller studio theatre upstairs. The theatre bar is where performers gather after all major productions, so the place for a late-night drink if you're keen to mingle with thespians.

The Fugard
Caledon Street,
District Six, East City, City Bowl
Tel: 021 461 4554
www.thefugard.com

Launching in 2010 with a season that includes The Train Driver, a Fugard world premiere, the West-End hit The Mysteries, and an Olivier Award-winning production of The Magic Flute, this looks set to become the new spiritual home of meaningful theatre in South Africa – an ideal tribute to Fugard, our greatest playwright. Housed in District Six's Sacks Futeran building – a textile and soft goods supplier in the early twentieth century – the theatre comprises two refurbished warehouse spaces and part of an old Gothic-style church. It's the brainchild of the acclaimed Isango Portobello production company: the world's largest black theatre company, and has earned an international reputation in artsy circles for its film U-Carmen eKhayelitsha, which won the 2005 Berlin Film Festival's Golden Bear Award, as well as its multi-award-winning The Magic Flute which ironically enough won far more critical acclaim in London's West End than it did at its 2007 premier at the Baxter.

Infecting the City
around the City Centre
www.infecting thecity.com
Festival happens annually in late-February

Curated by agent provocateur Brett Bailey, one of the most innovative minds to come out of Cape Town's theatre scene, the city's most exciting arts festival takes place over a one-week period, when a series of specially commissioned collaborative performances are staged in and around the public spaces of the inner city. Every year the shows, performed by a mix of local and international thespians, tackle a socially-relevant and potentially combustible theme designed to get people out on the streets and caught up in productions that are challenging without necessarily being overly highbrow. The result is often sensational. Some of the productions in the past (and this is a very young festival) have included mind-blowing spectacles such as seeing human actors dancing with mechanical forklifts, and witnessing a human effigy going up in smoke at the bottom end of Adderley Street. Join audiences on the sidewalks, in public squares and newly discovered spaces, and prepare for some unique insights into local culture. The programme, along with a map indicating the site of each performance, is found on the festival's website.

Kalk Bay Theatre
52 Main Road, Kalk Bay,
Southern Peninsula
Tel: 073 220 5430

www.kbt.co.za

Built as a church in 1876 this remains a hugely atmospheric venue – perhaps the most charming performance space in Cape Town – all white on the outside (although now with a few upbeat neon strips to lure potential audiences) and pure vintage antique on the inside. Cushioned beech wood reproduction Morris chairs edge onto a polished wooden thrust stage, no bigger than a modest-sized lounge, making this an exceptionally intimate space, seating fewer than 80 people in three raked tiers. Overlooking the auditorium is a gallery with tables and chairs for patrons of the theatre's fab little café-bar (with a proper menu). Performances are a mixed bag, but occasional gems make a visit truly worthwhile.

Labia

68 Orange Street,
Gardens, City Bowl
Tel: 021 424 5927
www.labia.co.za

Opened as a live theatre venue in 1949 by Princess Labia, this remains the oldest surviving independent cinema in the country, with four screens in the former ballroom of the Italian Embassy, located in the armpit of the bend at the top of Orange Street (practically next door to the Mount Nelson hotel). It is a true original, where the popcorn still smells the way popcorn did before the days of faux spicing, and you can purchase a glass of wine to wash it down with. The programme is a mix of new releases and festival fare, and while there are

occasionally some downright commercial products, the general tendency is for the more interesting titles to appear here. The sprinkling of tables in the outside terrace makes for a sociable pre- or post-film haunt, and the cinema benefits from a liquor licence and a bar and sweets counter operated by one or two of Cape Town's genuine old souls. (Note that the secondary Labia, in Kloof Street's Lifestyle Centre, has none of this old-style romance.)

Maynardville Open-Air Theatre

cnr Wolfe and Church streets,
Wynberg, Southern Suburbs
Tel: 021 421 7694
www.maynardville.co.za
Performances: Jan–Feb

A perennial favourite on the Cape Town summer entertainment calendar, Maynardville Park first hosted a performance of The Taming of the Shrew in the mid-1950s; since then the outdoor 'Shakespeare in the Park' has become an annual fixture, and draws large crowds (averaging around 20,000 each year) to witness an annual reinvention of one of the Bard's plays, often treated with a uniquely South African timbre. Each year a different local director is charged with breathing new life into an old favourite, and the cast typically includes a range of performers, from top-drawer stars to emerging student actors. Bring your own picnic (put together at Melissa's; see Snack), or order a hamper from The Picnic Company (Tel: 021 706 8470), and enjoy a glass of bubbly in the beautifully shaded grounds before this much-cherished Cape Town institution.

The New Space Theatre

44 Long Street, City Centre
Tel: 021 422 5522
www.newspacetheatre.co.za

One of South Africa's most famous (and infamous) theatre spaces, the original Space – founded by Brian Astbury and his actress wife, Yvonne Bryceland in 1976 – was heretically non-racial, which made it a target for ongoing harassment by the then Apartheid government, which banned many plays and even famously placed the theatre 'under house arrest'. Opening with Athol Fugard's 'Statements After an Arrest under the Immorality Act', the groundbreaking anti-establishment theatre saw almost 300 productions on its boards, including numerous premieres of some of the country's most astonishing theatre. Launched at the end of 2008, The New Space pays homage to this heyday with old posters on the walls, but the line-up of cabarets, musicals, revues and tribute shows appear to be more about gaining a younger audience than herding holy cows. Now with two separate performance spaces, this is a great venue if you value pre- and post-performance aperitifs: downstairs is Boo Radleys, while Daddy Cool and others are a minute's stroll away (see Drink).

On Broadway

88 Shortmarket Street,
City Centre
Tel: 021 424 1194
www.onbroadway.co.za

Feeling rather hidden away and suspiciously anonymous, On Broadway was for many years the most popular and prominent evening escape in Green Point's Pink Quarter. Today, in its inner-city locale, it remains a bastion of cabaret, cross-dressing divas, and light, frothy entertainments that work very well with the hearty meals and a full bar service that turns a night here into full blown rollicking fun. If men who look astonishingly good as women are in any way your cup of tea, don't miss the legendary Mince duo, Kieron Legacy and Lilly Slaptsilli, who regularly grace the boards with their sassy strutting, vocal miming, and lightning-quick costume-changes.

Oude Libertas Amphitheatre

Oude Libertas Centre, cnr Adam Tas and Oude Libertas roads, Stellenbosch, Winelands
Tel: 021 809 7473
www.oudelibertas.co.za
Performances: Nov–Mar

Providing a beautiful setting for high-quality entertainment under the stars, this is a lovely venue surrounded by oak trees and set on one of Stellenbosch's oldest wine estate, where it's possible to enjoy a picnic prior to your show. Launched in 1977, this open air stage – in design inspired by Spanish and Grecian outdoor amphitheatres – hosts a programme that is primarily sophisticated music, including international chamber choir recitals, respected local singer-songwriters, acapella groups, jazz and opera, but also has its moments of dance and serious drama. Since it's entirely outdoors, most shows happen during the summer season that commences late November and ends in March.

The Pink Flamingo

The Grand Daddy Airstream Trailer Park, 38 Long Street, City Centre
Tel: 021 424 7247
www.pinkflamingo.co.za
Screenings on Thursday and Sunday evening commencing around 7.30pm

It's Old School bioscope revived on the rooftop of the über-cool Grand Daddy hotel, stashed between the Airstream trailers that make up the city's most unusual lodging space (see Sleep). On Thursday and Sunday evenings, around 30-odd seats (including two leather sofas) are laid out facing a screen onto which classics, cult hits, and slightly off-beat old favourites are projected in front of an audience of Capetonians looking for a night under the stars and entertainment with a difference. Everyone gets a paper cone of candy sweets, and there's a non-stop supply of popcorn, as well as a free drink from the rooftop bar (which may get a little rowdy, even while the movie is playing). As with movie screenings of old, they even play a short cartoon (of the Looney Tunes ilk) to get you in the mood. Tickets tend to sell out, so go online to check out the schedule and secure your place (preferably a front-row sofa).

Theatre on the Bay

1a Link Street, Camps Bay, Atlantic Seaboard
Tel: 021 438 3300/1
www.theatreonthebay.co.za

One of the biggest names in South African theatre, Pieter Toerien is well-known as an astute and serious businessman, having produced the local versions of some of the world's biggest musicals, including most of Andrew Lloyd-Webber productions, several of which he has toured internationally. He also owns his own stand-alone theatre here in Cape Town, the aptly-named and flamboyant Theatre on the Bay; be sure to catch the sunset before taking your seats. It's a wonderfully intimate space where you'll very likely meet artists at the bar after the show, and is well located if you want to head out to any number of bars along the sunset strip afterwards. Although Toerien has staged the likes of Joseph and the Amazing Technicolour Dream Coat and Hair in this theatre, it's more often the domain of smaller dramas, comedies, and revues, with plenty of cabaret and stand-up comedy, too.

Vaudeville

11 Mechau Street, City Centre
Tel: 0861 787 737
www.vaudeville.co.za
Performances: Tues–Sat, seating by 7.45pm

Inspired by circus, burlesque, and some seriously naughty cabaret, this is Cape Town's most energetic live show, featuring svelte B-boys, lithe acro-adagio dancers, pink feather boas, platinum blonde wigs and lots of sweaty, toned muscles displaying raw talent. It's a multi-sensory experience, with risqué show tunes, and a fusion band playing an edgy Balkan gypsy-meets-beerhall sound, while bits of high-wire theatrics, rope-work, clowning, pole-dancing, and displays of pure athleticism keep your eyes popping. A megalithic old boat warehouse has been transformed into a magnificent baroque brothel, complete with cotton wool clouds, red velvet curtains, opera-style balconies, men in tights, one penguin on acid, and a five-breasted woman dancing through the sky, psychedelic video projections, jugglers, muscle men, and surreal characters sauntering about on stilts. Grab drinks at the bar before settling in at your table (the more expensive ringside seats and booths affords better views) where a set dinner is served through the evening. After the show, swing yourself up the steps to The Fez, an updated version of one of Cape Town's old favourites (see Party).

Wine Tasting

Cape viniculture, by European standards, is a fledgling industry (although, at 350 years, it's the second-oldest outside Europe and the Mediterranean), but in recent years it has grown in leaps and bounds, and is one of the region's huge successes, having reinvented itself significantly since the mid-1990s.

When South Africa became a democracy in 1994, some 250 Cape cellars were producing wine and less than 50 million litres was being exported; by 2008 this had increased to almost 600 cellars and export figures had risen to 400 million litres. This figure represents more than half the country's wine since we are not yet a nation of fully-committed wine drinkers (in 2008, South Africans consumed an average of only 7.34 litres of wine each, compared with 53.9 litres by the French). Recent years has seen the Winelands gearing up to high levels thanks to a wave of reinvestment, particularly by high-roll-

ers eager to have their fingers in what is a very sexy business. From retired Springbok rugby players and champion golfers (Ernie Els produces some of the finest, and priciest, wines in the Stellenbosch wine region), to hedge fund and entrepreneurial billionaires, owning an award-winning wine estate is clearly as sexy as owning a champion race horse used to be.

Well-organised and increasingly setting new trends worthy of international attention, facilities for experiencing wine in situ have thus broadened enormously, and while you can still enjoy an intimate tasting with the winemaker in his own cellar, you're more like to find yourself in a state-of-the-art tasting room surrounded by designer furniture and priceless artworks, fabulous architecture and breathtaking views. And these days, almost every estate boasts its own dining experience, each one more brilliant than the last. Wine-tasting may offer a cultural insight that's designed to provoke the tastebuds, but you can easily find yourself caught up in an all-round sensory adventure – and what better comfort on your return home than to find a few boxes of interesting vintages waiting for you (most farms will do this for you with almost no fuss at all).

Generally recognised as the premiere wine region in the country, Stellenbosch is also the biggest, with 157 wineries, and known for the excellence of its terroir. While here, do try pinotage, South Africa's very own varietal (a cross between the Pinot Noir and Cinsault); known for its barista character and either praised or sneered at for its chocolatey and coffee flavours, Pinotage is believed to achieve its apotheosis at Kanonkop (Tel: 021 884 4656, www.kanonkop.co.za), an estate on the lower slopes of Stellenbosch's Simonsberg Mountain; also here is the beautiful Muratie estate, a favorite as much for its wines as for its atmosphere. With a relatively benign climate the Cape's premier wine region attracts much comparison with Bordeaux, and some of its premier wines certainly back up such comparisons – venture towards Stellenbosch's Warwick estate (Tel: 021 884 4410, www.warwickwine.com) to sample the celebrated Trilogy ('07), a sublime blend of Cabernet Sauvignon, Merlot and Cabernet Franc. Or try the stable of red cultivars (and an excellent Shiraz-Cabernet Sauvignon blend) at Rust en Vrede (Tel: 021 881 3881, www.rustenvrede.com), an estate dating back to 1694, and well-known as a favourite of former president Nelson Mandela.

Others well worth earmarking, all gorgeous estates producing mind-blowing wines, are: Meerlust (Rubicon being probably the Cape's most iconic wine), Waterford, De Trafford, Vriesenhof, Rustenberg, Grangehurst, Le Riche and Plaisir de Merle – and that's just our top selection in Stellenbosch!

With so much to choose from, it's difficult to know where to start. You could start by chatting to a sommelier, who may point you towards some hidden gems, or purchase the John Platter Wine Guide, annually updated, and work your way through the 5-stars, or just pick up a couple of wine route maps and venture forth, turning off whenever you spy a "WINE TASTING" sign on the side of the road.

Better still, particularly (but not exclusively) if you love your wine, is to book a tour with a specialist (this automatically also takes care of the driving!). Former Chairman of the Wine Tasters Guild of South Africa and current leader of the Cape Town Slow Food Convivium, Stephen Flesch offers exceptional tailormade tours – tell him your varietal or regional preference, or leave it up to him; either way he will come up with a personalised itinerary that will cover a widest possible tasting experiences, topped with a luncheon at one of the best restaurants in the Winelands (Tel: 021 705 4317; www.gourmetwinetours.co.za). Alternatively, Racontours (Tel: 021 794 6561; www.racontours.co.za) offer pretty decent wine estate and cellar tours.

Finally, for anyone harbouring fears or potential pretentions when it comes to embarking on a wine-tasting expedition: There are no rules when it comes to wine-tasting. Except that the driver should spit. And whatever you do, don't plan on visiting too many estates in a single excursion – 4 or 5 is the max we recommend.

Boekenhoutskloof *(left)*
Excelsior Road, Franschhoek,
Winelands
Tel: 021 876 3320
www.boekenhoutskloof.co.za
Open for tasting: 9am–5pm Mon–Fri

In the most far-flung corner of the
Franschhoek Valley, this historic estate is named for the Cape beech tree
(boekenhout), which was used extensively in the production of Cape furniture. Most of the vintages available for
tasting are from the midlevel Porcupine
Ridge range, but every tasting includes
a few swigs of The Chocolate Block, a
famed red notable for its distinctively
chocolatey flavour, and one cultivar
from the more exclusive (and in all other respects, sold-out) Boekenhoutkloof
Collection. The delightfully laid-back
unpretentious setting and warmth of
the tasting experience makes this a
particularly memorable outing.

Cape Point Vineyards *(middle)*
Noordhoek,
Southern Peninsula
Tel: 021 789 0900
www.capepointvineyards.co.za
Open for tasting: 9am–5pm Mon–Fri;
10am–5pm Sat; 10am–4pm Sun

An unexpected surprise at the 'other'
end of Chapman's Peak, just outside
Noordhoek, close to the seemingly
endless white dunes of Long Beach
(see Play), and a useful stop en route
to Cape Point itself. Wines tasted here
come from grapes grown on a postage
stamp-size estate that is the only mem-
ber of the Cape Point wine district; apparently, the sea breezes from the Atlantic on both sides, and the elevation,
creates a distinctive environment and
three varieties of soil substrate that, ultimately, contribute to the award-winning wines produced by surfer-cum-
winemaker, Duncan Savage. Tastings

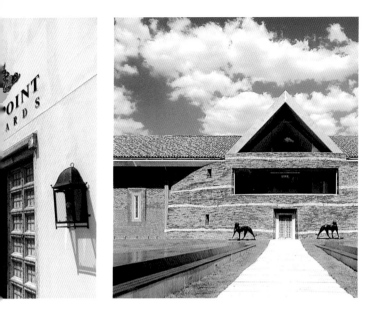

don't happen on the estate itself, but in a renovated mine building on top of a filled-in kaolin mine; the whites are consistently rated amongst the best in the country, and you'd better not miss Duncan's sublime Sauvignon Blanc/Semillon blend, Isliedh.

Graham Beck *(right)*
Franschhoek Estate
on the R45 to Franschhoek, Winelands
Tel: 021 874 1258
www.grahambeckwines.co.za
Open for tasting: 9am–5pm Mon–Fri; 10am–4pm Sat–Sun

On the outskirts of Franschhoek, just down the drag from L'Ormarins, this immaculate, modern estate (one of several in the Graham Beck portfolio) features manificent landscaping, slick modern architecture, and a tasting room with a dramatic view into the gleaming bottling plant through the massive glass wall. Graham Beck's wines are fine-drinking, and the list of awards garnered is immense. With grapes from four different wine farms, each with its unique terroir qualities and climate conditions, the winemaker has the benefit of considerable range when it comes to producing distinctive notes and character in the wines. It's the Graham Beck Brut sparkling wine which is widely considered amongst the nation's top 10 exports, but that doesn't mean there aren't several surprises to be found amongst the long list of non-bubbly vintages produced here; the Old Road Pinotage is making considerable waves.

culture

Muratie *(left)*

off the R44, between Stellenbosch and Paarl, Stellenbosch, Winelands
Tel: 021 865 2330/6
www.muratie.co.za
Open for tasting: daily, 10am–5pm. Closed Christmas Day and Good Friday.

With centuries worth of tartaric acid stuck to its cellar walls and cobwebs layering the dusty bottles, grapes picked exclusively by hand and an ancient oak tree planted by the original owners, this late 17th-century estate conjures up the most romantic notions of wine farming. Muratie's history is hardly unique to this region, but the tale of how the original owners – a German soldier and his slave girl wife – saw out their love affair against the odds is part of the great irony of South African race history. Muratie's layers of history are visible everywhere, making this one of the more evocative estates anywhere in the Cape; and if you're looking for a vintage-related conversa-tion opener, it was here that the first Pinot Noir grapes were planted in 1927. Cellar tours – recommended for the chance to soak up the deep history – happen at 10.30am and 2.30pm.

....

Solms-Delta *(middle)*

on the R45 to Franschhoek, Winelands
Tel: 021 874 1852
www.solms-delta.co.za
Open for tasting: daily, 9am–5pm

Besides the fact that there's a fabulous tale behind each label at this recently revitalized estate that enjoys partial ownership by the resident community, the pleasure of a tasting here is the intimate and lively explanation that accompanies each varietal. The guides, who can also take you on a brief (or not-so-brief) tour of the small museum, reveal the mysteries and potentialities of each bottle with considerable charm and enthusiasm, making you feel more like you're sharing a moment with a wine-loving friend than

someone who's simply going through the motions. Once you've tasted a few, however, you'll probably want to stay on for a picnic on the grounds, supplied – along with a bottle of wine – by Fyndraai, the estate's restaurant (see Snack).

....

Vergelegen *(right)*
Lourensford Road, Somerset West, Winelands
Tel: 021 847 1334/7
www.vergelegen.co.za
Open: daily, 9.30am–4pm. Closed Christmas Day, Good Friday and Workers' Day.

Because it's become such a built-up town, Somerset West is seldom considered amongst the Cape's mainstream wine tasting destinations, yet is home to one of the country's most beautiful wine estates, and one which is consistently rated the best winery in the country (not to mention 2005's New World Winery of the Year, according to Wine Enthusiast magazine). Vergelegen (meaning 'Far Location') is an estate of epic beauty, its Cape Dutch buildings set amidst ancient oak groves and stunning gardens where luxurious picnics are served. The original homestead is a great example of Cape Dutch architecture, complete with thatch roofing and elaborate gables; the five trees that grow around its entrance are Chinese camphors, planted by Willem Adriaan ven der Stel – the original owner of the estate (and a cad at that) – between 1700 and 1706. If you are looking for an estate with similarly sublime historic value (well, just about), but without the time-consuming detour into Somerset West, do not miss a stop at Vergenoegd (Tel: 021 843 3248, www.vergenoegd.co.za) which has the added advantage of being family-run (in fact the current winemaker, John Faure is the sixth generation Faure to farm on this estate) and responsible for some truly melt-in-the-mouth reds.

shop...

It used to be that the only way a Capetonian could reach shopping nirvana was to book a seat on a long-haul flight to London, Paris, New York – anywhere 'connected'. That was a decade ago. With the shedding of our pariah status came a slow awakening that our so-called parochial backwaters nurtured some extremely talented designers, artisans and artists, and the phrase 'local is lekker' (delicious/ delightful) was embraced with relish. There's still plenty of traditional beadwork and wooden carvings (the latter imported from elsewhere in Africa), but the sophisticated blend of Afro-Euro – particularly functional decor items with superb local twists – is what's finding its way into photographic books and design-savvy shops all over the world.

Aiming to be the World Design Capital in 2014, the city fathers are pioneering a variety of projects to help nurture the creative and design community that is mostly concentrated in the City Centre, Woodstock and Green Point areas (a compact district within a 2km radius of one another). To fully understand the breadth and wealth of the city's burgeoning talent, make every effort to queue up with the international buyers at the annual Design Indaba (www.designindaba.com), held over a weekend in February at the Cape Town International Convention Centre, in the Foreshore area. Not only does the Design Indaba showcase the country's premiere design talent, but the international speakers are top calibre, including interesting choices such as Ferran Adrià, the designer chef at the helm of El Bulli. If you're not here during February, serious shoppers keen to take in the most they can within the shortest time span should consider contacting Sandra Fairfax of Blue Bayou (Tel: 083 293 6555 or 021 762 5689; www.bluebuyou.co.za). Sandra will put together a highly personalized shopping tour that takes into account your particular interest, budget and taste; she'll pick you up at a time convenient to you and then take you on a whirlwind visit to the city's interesting outlets, as well as (if you're interested) introduce you to some of the most successful designers, artists and shop owners.

If you're more of a spontaneous browser, preferring to stroll off a meal by peering into shop windows, or like to plunder with plenty of cappuccino pitstops along the way, then the City Centre/Bowl and De Waterkant is where you'll want to head. One-way Long Street becomes two-way Kloof Street as it clambers up the mountain slope – these are the top City choices, with Victorian buildings, distinguished by their cast-iron balcony railings (colloquially known as *broekie lace*, or knicker lace), outnumbering modern monstrosities, a community feel, and numerous cafes and restaurants to refuel in. The top end of Long Street, a backpacker precinct, still has a slightly grungy feel, with everything from gun shops and porn outlets to second-hand clothing and art galleries; you can either continue up Kloof, where the proximity of City Varsity has produced plenty of edgy youth-fashion

boutiques, or head towards the harbour, walking all the way to Shortmarket Street to Greenmarket Square, a lively trading area dealing in mostly African curios. Also off Long Street (just before Greenmarket Square) is Church Street, a pedestrianized cobbled walkway that attracts casual traders dealing in antiques and trinkets, and lined with some interesting shops. Time allowing, don't miss Bree Street, which runs parallel to Long, parts of which has enjoyed regeneration, particularly around Heritage Square – some have even taken to call it the 'thinking man's Long Street', a mish mash of industrial spaces, designer boutiques, trendy bars and eateries, alongside longstanding mechanics and panel beaters.

The city streets provide in some ways the most authentic shopping experience, but when it comes to dropping into a one-stop shopping area, with the most sophisticated wares in the city, De Waterkant is the indisputable top choice. A small gentrified precinct of cobbled streets, a fine square and a brand new mall, De Waterkant is exceptionally easy to explore, though the plethora of choices could have you stuck here for a week. Make sure you stroll the original fine square (Cape Quarter) as well as Jarvis and Waterkant streets but the piece de resistance – at least from a shoppers point of view – is the mall, which the owners have cleverly opted to stock with independent local-only shops – no chains or international brands welcome.

The opposite is true of the Waterfront (www.waterfront.co.za), which for the most part is just a glam mall with a famous location filled with the usual suspects; names you're likely to encounter at duty free, not to mention home turf. There are a few exceptions (we've listed a few worthwhile stops on the following pages), and if you want to remember your Cape Town vacation with a Louis Vutton bag, a Gant shirt or a pair of Paul Smith socks, by all mean spend the day shopping here. But we'd like to encourage you to spend your money on one-offs, the kind of thing that everyone back home will want (and won't be able to get). Because local really is lekker.

Mall rats note: If you simply can't resist huge shopping centres with loads of parking, the following three are the city's best malls: Canal Walk, the southern hemisphere's biggest shopping mall (www.canalwalk.co.za); Cavendish Square, in Claremont (southern suburbs; www.cavendish.co.za; incidentally, this is the only place in Cape Town to browse the funky collection at The Space, a real SA designers emporium, co-owned by talented designer Amanda Laird Cherry), and Willowbridge Mall, an attractive open-air mall (www.willowbridge.co.za), located in the northern suburbs. If you like the idea of shopping outdoors, closer to home is The Montebello Design Centre (31 Newlands Ave, near Kirstenbosch), where a number of excellent designers and artists have set up studio under the trees; pop in to view award-winning ceramicist Louise Gelderblom at work and take a turn at the Mielie Shop for arts and crafts.

City Centre & Bowl

▦ Long Street

Tribal Trends (72–74) showcases a good (but pricey) selection of African-inspired designs

Pan African Market (76) probably the best place to pick up African crafts in Cape Town, with a variety of traders having stuffed every room to overflowing with goods from all over Africa; stop by here before you do Greenmarket Square

Mungo & Jemima (108) local designerwear and accessories that are worth a look in

A-List (110) forgot to pack your little black dress? Here's the place to pick it up. Sexy womenswear.

Miyabi (111) you'll find Durban-born Eastern-inspired Sandaline's colourful and feminine clothing at other outlets, but this is the home of her casual designer wear

Imagenius (117) one of the best most intelligent selections in the whole city, with irreverent, eclectic functional art (ceramics, lamps, artworks, furniture, novelty gifts) spanning three floors of a refurbished turn-of-the-century building

Mememe (117A) contemporary South African fashion for women - light and lovely stuff

African Music Store (134) comprehensive collection of African music

Darkie (159) known for its signature Afro-comb, this is one of SA's most popular streetwear and sportswear brands (looking for a pair of bellbottoms?), designed by the very cool Themba Mngomezulu

Wildfire Tattoos & Piercing (192) take home a souvenir you'll never forget, with a wide variety of designs on display, this is where you'll find the city's finest tattoo artists

Second Time Around (196) has been here for almost as long as the vintage apparel available for sale or hire

Clarke's Bookshop (211) established since 1956, this is for book collectors (not a Jackie Collins in sight), particularly for those interested in SA art, located in a wonderful old-fashioned shop, ideal for a a few minute's break from the hubbub of Long street

210onLong (210) young designers' market, comprising around 8 stalls; look into Jellyfish for contemporary crafts and gifts and cool Ts from Gravy (look for the Electric Zulu label, designed by Craig Native)

Misfit (287) as the name suggests this female fashion boutique is for strong women who don't intend blending with the crowd.

So You Wearable Vintage (303A) separates the vintage from the second hand.

▦ Kloof Street 19

O.live (Buitenkloof Studios) quirky very individualistic décor shop with an Afrikaans sensibility that mixes vintage pieces (porcelein buck; 70s coffee set; enamel tin) with gorgeous current items, some of them bespoke

laLESSO (Buitenkloof Studios) cool beach gear for girls who want to flaunt their African credentials, with innovative use of the East and South African kanga fabrics in bikinis, skirts and dresses

Cape Storm (Buitenkloof Studios) serious no-nonsense clothing and gear for the outdoor enthusiast, from good quality fleece coats to cycling shorts; lightweight camping plates to whatever-you-need-to-get-out-and-stay-fit

Nap Living (41) pick up the classic classy Cape Town look here; Kloof being one of 4 outlets of this gorgeous design emporium, with décor to die for, bits of beautiful jewellery and a small but perfect selection of simple classic leisure clothing in neutral shades – the kind you want to wear while lounging around your beach house in Clifton or Camps Bay

The Lot (Beckham House) funky 'rock 'n roll' men and women's clothing and hats; the women's fashion section is better. Aimed at the young woman who wants to make a statement and not afraid to show a bit of skin.

Wardrobe (45B) feminine but modern take on looking and feeling cool, with thin fabrics featuring plenty of florals; most of the female designers showcased work exclusively for this one-off store

Poppa Trunk's (45D) edgy menswear 'youth' shop, with, amongst other things, the coolest collection of belt buckles south of the equator. Good T's.

Hi-Five (Mooikloof Centre) rare independent music specialist stores, selling music (CDs & vinyl) and DJ equipment, but we also love the great selection of funky T-shirts

Xupa Xupa (Mooikloof Centre) fabulous kitsch and naughty gifts, as well as a few cool items, all at ridiculously low prices, the perfect place to pick up a joke gift and have a laugh at your dinner host's expense

Astore (Lifestyle on Kloof Centre) local designers like David West and Citizen Brand alongside Limited Edition Adidas and design books – a one-stop shop specializing in A-list cool

Blue Collar White Collar (Lifestyle on Kloof Centre) the owner of the fab unisex shirt shop (bias towards men) with a sideline in great fabric swimming trunks, has been in the clothing industry for almost four decades and he knows his shit

Baroque (Lifestyle on Kloof Centre) girly gorgeous, with lots of silk 'n chiffon 'n lace, and flowing lines at the aptly names Baroque. Plus arguably the best collection of glittering costume jewellery in the city. Even the strappy sandals (a few on show) are faux jewel encrusted.

Wine Concepts (Lifestyle on Kloof Centre) regular wine tastings and a great selection of South African wines, plus an intelligent salesperson to guide you through the plethora of choices. What's not to like?

Wellness Centre (Lifestyle on Kloof Centre) health shop 'supermarket' in Cape Town, with a chemist, deli/café, beauty therapists, books and various other sections for a great one-stop shop for health nuts and others

Amulet OK not strictly Kloof Street but a short stroll up Lower Kloof towards Kloof Nek and definitely worth it – a female design duo who make well-priced soulful jewellery pieces that suit both hippy and hip — the perfect gift for a woman you love

LIM (86A) stands for Less Is More and that's evidently owner Pauline's mantra, going by her classy collection of modern-organic homeware items (pity the paper-thin Shapiro bowls are so breakable), hide bags, lamps, furniture and affordable jewellery; her great eye is evident throughout

Klooftique (87) too big to fit in the

suitcase but this range of bespoke furniture is worth checking out, and worth waiting for your shipment to come in

Melissas (94) great place to pick up a treat for a dinner party host or edible gift for someone back home — check out the Afro tea selection (also an outlet at Waterfront and other locations).

Stefania Morland (153) Stefania worked in costumes before she opened her design shop with clever constructions that manage to meld feminine wiles with intellect. Very individualistic head-turning stuff.

Stock Exchange (116) specialising in pre-owned designer wear, allowing the rich well-travelled City Bowl ladies to treat it like one vast revolving wardrobe. Thrilling bargain hunting, if you find your dream item in your size.

Loft Living (122) beautiful décor shop at the top of Kloof; large item furniture but worth shipping home

....

🏁 Shortmarket Street

Greenmarket Square between Shortmarket & Longmarket Streets. A great place to browse for African crafts as much for the atmosphere as the architecture surrounding this cobbled square.

Erdmann Contemporary (63) Heidi Erdmann has a knack for unearthing new talent – she also handles work by brilliant talents like Conrad Botes and Varenka Paschke

Gregor Jenkin (84) South Africa's most talented contemporary furniture designer, with pieces gracing the most elegant Parisian and London homes, purchased from Conran Shops

Streetwires (66) best place to shop for wire and bead crafts, this is where a large team of craftsman produce and

market their wares direct to the public; work is generally more sophisticated than what you'll find at say Monkeybiz.

....

🏁 Loop Street

Joào Ferreira Gallery (70) small chic gallery, with interesting solo exhibitions by the up and coming and the well known, this is well worth popping into

iArt Gallery (71) well-established gallery, showcasing some of the country's best known artists upstairs, while slightly edgier less discovered stuff is featured downstairs

Casamento (74) retro-vintage furniture in a mix of masculine lines and feminine textures, from clothing to furniture

Spaghetti Mafia (199) ok it's all imported from Italy but if you're looking for affordable quality menswear, this is the place

....

🏁 Bree Street

The Bell-Roberts Gallery (89) excellent gallery worth checking out for both art and photography

Cape Originals (97) stockists of locally-produced functional art pieces, like Avoova – a range of ostrich eggshell designs (made by formerly disadvantaged community in Prince Albert) in which egg shells, discarded by ostrich farmers, are used to decorate anything from vases and mirrors to bowls and bangles. Very pretty.

Miseal (103B) 'create the object that you have always wanted to make and are passionate about making but wondered whether it would find an audience' is how Michael Haerens and Ivano Gelio briefed local artists and designers; don't miss their ongoing 'exhibition' of one-off or limited edition pieces

Blue Blood (104) if denim is your preferred uniform you won't leave this specialist denim shop empty handed

DVD Nouveau (166) by far the best DVD rental shop in the city, located next door to Boss Models in a converted home; four separate rooms, each showcasing a different theme/genre, from foreign films (all the classics) and documentaries to just about every series ever made.

Vintage Clothing (243) what used to be second hand is now bespoke vintage.

▨ Bo-Kaap

Olive Green Cat Jewelry, Studio 51 Wale Street. Brilliant local jewellery designers Phillipa Green and Ida-Elsje, along with architect and diamantaire Gregory Katz, showcase and create here. Philippa's perspex cuffs, which she embellishes and inlays with stones, buttons, rubber and silver, are just beautiful; Ida-Elsje specialises in custom-designed engagement rings and earrings; both do innovative resetting of old jewellery pieces in new, or combine precious stones with resin.

Shine, 45 Lewen Street. Gorgeous handbags in eye-catching colours and designs.

Rhubarb Room, 142 Buitengracht St. Gifts and designerwear in gorgeous coffee shop atmosphere.

Monkeybiz Bead Project, 43 Rose Street. This is a non-profit organisation that provides self-employment for bead artists; all profits go right back into the communities from which the crafts came.

▨ Roeland Street (East City)

g-mo (18) Grandt Mason's unique g-mohawk backwing shoes and slippers made from recycled fabrics; all handmade and each pair of shoes is utterly unique – a true one-off, at least until he's discovered

Book Lounge (71) independent book shop created by and for true book lovers, with staff that really know their stock, from coffee table tomes to airport thrillers

Orms (5 Roeland Square) best camera shop in Cape Town – not only for purchasing equipment but this is where professionals have their shots developed (you can definitely see the difference).

▨ Woodstock

The Old Biscuit Mill, 373-375 Albert Road. Site of the weekly Neighbourgoods Market (Saturdays; see Snack), it's worth your while to pop in here during the week to check out the small retail section adjacent. If you haven't seen them at Cape Quarter, don't miss Imiso Ceramics and Heartworks. Plush Bazaar always has an interesting collection of found objects for the home, Decadence Couture make the most beautiful one-off lampshades you have ever seen, and Bead Boyz has a great selection of beads to custom-make your own jewellery. Whatever you do, don't miss

The Mobile Boutique, a collection

of the coolest South African designers (look out for Amanda Laird Cherry), a step above the now rather commercial and tacky YDE (see Waterfront).

Whatiftheworld Gallery, 208 Albert Road. There are a lot of top-end galleries in Woodstock now, but this gallery got here first. It leads the way in terms of curation too – young and edgy, Whatiftheworld has kickstarted the careers of several rising stars.

The Bromwell, 250 Albert Rd. A 'shopping concept' store, with not a single shopping assistant, just computers into which you press the number of whatever you're investigating. And you are likely to be investigating a lot – not unlike an overstuffed museum, just about every piece here is fascinating and probably overpriced. I guess that's the price you pay for truly 'unique'.

Rewardrobe, 89 Sir Lowry Road. Refashioned and recycled second-hand garments and accessories, Rewardrobe specialises in giving old items new life. Every Sat there's a sale of stock that's been on the rails for more than a month.

Vamp Cnr, Albert Road and Treaty St. Vintage furniture, décor and homeware products sensitively restored and revamped, often in bold and unusual colours.

Greenpoint, De Waterkant & Cape Quarter

▨ Green Point

Klûk & CGDT, Portside Centre, Main Road. Malcolm Kluk and Christian Gabriel du Toit are at the cutting edge of contemporary SA fashion; they also sometimes turn their hand to refashioning old items of furniture.

Wallflower, Portside Centre, Main Road. Great selection of quirky, pretty homeware and gifts.

Helon Melon, 399 Main Road. Ok, technically this is Sea Point but it's worth trekking down the main road to browse through this delicious range of sleepwear and linen.

▨ De Waterkant

Hawksmoor Antiques, 125 Waterkant St. If you liked the Cape-meets-European design aesthetic of Hawksmoor House, here's where you can get the kit to recreate it at home. (Their scented candle is worth sniffing out too.)

Beatnik Bazaar, 111 Waterkant St. With its selection of quirky hand-crafted retro-style items, this was named by Time magazine as one of the top 10 best reasons to visit Kalk bay; like all the top Kalk Bay shops, BB has moved into swanky new De Waterkant premises.

Africa Nova, 72 Waterkant St. This is a definite must-see, the best African craft shop in the country, chosen with a real eye by Zimbabwean Margie Murgatroyd; it's where craft really starts to meet art, and where Conran was inspired to celebrate SA design.

Out of this World, 72 Waterkant St. Also worth popping into for their selection of African artefacts sourced locally and across the continent.

Kingsley Heath, 117 Waterkant St Referred to as the South African Abercrombie & Finch, this is where you shop for sophisticated-on-safari look.

Fibre Designs, 16 Dixon Street. Taking carpets to new heights ('bespoke hand-woven floorware', to be exact), with classic and exciting designs in wonderful colour combinations.

Living Leather, Jarvis House, Jarvis Street. Beautifully hand-tooled leather items.

....

▨ Cape Quarter Square
Anpa another reason to drive to Kalk Bay just moved to the Cape Quarter. Distinctive jewellery for women who like strong individualistic pieces using unusual materials. Unbelievably good value too. Commissioned work is fast.

Big Blue funky T-shirts and gorgeous feminine bo-ho womenswear; one of our favourite clothing shops (also in Kalk Bay).

Heartworks Margaret Woermann's unerringly good eye (and warm heart) brings you100%-local small collectibles, decorative and functional (best embroidered teddies); very affordable and a great place to shop for gifts (there is also an outlet on 98 Kloof Street)

Galeria Gibello photographic gallery, owned by travel photographer Caroline Gibello, whose lens is worth looking into

Imiso ceramics Andile Dyalvane, Abongile Madabane, Zizipho Poswa and Mlamli Charles Mayosi are the hip ceramicists producing a range of cups, bowls, mugs, vases and plates that have been snapped up by international buyers – don't miss this

JQ Designer Collections designerwear sourced from across the continent. Clients can customize garments and there are a range of accessories to ensure you leave with the full look.

Just Cruizin 100% pure cotton (or cotton-linen mix) in muted tones for casual floppy beach/yoga/meditation wear; very affordable

Nap Living latest outlet of this gorgeous design emporium (see Kloof Street), with décor, beautiful jewellery and a small covetable selection of classic leisurewear that will have you looking and feeling like a Capetonian

Pierre Cronje Shop master craftsman Pierrie Cronje makes contemporary and classic furniture items destined to be heirlooms

....

The Waterfront

African Trading Post, Pierhead, Dock Road. In the old offices of the Port Captain (on the way to the Clock Tower), spread over three stories, this is an excellent selection of sculptures, jewelry, tableware, textiles, ceramics, and furniture.

Caroline's Fine Wine Cellar, KWH8 Victoria Wharf. The best wine boutique in the city; Caroline is passionate about finding those out-of-the-way gems and will arrange all shipping. Tastings on Thurs & Fri evenings. (also 62 Strand St in town).

Carrol Boyes, 6180 Victoria Wharf. Her pewter, stainless steel and chrome homeware items are stocked all around the world but they are a great deal cheaper here.

Cape Union Mart, 142 Victoria Wharf. Unpretentious safari and camping gear, from cool clothing and climbing boots to torches and lightweight tents (the latter ideal if you decide to kit up for one of the weekend trance parties (see Party).

Christoff, 7217 Victoria Wharf. Top-end top-quality jewellery, classier than the better publicized Shimansky.

Everard Read Gallery, 3 Portswood Rd. One of the best galleries in the country, with serious investment value artists. Bring a gold card.

Exclusive Books, 6160 Victoria Wharf. Yes, it's a chain, but this outlet has a great selection, with plenty of books on and about the continent and the country for tourists as well as usual airport tat.

Extreme Eyewear, Victoria Wharf. Someone stolen your sunglasses? Get a new pair here; best selection of funky eyewear in the city.

Fabiani, 272 Victoria Wharf. All imported menswear collection but the best in the Waterfront and a must stop shop if you're looking for a shirt that will make you look and feel like a million dollars.

Joubert & Monty, next to Vida, Victoria Wharf. This is a chain of reliable biltong suppliers, the traditional healthy SA snack (strips of meat, spiced, cured and air-dried) —ask for a piece of beef with a slight bit of fat, slightly moist, and have it sliced.

Love@the Waterfront, Victoria Wharf. Funky local stuff.

Out of Africa, 125 Victoria Wharf. This is the best selection of African arts, crafts and furniture in the Waterfront. Gorgeous but pricey.

Pure Solid, 6248 Victoria Wharf. For Eastern-inspired curiousities and clothing.

Red Shed Craft Workshop, A large indoor market open 7 days a week. This is where you get locally produced stuff in the Waterfront but selection is hit and miss

Sun Goddess, 243 Victoria Wharf. 100% authentic African designerwear, worn by local politicians and new-money BEE wives.

Woolworths, This is the best grocery chain in South Africa (you'll see the large W everywhere in the city) and the best place to stock up on food (wine selection is poor). Clothing and shoes at the Waterfront Woolies aren't bad either: Look out for the W Collection as well as Country Road and Trennery labels – the latter imported from Australia but very South African.

YDE, 225 Victoria Wharf. Young Designers Emporium is just what it says (small lines; young designers), but since swallowed by the big WoolTru group not quite as cutting edge as it used to be. Still, worth rifling through the racks.

play...

With a beautiful coastline washed clean by the wild waters of the Atlantic, a string of fabulous mountains in their backyard, and a temperate climate, Capetonians are truly spoilt for choice when it comes to staying active.

Stretching northwards from jagged Cape Point, all the way to the city's Signal Hill (the looming rump which swells up behind Bo-Kaap, then descends into Green Point and Sea Point, and culminates in the granite mane of Lion's Head), Table Mountain National Park is a vast and fascinating playpen, sheltering the world's highest concentration of plant species, troops of chacma baboons, Cape clawless otters, Cape fur seals and African penguins. Keen walkers explore its length on the Hoerikwaggo Trail – a fully-portered and catered one to five-night trail, while riders gallop the length of Noordhoek's deserted wind-swept beach. Squadrons of cyclists tear around the contour roads of the peninsular coast, while solitary types career down dirt tracks on the mountain's lower slopes. Wetsuit-clad surfers bring just the right degree of sexy-cool to even the most laid-back villages of the Peninsula, while kite-surfers and engine-propelled boatmen get high on speed. What's not to like?

You can jump off Lion's Head attached to a pro-paraglider – probably the finest way to see the city; scramble down the uppermost cliff-face of Table Mountain in the world's highest commercial abseil; fly down dunes attached to a sandboard, or simply don a pair of trainers for a jog along the Seaboard promenade that snakes from Mouille Point to Bantry Bay, and then hugs the cliff to Clifton. Climb into a steel cage and eyeball great white sharks in their hunting grounds, or ease into a pair of boardshorts to swim amongst the penguins at Boulders beach. Or set sail in the world's fastest wind-powered sea-going vessel, looking out for whales breaching, then see the entire Cape Peninsula from the seat of a helicopter. If that sounds tame, take to the skies at 2,400km per hour – Thunder City (tel: 021 934 8007) owns the largest collection of former military fighter jets in the world available for civilian use, though only civilians with extremely deep pockets need apply. In short: there are a myriad ways in and around Cape Town to get your heart rate racing: for a one-stop adventure company specializing in extreme sports, contact Extreme Scene; tel: 079 666 9789 or 072 538 1574, www.extremescene.co.za). But adrenaline junkies note: for a real leap of faith, you'll need to travel the Garden Route – a beautiful 5-hour drive, which you should spread over a few days to make the most of it, travelling via Route 62 to start the route in Wilderness – and take the world's highest bungy jump, a 216m heartstopping drop off the Bloukrans Bridge, 40km east of Plettenberg Bay (tel: 042 281 1458, www.faceadrenaline.com).

Of course your ideal play date may be one spent lazing on a soft sand, watching the sun glisten off the sea – if so, Cape Town's coastline offers amongst the most sensational urban and semi-urban beaches on earth: white sandy shores interlaced with gigantic sculptural boulders, lapped by brilliant azure waters, and set against a backdrop of cliffs and craggy mountains. While swimming itself can take a bit of courage – waves can be mean and temperatures freezing – there are relaxed tidal pools where even non-swimmers can comfortably enjoy the refreshing, biting, depression-curing waters of the Atlantic Ocean.

And, finally, when the weather refuses to cooperate – usually in the form of raging, unrelenting wind – there are plenty of world-class spas offering treatments to soothe, relax, heal and restore. Ready to play?

Abseiling, Climbing & Kloofing

One of the most popular descents is the abseil experience right off the top of Table Mountain; you don't go all the way down, but the few moments spent clambering down the uppermost 100-or-so metres is certainly enough to get the blood pumping. But for real thrills, Capetonians go kloofing. Also known as canyoning, kloofing is the adrenaline-pumping art of getting yourself down a river gorge by hopping between boulders, swimming, climbing, wading, and jumping off cliffs. It's like a hardcore obstacle course designed by nature – you need to be reasonably fit and rather fearless.

Abseil Africa

Long Street, City Centre
Tel: 021 424 4760
www.abseilafrica.co.za

You have to find your own way to the top of the Mountain, but once you're up (either by cable car or on foot), this experienced outfit will happily attach you to one end of a rope and send you back over the edge. A basic 100m abseil costs R595 (excluding cable car fees); R750 combines a guided hike to the summit with an abseil session. The Kamikaze Kanyon Kloofing is a great day trip scrambling down the faces of a river gorge, culminating with a 65m waterfall abseil – the full day out costs R795.

Frixion Adventures

Tel: 021 447 4985,
082 855 6271, or 082 378 8853
www.frixion.co.za

This small operation specializes in kloofing adventures, with excursions to some of the most exhilarating mountain ravines, with amazing waterfalls and the chance to do some extreme cliff-jumping. Suicide Gorge (R450) is one of the more popular excursions, but real thrill-seekers will want to opt for Sluicegates, a journey into the Hawequas Mountains with more than twelve waterfalls and tremendous drops that will scare the bejeezers out of anyone with even the slightest fear of heights; it will cost you R1,650 (and every ounce of bravery).

Venture Forth

Tel: 086 110 6548 or 082 770 7876
www.ventureforth.co.za

This is a serious outfit (it's also an accredited mountaineering training school) offering guided climbing excursions up Table Mountain by qualified mountain guides; Venture Forth also offers climbing, abseiling, canyoneering and mountaineering trips all over the country.

Beaches

A number of Cape Town beaches have Blue Flag status (www.blueflag. org), including Big Bay (Bloubergstrand), Camps Bay, Clifton 4th Beach, and Muizenberg. If you're keen on spending a little more time in the water as opposed to simply posing on the shore, you should consider one of the beaches around False Bay where the water is a good three to four degrees warmer. Of these the most interesting choice is Boulders, where the proximity of the 3,000-strong penguin colony is an opportunity to bathe with unusual swimming partners. False Bay's beaches tend to be more easy-going, with less of the bling-style posing that you inevitably find around Clifton and Camps Bay, where proximity to the city centre (10 minutes) means that the beautiful people and their hangers on are more inclined to order a sun-loungers and a beach massage.

Be aware that white sharks are present and active and are particularly predatory in False Bay. A shark-spotting programme is active throughout the year in Muizenberg, St James, Noordhoek and Fish Hoek, and over weekends, public holidays, and the December/January summer season on other selected beaches (www.sharkspotters. org.za). If there's no spotter, pay attention to obvious signs, such as when no-one else is in the water, or where there have been recent reports of sharks in the area. Don't swim at night, near river mouths, near fishing activity, or in the vicinity of birds, dolphins and seals that might be feeding. Avoid swimming on your own and do not swim beyond the breakers. Pay careful attention to signage on the beach and if you're in any way uncertain of conditions or potential hazards, ask local officials or life-guards – or speak to the surfers. Note, too, that seals have been known to attack.

Bakoven
Atlantic Seaboard

Comparatively undiscovered, this pair of tiny beaches surrounded by gigantic boulders at the outskirts of Camps Bay is an ideal choice for sundowners if you want to avoid the crowds and the beach clichés.

Blouberg
Not recommended for either swimming or sunbathing (winds are fierce), Blouberg attracts primarily wind- and kite-surfers, as well as paddle skiers.

Boulders
M4, Main Road, Simons Town, Southern Peninsula

As described in Culture, this beach is home to a colony of Africa penguins and located just outside the naval town of Simon's Town.

Camps Bay
Atlantic Seaboard

The most accessible beach to the city is also one of its prettiest – a palm-lined curve of sand overlooked by bars and restaurants. The curvaceous beach is immaculate until the hordes show up, some of them setting up camp on the struggling, sprawling patch of lawn that spreads between the beach and ever-busy Victoria Road.

Clifton
Atlantic Seaboard

Considered amongst the world's top ten beaches, enormous natural granite boulders divide Clifton into a string of four wind-sheltered beaches. Thanks to the many steps you need to climb to get to them, it's not nearly as popular as nearbyCamps Bay. Clifton's Fourth Beach has Blue Flag status and is probably the premiere spot to unfurl your beach towel; First and Second are harder to get to (more steps), but they tend to attract a local crowd, with surfers opting for First Beach. Third Beach is popular with gay men (although by no means exclusively so) where members of a model-like crowd flaunt package-hugging Speedos.

Glen Beach
Atlantic Seaboard

Remarkably undiscovered, yet right next to Camps Bay, Glen Beach is often dotted with surfers, suppers, and other board sports enthusiasts. It's a tiny, idyllic cove backed by a number of pretty bungalows and a promenade, and protected on either end by massive boulders.

Hout Bay
Southern Peninsula

By no means a recommended swimming beach, Hout Bay suffers because it is a fishing port, and evidence of nearby sharks may be found in the form of half-chewed seals washed up on shore. Still, if you simply want to escape the crowds and laze on the beach, there's plenty of space to do so here, and the restaurants and bars at the edge of the beach are far less pretentious than those at Camps Bay.

Llandudno & Sandy Bay
Atlantic Seaboard

Although parking is always a problem, finding a spot on the white sand between Llandudno's sculptural boulders is bliss. Nearby Sandy Bay has long been famous as the city's unofficial nudist beach; it's surrounded by boulders and thick fynbos vegetation so there's a good sense of seclusion (and protection from the wind), aided by the effort and time – along a very long, narrow path – taken to get here. That doesn't mean that women aren't vulnerable to shameless voyeurism, while for gay men, the far end of the beach is a known cruising hub.

Long Beach/Noordhoek
Southern Peninsula

Around eight kilometres of powdery white sand makes this one of the prettiest beaches in Cape Town, popular with surfers, hippies and horseriders. It stretches from the laidback village of Noordhoek at the end of Chapman's Peak Drive to laidback Kommetjie.

Muizenberg
Southern Peninsula

Victorian beach huts painted in bright colours line the shore at this beach that's a favourite with beginner surfers and families, thanks to its gentle waves.

Platboom
Cape Point, Southern Peninsula

Literally translates as 'flat tree', possibly referring to the power of the southeaster – if the wind doesn't, the gorgeous white dunes and seeing ostrich or eland crossing the beach will blow you away.

Scarborough
Southern Peninsula

Neighbouring Cape Point Nature Reserve, this pristine white sandy beach is backed by one of the most laidback villages on the Peninsula – with just 450-or-so houses, of which only 120 are occupied throughout the year, they don't even have streetlights here.

Smitswinkelbaai
near Cape Point, Southern Peninsula

This tiny gem is known almost exclusively to the few who have houses here. It's a stiff walk down but once there it's bliss.

St. James
Southern Peninsula

Like neighbouring Muizenberg, tiny St James still has its collection of Victorian bathing houses. There's also a tidal pool here that's popular with old timers who like to kickstart their day with an early morning dip. It's a relatively tiny beach, though, and can get extremely crowded during the busiest part of summer. You can walk here from Muizenberg along a pedestrian-dedicated boardwalk.

Canoeing & Kayaking

Meandering along the shore under paddle power for uninterrupted views of the mountains; if you're lucky, you'll find yourself accompanied by a curious seal or dolphins. Several kayaking outfitters offer guided kayak tours, with equipment included.

Coastal Kayak
179 Beach Road, Three Anchor Bay
Tel: 021 439 1134
www.kayak.co.za

This outfit, based right on the beach at Three Anchor Bay (between Green Point and Sea Point) specializes in guided trips along the Seaboard and around Table Bay. Typically, their two-hour trips set off towards Clifton, where you take a break on the beach before the return leg. Experienced paddlers can opt for longer tours.

Real Cape Adventures
Tel: 021 790 5611
www.seakayak.co.za

You'll have plenty of choice with this outfit, since they cover almost every sea-kayaking route on the western and southern coasts – request a trip to the rugged coastline of Cape Point. Two-hour kayak trips start from R250 per person.

Casinoes

South Africa's gambling culture is seldom associated with class or prestige but rather wannabe Vegas knock-offs, attracting the widest possible variety of people.

....

GrandWest Casino

1 Vanguard Drive, Goodwood
Tel: 021 505 7777
www.suninternational.com

Located in Goodwood, one of Cape Town's insalubrious Northern Suburbs, this is the only real casino in the city – an extensive complex with slot machines, tables, cinemas, an ice rink, restaurants and an children's entertainment centre. An outing here is more a study in social anthropology than anything else, although the 5,000-seater theatre gets in some top-calibre acts.

....

Cruises & Boat Trips

It's worth every effort to head out on a sunset cruise – the spectacle of the city backed by Table Mountain is unforgettable as is the sun slowly disappearing, turning the water to molten lava while the glittering lights of the city are switched on.

The Royal Cape Yacht Club (tel: 021 421 1354, www.rcyc.co.za) is where South Africa's America's Cup team, Shosholoza, is based, but you have only to roam around the marinas at the V&A Waterfront to get a sense of how the high-rollers play when they're out to sea. Fortunately, you needn't own one to cruise the Seaboard.

Atlantic Adventures

Tel: 021 425 3785
www.atlanticadventures.co.za

If it's speed more than views that you're interested in, sign up for a 130kmph rubber duck jaunt across Table Bay. They charge R350 per person per hour and the inflatable craft takes up to 11 passengers. They also offer gentler cruises, including whale-watching.

....

Cruise iQ

Victoria & Alfred Waterfront
Tel: 021 421 5565
www.cruiseiq.co.za

This is Cape Town's sexiest cruising option – the newest, slickest sailing vessel in the city, this custom-built catamaran features cocktail seating and a bar serviced by a cool crew of genuine sailors and reaches up to 26 knots under sail. With four trips each day (conditions allowing), each lasting 90 minutes, you can choose between the (R130) daytime cruise, the (R150) early evening 'Happy Hour' cruise, or the (R200) recommended Sunset Cruise, with complimentary sparkling wine. Or charter the entire boat for R4,100 per hour.

If you prefer to be aboard something a great deal faster, then opt for cruise aboard the Adventurer, a state-of-the-art wave-piercing trimaran which was originally custom-built for a trip around the world and holds the record for the fastest circumnavigation (round-the-world in 74 days). A two-hour daytime cruise costs R250; sunset costs R300.

....

Drumbeat Charters

Tel: 021 791 4441
www.drumbeatcharters.co.za

For trips to see the Cape fur seals on Duiker Island, choose this outfit based in Hout Bay harbour. The return journey takes around 40 minutes and costs R60. They set off every day during season, but excursions are highly weather-dependent.

Splash Rentals

Tel: 073 727 7628 or 073 727 7511
www.splashrentals.co.za

Specialists in the high-end rental of just about any kind of ocean-going vessel, Splash provides yachts, catamarans, dinghies, canoes, kayaks, motorboats and inflatables primarily for use in the film industry, but also available for you to live out your deepest seagoing fantasy.

Simon's Town Boat Company

Tel: 083 257 7760

Specialising in trips to Seal Island, some 16km from Simon's Town, a highlight of a trip with this company is the chance to spot dolphins, humpback whales, Brydes whales throughout the year, whilst southern right hales are regularly spotted between July and November. During winter there's a high chance of seeing great white sharks in action feeding on seals around the island. Breeding season for the Cape fur seals – 75,000 of which make their home on Seal Island – is in November and December.

Waterfront Boat Company

V&A Waterfront
Tel: 021 418 5806
www.waterfrontboats.co.za

During summer, there's a daily 90-minute sunset cruise starting from the V&A Waterfront and following the coastal contour as far as Clifton Bay. Cost is R200 per person. The company also has a whale-watching license, offering specialised trips in season. Also part of their inventory are two gaff-rigged schooners – the Spirit of Victoria and Esperance – which set off on regular trips across Table Bay and towards Blouberg.

Cricket

This is the top summer team sport in the country, although if you go by attendance at stadia, it would be safe to assume that Capetonians prefer to idle in front of the television rather than turning up for a live match.

Newlands Cricket Ground

146 Campground Road,
Newlands, Southern Suburbs
Tel: 021 657 3300
www.wpca.co.za

With a majestic mountainous backdrop this is a great place to enjoy a bit of cricket under the warm African sun – although it's worth checking out the local Cape Cobras in action, local fans are mostly interested in international test matches.

Cycling & Mountain Biking

The 109km Cape Argus Pick n Pay Cycle Tour (www.cycletour.co.za) is the world's largest timed cycling race, with over 35,000 participants in March 2009 (including Matt Damon). It's a serious test of stamina – particularly challenging when the wind gathers momentum – but attracts a wide range of entrants, from teenagers to Lance Armstrong, due to participate in 2010. If you prefer a more laidback approach, there's great cycling to be had throughout the Cape Peninsula and in the Winelands – make every effort to ride Chapman's Peak, often acknowledged as the world's most beautiful drive, with exhilarating views and a chance to marvel at some of the country's most technologically innovative and spectacular road engineering. Be wary of engine-powered vehicles however, whose drivers ensure a disturbingly high incidence of accidents.

With no cars to contend with, mountain biking is generally safer, and a great way to explore Table Mountain and the Winelands (call Manic Cycles, tel: 021 876 4856, to hire bike); you'll find some of the best routes through the Tokai Forest network and the Constantiaberg trails. Contact the outfitters below for both bike hire and guided bike tours. If you're the competitive type, the annual eight-day Cape Epic (www.cape-epic.co.za), which happens towards the end of March and start of April, is truly that, taking serious mountain bikers through 800km of unspoilt natural wilderness.

Day Trippers
Tel: 021 511 4766
www.daytrippers.co.za

Besides organizing training sessions for cyclists who come to Cape Town to take part in some of the major cycling events (including the Argus and the Cape Epic), Day Trippers runs guided bike tours of Cape Town and much farther afield. Their website provides full details of their routes; a typical Cape Point and Peninsula tour costs R545. You can bring your own bike, or rent one of their good quality 21-speed machines.

Downhill Adventures
Tel: 021 422 0388
www.downhilladventures.com

These adventure specialists will put you in the saddle for a day, and provide you with a guide to explore the Winelands and Cape Point; the cost is R655. Or you can rent a mountain bike from them (R140) and spend the day checking out the network of dirt trails on the slopes of Table Mountain; be sure to ask about routes.

Diving

Although the cold water means thick wetsuits are essential, the waters around Cape Town are popular especially for wreck dives – it's not known as the Cape of Storms for nothing, and there are consequently many coral-covered wrecks to explore. Precisely where you end up will depend on weather and water conditions, best left to local experts.

One place where the weather won't decide when and how you dive is at the Two Oceans Aquarium (tel: 021 418 3823, www.aquarium.co.za) where experienced scuba divers have the chance to spend half an hour in the Predator Tank amongst the ragged tooth sharks. There are three such dives per day (booked in advance), costing R485 per session.

Dive Action
22 Carlisle Street,
Paarden Eiland, Cape Town
Tel: 021 511 0800
www.scubadivecapetown.co.za

Arguably Cape Town's top dive company, offering PADI-certified courses all the way up to Rescue Diver level, as well as a Nitrox course, under highly qualified and experienced instructors. Part of their dive training happens in Sea Point's public swimming pool, and they have some of the best available equipment on hand for new and experienced divers. Regular dive trips take them to prime locations around the Southern Peninsula, including the top-rated Smitswinkel Bay wrecks and The Lusitania, which struck Bellows Rock at Cape Point in 1911.

Pro Divers
Shop 88B, Main Road, Sea Point
Tel: 021 433 0472
www.prodivers.co.za

Also offering PADI dive instruction,

Pro Divers offers a number of specialized courses, including National Geographic, dry-suit and underwater photography programmes. Experienced divers can sign up for wreck dives, diving with seals, night dives, and kelp forest dives. They offer both shore and boat dives.

Fishing

Cape Town's waters afford the opportunity to land longfin tuna, Dorado, shark and marlin – we don't need to tell you to only do so with a catch-and-release operator. Note that the tuna season runs from September all the way through June.

For fly-fishing and the chance to bag trout in the Franschhoek Valley in the Winelands, contact either Dewdale Fly Fishery (tel: 021 876 2755) who can advise on most essential details, including permits, or La Ferme (tel: 021 876 0120).

Cape Sea Safaris
Tel: 0861 266 524 or 079 519 4676
www.capeseasafaris.com

Besides offering sunrise and sunset cruises that set off from the Radisson Hotel (near the V&A Waterfront), this upmarket boat company charters various catch and release fishing trips. Half a day of inshore fishing costs R3,500–R6,000, full day R4,500–R7,500. A full day of offshore fishing, where you have a good chance of landing tuna and dorado, costs R12,500

Hooked on Africa
Hout Bay
Tel: 021 790 5332
www.hookenonafrica.com

These guys operate out of Hout Bay harbour and offer both deep-sea tuna and light tackle in-shore fishing, with the option of adding an excursion to Seal Island at the end of your trip. A full charter costs upwards of R8,000.

Football (Soccer)

Although the majority of white South Africans will, ignorantly, tell you that rugby and cricket are the mainstay of the South African sporting environment, there's no denying that, statistically, soccer (local parlance for football) is played and enjoyed by a far greater number of people here than any other team sport. Naturally it has also enjoyed more widespread support since the announcement that the country is to be the first African nation to host the FIFA World Cup championship in 2010.

Cape Town's two Premiere Soccer League team are Santos FC (www.santosfc.co.za), based at Athlone Stadium, and Ajax Cape Town (www.ajaxct.com), which has, until the completion of the new soccer stadium in Green Point, played home tournaments at Newlands Rugby Stadium. Cape Town, prior to the World Cup, has not been a hotspot for international football, but when either of the country's two biggest teams – Orlando Pirates and Kaizer Chiefs – are in town, support can be fierce – you might want to bring earplugs to stem the onslaught of the *fufezela*, the wind 'instrument' that soccer fans traditionally blow at live matches (and sometimes in the streets).

Other than catching a match in the new 68,000-seater football stadium in Green Point (www.greenpointstadiumvc.co.za), you can learn more about Cape Town's soccer culture by joining one of Coffeebeans Routes' Soccer Tours (see Culture) which introduces you to the city's premiere league teams, giving you insight into the local players and their teams, as well as the stadia where local premiere league teams are based. It also gives you a chance to play a game with some local youths in the black township of Khayalitsha, where you will get to experience the energy, colour and vibe of a very different Cape Town.

Golf

Royal Cape
Tel: 021 761 6551

A regular host of the South African Open.

Milnerton Golf Club
Tel: 021 552 1047
www.milnertongolf.co.za

This the only true links course in the Cape, with magnificent views of Table Mountain; best avoided when the wind is blowing.

Clovelly Country Club

Clovelly Road, Clovelly, Fish Hoek
Tel: 021 784 2111 or 021 784 2100
www.clovelly.co.za

Located in the beautiful Silvermine Valley, this is a tight par 73 course with handsome surrounds. Take your swimming gear along for a dunk in the waters of False Bay after you've played the 18 holes.

Erinvale

Lourensford Road, Somerset West
Tel: 021 847 1144

In the dull Winelands town of Somerset West, this Gary Player-designed 18-hole, par-72 course is considered one of the very the best. It has a very well-maintained rough, broad fairways, and water on six holes.

Pearl Valley Golf Estate

Franschhoek Valley
Tel: 021/867-8000
www.pearlvalleygolfestates.com

Designed by golfing hero Jack Nicklaus, this top-drawer course hosts the South African Open for the third time in 2010. Great views throughout your game, and an especially memorable 13th hole.

Gyms

Not only is staying in shape a part of the local culture, but the city is home to a disproportionate number of modeling agencies so you'll get a work out for

your eyes as much as anything. The biggest and best chain is Branson-owned Virgin Active; you're looking at around R170 for single-day usage, so it may be worth considering a contract if you're planning on being here for a while. You'll find a Virgin in just about every suburb these days but the Point is perhaps the most conveniently located (within spitting distance of the Sea Point Promenade and the Green Point Stadium).

Virgin Active Point

Bill Peters Drive, Green Point
Tel: 021 434 0750
www.virginactive.co.za
Open: 5am–10pm Mon–Thurs;
5am–9pm Fri; 7am–9pm Sat–Sun
and public holidays

This split-level, open plan gym gets particularly busy during peak hours, before and after standard office hours, so try to avoid these times, unless you're especially keen to share your training session with a toned crowd. There is a daylong programme offering everything from Iyengar yoga to pilates, a large indoor pool, squash courts, sunbeds, sauna and steam rooms, and outdoor beach volleyball courts. The club is close to the Sea Point Promenade, so you may opt for a glorious outdoor run, rather than wait in line for one of the ever-busy treadmills.

Helicopters Flips

Surely the ultimate way to see a lot of Cape Town quickly and effortlessly (albeit noisily) – flights depart from the Waterfront, or you may arrange a pick up from the 12 Apostles Hotel helipad.

The Huey Helicopter Company
V&A Waterfront Helipad
Tel: 021 419 4839
www.thehueyhelicopterco.co.za

Turning history into novelty, this company operates a restored Vietnam veteran military chopper for leisurely commercial flips over the Peninsula. Their shortest flight is 15 minutes, and their most exhilarating is a simulated combat mission that involves low-flying over the beach.

NAC Makana Aviation
East Pier Road, Victoria & Alfred Waterfront
Tel: 021 425 3868
www.nacmakana.com

Private tours cost from R2,205 for 20 minutes in a three-seater, and up to R13,200 for an hour in a six-seater; shared flights start at R735 per person for 20 minutes, and R2,200 per hour. The basic 20-minute flight takes you along the Atlantic Seaboard as far as Hout Bay, where you spy Seal Island form the sky before returning to the Waterfront. To get as far as Cape Point and Simon's Town, you need to sign up for an hour. It is also possible to arrange for trips to specified points.

Hiking

With around 300 trails, Table Mountain (tel: 021 701 8692, www.sanparks.org) is said to be the most hiked in the world. Since the cliffs around the summit of the mountain are steep, there aren't too many ways of ascending the Table directly; the most popular is Platteklip Gorge, which runs up the centre of the main mountain face – it's a pretty straightforward route and can take between one and three hours to make the ascent. Ascending via the 'back' of the mountain takes longer, but routes such as Skeleton Gorge, commencing from Kirstenbosch Gardens, are recommended. Other starting points at the 'back' include Rhodes Memorial and Constantia Nek.

Many visitors choose to take the cable car to the top and then take advantage of free guided hour-long walks at 10am and noon each day; or it's possible to hike solo to the mountains highest point, Maclear's Beacon, a trigonometrical stone cairn built in 1865 towards the eastern end of the plateau. At 1,085 meters above sea-level, it takes about an hour to get there from the upper cable station. One of the best-kept secrets on Table Mountain is the Tranquility Cracks walk, where you get to meander through an underground yellowwood forest. And if you want to get your heart racing (although without using any ropes or technical climbing ability), it's possible to walk inside the Mountain on the cliff face just below the upper cable station; known as the Right Face-Arrow Face Traverse, it's a gutsy hike, not for the faint of heart.

Be warned: Table Mountain is renowned for her swift mood swings that turn a sunny day to rain, or fill clear skies with unexpected fog. If you are attempting to hike one of the less-travelled routes, start early, wear the correct gear (prepared for weather swings), carry plenty of water and hire a guide (14 Hoerikwaggo Trail Hiking Guides are available). Many people are injured from falls (and on average one person is killed each year), while others spend a frightening night on the mountain due to losing their way – it may look semi-urban but it is in fact a wilderness area.

Besides hiking Table Mountain, you can also climb Lion's Head, a very gratifying sunset outing, and particularly popular on full moon nights when you can watch the sun set and the moon rise, along with spectacular views of the city, the sea, and neighbouring Table Mountain, too.

Of the easier walks around the Peninsula, the Chapman's Contour Path, with brilliant views over Hout Bay is highly recommended. Another popular and beautiful hike is through the *fynbos* landscape of Silvermine, also part of Table Mountain National Park, in the Southern Peninsula, accessible off Ou Kaapse Weg; Jonkershoek Nature Reserve in Stellenbosch has some great trails if you're based in the Winelands.

Hoerikwaggo Trail
Tel: 021 465 8515/6
www.hoerikwaggotrail.org

The Hoerikwaggo Trail – due to be completely operational in June 2010 – is a five-night, six-day 97km trail from Cape Town city to Cape Point. Hikers can book sections of the overall trail; the trail is fully portered and catered, and accommodation is in permanent camps that are pretty luxurious given

that you are in the middle of a wilderness.

Table Mountain Explorations
Tel: 021 438 6073 or 083 683 1876
cauaburi@yahoo.com

Considered one of the finest Table Mountain hiking guides working today, rock climber and trekker Riaan Vorster offers a large variety of routes, and will point out the mountain's specialized flora and fauna, and tell you about the history and geology along the way. Prices depend on the number of people in your group, with a half-day costing R600 if you're going solo, or R800 for a full day of Riaan's time. Riaan's hikes are personalized to match your level of fitness, experience, and ability.

Venture Forth
Tel: 086 110 6548 or 082 770 7876
www.ventureforth.co.za

Not quite as personalized as Riaan Vorster, but a safe way to explore off the beaten track, with a range of hiking and rock-climbing adventures offered along with qualified guides.

Horseback-riding

Cape Town has in recent years recruited horses into its Metro Police force and you'll see the mounted cops patrolling the streets of the city and Seaboard suburbs. If you want to climb into the saddle, you'll be best off in the Winelands (where it's possible to ride amongst the vineyards and even do a winetasting tour on horseback; contact Paradise Stables, tel: 021 876 2160) or in the villages of the Southern Peninsula, Noordhoek, in particular. The best city ride is along the 8km stretch of Long Beach, gambolling through the waves and over the sand dunes. A two-hour ride will cost upwards of R350. Advance booking essential.

Sleepy Hollow
Noordhoek
Tel: 021 789 2341
www.sleepyhollowhorseriding.co.za

Based in the laidback village at the foot of Chapman's Peak, Noordhoek's best-known equestrian outfit is a well-organized operation with well-schooled horses available for rides that include trotting and cantering on the beach. For the best experience, secure an early-morning (9am) or sunset ride (commencing 4pm in winter and 5pm in summer); each ride lasts two hours and costs R300.

Wine Valley Horse Trails
Tel: 083 226 8735
www.horsetrails-sa.co.za

As the name implies, this outfit offer rides within the vineyards, commencing on Rhebokskloof Wine Estate.

Horse-racing

One of the most anticipated social events in Cape Town's busy calendar is the annual J&B Met (www.jbmet. co.za), when dressing up for a full day and long night of partying takes precedence over paying any kind of serious attention to events on the race track. The Met is held at the Kenilworth Race Course (Rosmead Avenue, Kenilworth; tel: 021 700 1600) in January each year; it's exceedingly popular and almost impossible to find parking, so consider pre-booking a taxi to and from the event. General entrance tickets cost R150, which includes a R10 betting ticket and access to the full ten-race event – races kick off just before noon and go on until early evening, and from 7pm there's a swinging after-party till midnight.

Jogging & Running

If a daily jog or run is part of your routine, you'll be spoilt for choice just about anywhere in and around the city and the Peninsula – the scenery along just about any route is captivating. Our favourite city route is the cliff-hugging promenade between Camps Bay and Bantry Bay, with epic sea views all the way; you can extend this all the way to Moulle Point along the Sea Point Promenade.

Hardly surprising then that the 56km Two Oceans Marathon (www.two-oceansmarathon.co.za) is said to be the most scenically beautiful road race on earth. Part and parcel of Cape Town's Easter weekend festivities, the race attracts well over 25,000 participants, a far cry from the 26 runners who launched the event in 1970. You'll need to apply in advance to take part in the ultra-marathon event or the 21km half-marathon that happens at the same time (the latter is capped at 11,000 so you'll need to enter before February) – and will need to qualify by completing a number of shorter races beforehand; alternatively, sign up for one of the two short fun run events that add to the festivities on the day.

Kite-surfing & Windsurfing

When the wind blows in and around Cape Town, everyone moans – except for one tribe. Cape Town is one of the finest kite- and windsurfing destinations in the world, attracting multitudes of so-called 'Euros' who descend on Big Bay (Bloubergstrand) and Langebaan (West Coast, about an hour north from Cape Town) each year. Coupled with good waves and the iconic view of Table Mountain (the one pictured in just about every travel brochure), the consistently windy conditions makes Big Bay highly sought after – to the extend that it can feel a little crowded out there on the water. Things get even busier during the annual Langebaan Downwind Dash, a wind-powered event that's been going since 1984 and is widely considered the biggest kiteboarding event in the world. The Dash covers a 17km stretch between Langebaan and Saldanha, and is where you'll catch many of the sport's top names competing. A few other popular spots for windsurfing include the Milnerton Lagoon and Platboom, en route to Cape Point.

Cabrinha
Marine Promenade, Porterfield Rd.,
in Table View
Tel: 021 556 7910
www.cabrinha.co.za

Based on Blouberg's world-famous 'Kitebeach' – considered one of the premiere kitesurfing spots on the planet – Cabrinha offers lessons and equipment rentals, and is widely considered the top outfitter of its kind. A two-hour lesson (with no more than two students per instructor) costs R495, you'll probably need three sessions before you're feeling confident enough to go it alone.

Motorcycle & Side-car Adventures

The advantage of zipping around Cape Town and the Peninsula on two wheels is that you can outmanoevre the often-congested traffic that plagues prime locations during peak season. The downside is that you are vulnerable to other motorists and the weather.

Cape Sidecar Adventures
2 Glengariff Rd.,
Three Anchor Bay, Sea Point
Tel: 021 434 9855/6
www.sidecars.co.za

With a fleet of 25 sidecars – modeled on 1938 German BMW sidecars and manufactured for the Chinese Red Army from the mid-1950s – Tim Clarke's innovative venture puts an alternative spin on sightseeing. You can travel in the sidecar with a chauffer-guide for around R1,785, or motor yourself with your partner in the sidecars. Overnight and multi-day rentals are possible.

. . . .

La Dolce Vita Biking

13D Kloof Nek Rd., Gardens
Tel: 083 528 0897
www.ldvbiking.co.za

It's quite fashionable to charge around the city on a scooter; specially useful for getting to the beach (where parking can be a major issue). La Dolce Vita charges R110–R165 per day (including unlimited mileage, a helmet, and insurance); they also rent proper motorbikes if you prefer more power between your legs (R140–R280 per day).

. . . .

SA Motorcycle Tours

Tel: 021 794 7887
www.sa-motorcycle-tours.com

Only BMW bikes are available at this quality-oriented outfit. Prices start at R1,784 for their Cape Peninsula Tour, which includes a guide and the hire of your bike. Some tours stop to take in major attractions (like the penguins at Boulders), but for most you're touring some unparalleled landscapes. A number of multi-day bike tours are also on offer; no bikers under 28 years need apply.

. . . .

Harley-Davidson Cape Town

9 Somerset Road, City Centre
Tel: 021 446 2999
www.harley-davidson-capetown.com

This is the largest factory-authorized Harley rental outlet outside the USA, with over 20 Twin Cam bikes; they upgrade their entire fleet every year with brand new bikes, and all the machines are equipped with standard frills, including passenger seats. A regular Harley motorcycle breakfast run to the Winelands happen on Sunday mornings; ask about these when you pick up your rental. Bikes rent for R1,100–R1,500 per day, or R3,250–R4,400 for a weekend.

. . . .

Paragliding

A tandem leap off Signal Hill, floating effortlessly above the city before descending on Camps Bay beach – with nothing but thermals between you and the city below, this is amongst the most exhilarating ways to see and experience Cape Town. No previous experience is necessary if you fly tandem, while solo flying is possible after a short introductory course.

The most reliable jump point, from a weather point of view, is Signal Hill, but for the chance of landing on Camps Bay Beach or at La Med, right by the bar, nothing beats soaring from Lion's Head, where you can often hang on the thermals for a prolonged period.

Because paragliding is so highly weather-dependent, it's best to make contact with an operator as soon as you arrive in Cape Town and ask them to contact you as soon as there's a possibility of jumping; it's essential to have a mobile phone so that the operator can contact you as soon as conditions are right for flying.

Birdmen
36 Champagne Way, Table View
Tel: 021 557 8144 or 082 658 6710
www.birdmen.co.za

With over 2,500 flights to his credit, Barry Pedersen is amongst Cape Town's most experienced tandem pilots and instructors; his inspiration to become a 'birdman' came from his uncle, who was the first hang-glider to launch off Table Mountain. He offers flights off Signal Hill, Lion's Head, Chapman's Peak, and in the Winelands; a basic tandem flight will cost R950. Barry also runs a paragliding school through which you can acquire your South African paragliding licence – a lengthy course (minimum three weeks) during which you do up to 50 solo flights (with radio instruction) and walk away with no fewer than five hours flying time; The course costs R7,800. If you're pressed for time, but want to get some idea of what flying solo might be about, there's also a one- or two-day introductory course (R1 800 per person).

Rugby

For many, rugby is synonymous with South Africa, and as much a part of the white man's cultural diet as beer and *braaivleis* (barbequed meat). You'll catch Capetonians dabbling in a friendly game of touch rugby on the beach, practicing their skills (developed at school) in parks, or watching the game in dark pubs, but for a real cultural eye-opener you need to catch a major match in a proper stadium – hanging out with the *manne* (men) in manic support for a favourite team (and it's considered sacrilege to support anyone other than the local side, in this case known as the Stormers; www.thestormers.co.za) is fun; if the game is important it's also likely to be one of the few events where you'll see grown South African men in tears.

Newlands Rugby Stadium
11 Boundary Road, Newlands
Tel: 021 686 2150
www.iamastormer.com

One of South Africa's premiere rugby venues, this is the second-oldest rugby stadium in the world and – for fans, at least – a place of legend, where some major international scores have been settled. Getting to Newlands can be a real test of will power since traffic inevitably starts clogging up from early, so if you're determined to join the crowds, make plans well in advance, and don't plan on getting away in a hurry at the end of it, either. Of special interest will be any international test match, particularly a Tri-Nations game (against arch rivals New Zealand and Australia) or six-nations test match.

Sandboarding

This warm weather alternative to snowboarding happens on the high sand dunes of Atlantis, around 40 minutes from the centre of town. It's slower than snowboarding, and the sand can get darn hot!

Downhill Adventures

Tel: 021 422 0388
www.downhilladventures.com

Specialists in many of the Cape's adventure activities and extreme sports, this outfit will key you in to the basics of the sport, provide tuition, and rent you a board. Expect to spend around R700 for a full day on the dunes, with the benefit of an instructor.

Shark Cage Diving

Forget tawdry images of razor-toothed monsters chomping at metal bars – viewing great white sharks in their natural habitat is as much myth-dispelling as it is a riveting opportunity to get up close and personal with one of the earth's most ancient creatures. Most South African shark-cage diving companies adhere to a strict code of conduct and many are involved in eco-research aimed at helping save the endangered great white from imminent extinction. If you're at all fascinated by creatures of the deep, this day excursion is worth it.

White Shark Projects

Tel: 021 405 4537
www.whitesharkprojects.co.za

Like many of the operators, this company conducts morning and afternoon dive sessions, with Cape Town hotel pick-ups starting very early in the morning in order to get to Kleinbaai, known as the Great White Shark Capital of the World, two-hours from the city. Nowhere else on the planet can you get to the sharks with so little effort and with such favourable odds of actually seeing them. In winter, you'll head out to a spot near Geyser Rock – the preferred winter breeding ground for 60,000 Cape fur seals, who in turn provide an endless supply of meals for the sharks. You're supplied with everything you need for the dive, but take warm clothing along (the water is icy and the onboard breeze will chill you to the core); unless you're regularly at sea, consider taking sea-sick medication (ask you doctor). You can also purchase underwater cameras, or purchase the boat's crew excellent video of the entire outing (R300 per DVD).

Skydiving

As long as you weigh less than 105kg, you can propel yourself out of an airplane some 3,600m above the earth and enjoy up to 30 seconds of freefall, before your chute opens and you drift back down to earth.

Skydive Cape Town

Tel: 082 800 6290
www.skydivecapetown.za.net

Based some 35 minutes outside the city up the West Coast, this longstanding company offers daily tandem dives as well as static line and accelerated freefall courses under expert supervision. If you dive attached to an instructor it will cost R1,450 per jump; the introductory static-line course (where your chute opens immediately after you launch yourself from the airplane), costs R900 and includes a day of training, followed by your first solo jump. Experienced jumpers can rent equipment.

Spas, Steamrooms & Leisure Baths

During summer, certain spas even have mini-stations on a few of the most popular beaches; most top-end hotels have in-house spas open to the public (the exceptions are the exclusive Ellerman House and Cape Grace, both available to hotel residents only).

Agsana Spa

The Vineyard Hotel, Colinton Road, Newlands, Southern Suburbs
Tel: 021 674 5005
www.vineyard.co.za

There's good reason the ladies of leisure spend so much time traipsing in and out of here – this is some of the best attention your muscles are going to receive in Cape Town. Thai and Asian therapies performed by excellent Thai and Asian therapists are a key ingredient at this busy, no-nonsense spa in the heart of the Southern Suburbs, where most of the clientele are regular returnees. Treatments are performed in a sanctuary-like space with rooms facing onto a luscious garden.

Equinox Spa

Cape Royale, 47 Main Road, Green Point
Tel: 021 430 0511
www.equinoxspa.co.za
Open: 8am–8pm Mon–Sat; 9am–6pm Sun

A handsome, moodily-lit space within the confines of the pseudo-luxurious Cape Royale hotel practically across the road from Green Point Stadium.

Their signature massage is a chakra-balancing rubdown involving colour-coded soy candles that are melted and then applied to your skin with relaxing, rhythmic strokes so the nourishing oils can feed your skin.

Glasshouse Rejuvenation for Men

Unit 11A, The Foundry, 74 Prestwich Street, Green Point
Tel: 021 419 9599
www.glasshousemen.com
Open: 9am–7pm Mon–Fri; 9am–5pm Sat and public holidays

The only classy joint in town that has no qualms about offering a 'back, crack and sack' wax, this elegant men-only spa will tend to all your grooming requirements. Bar service and large-screen televisions keep you distracted from the work being done on your nails or toenails; great for invigorating post-flight rubdowns, they also get the skin smooth with body scrubs and the blood circulating with reflex-action foot massage.

Jiva Grande Spa

Taj Cape Town, cnr Wale Street and St. George's Mall, City Centre
Tel: 021 819 2000
www.tajhotels.com/capetown
Open: daily, 8am–8pm

Bringing authentic Ayurvedic treatments to Cape Town, this spa is an oasis of calm in the midst of the city centre. With mosaic-encrusted wet areas and light-filled, spacious treatments rooms, it's a harmonious blend of modern design and ancient thinking, with a full range of Ayurvedic treatments by imported Indian doctors.

The Hothouse Steam & Leisure

18 Jarvis Street, De Waterkant
Tel: 021 418 3888
www.hothouse.co.za
Open: noon–2am Mon–Wed,
noon–4am Thurs, open 24 hours at
weekends

With a trendy-looking lounge, bars
and a restaurant, this steam-bath and
sauna complex is designed as a meeting spot for gay men – there are even
private cabins and video lounges for a
totally different kind of grooming.

Librisa Spa

Mount Nelson Hotel, 76 Orange
Street, Gardens, City Bowl
Tel: 021 483 1000
www.mountnelson.co.za

Located in the gardens of the gracious Mount Nelson, this is an elegant, feminine spa, done with the
same modern-Victorian sensibility
that permeates the hotel. It's ideal for
ladies who feel like being pampered in
a choice of beautiful rooms (and are
bored rigid with the modern-Asian
aesthetic); they even have a kiddie spa
menu for little hedonists-in-waiting.

One&Only Spa

One& Only Cape Town, Victoria &
Alfred Waterfront
Tel: 021 431 5810
www.oneandonlycapetown.com
Open: daily, 8am–8pm

The city's largest and most attractive
spa, situated on a manmade Spa Island
on a manmade marina on the outskirts
of the V&A Waterfront. The signature
Essence of Earth and Ocean Experience is an invigorating, skin-tingling,
muscle-revitalising ritual that draws on
the ancient practices of the San people
using local therapeutic plants in a series of treatments – packaged into a
wonderful two-hour session that leaves
you feeling light-years younger.

Sanctuary Spa

Twelve Apostles Hotel and Spa,
Victoria Road, Camps Bay
Tel: 021 437 0677
www.thesanctuarygroup.co.za
Open: daily, 8am (9am winter)–8pm

A love it or hate it environment, this
spa is designed to mimic a subterranean cave, complete with fake rocks
and water features, and lit by neon
and candlelight, like entering the lair
of one of James Bond's archrivals.
The three-hour Moonlight Treatment starts with sparkling wine and
a picnic basket and ends with a stone
massage, all by moonlight. They have
Cape Town's only Rasul Chamber, and
there's a salt water floatation tank, too.
It can feel a touch claustrophobic if
you prefer light-filled, open-air spaces,
but to compensate, two glass-enclosed
massage gazebos have been erected
amongst the *fynbos* vegetation on the
mountain slopes.

Mansion Spa and Leisure Club

15 Jarvis Street, De Waterkant
Tel: 021 801 0501
www.mansion.co.za

A cushy sanctuary done out in crocodile skin tiles, with plans to host botox parties and other surface-adjustment excuses to socialize. This is an elegant and smart space to come for a leisurely rub-down, prolonged steam, and chance to cosy up to someone you just met at the bar upstairs. It's located in the cobblestone heart of Cape Town's Gay Village, so the idea is to combine muscle-tingling treatments with a chance to hang with the boys.

Supping (Stand-up Paddle Boarding)

A hugely popular new watersport, with Cape Town one of the core location for what is something of a hybrid between paddleskiing and surfing. Supping requires a specialized paddle board which is wider and longer than a standard longboard, designed to provide more stability; the accompanying paddles are made of wood, fiberglass or carbon and are around 15 to 25cm taller than the paddler using them. Coreban (tel: 021 553 0172, www.coreban.co.za) is a major producer of paddle boards and runs a summer series supping event in Cape Town in December.

Surfing

Now an annual event, the Wavescapes Surf Film Festival (www.wavescape.co.za) kicks off in the first half of December with a big screen showing on Clifton Beach. One look at the size of the crowd that shows up will give you some idea of the size of Cape Town's surfing community. The festival includes new, classic and cult documentaries as well as fiction films with surf culture as their key ingredient; further performances happen at various venues in the city, and as far out as the Brass Bell in Kalk Bay.

Surfers will find many spots around the peninsula with perfect breaks. Top spots include the waters off Kalk Bay reef and Long Beach (Noordhoek), while consistent waves at Muizenberg (Surfers' Corner) and Blouberg's Big Bay (take the R27 Marine Drive off the N1) make these popular training grounds for new surfers (with surf schools at both); all of these can be crowded, however, and you might prefer to seek out quieter beaches. Llandudno is a good call, whilst those who value a sense of solitude combined with stunning scenery tend to pitch the beaches within the Cape Point Nature Reserve as the ultimate surf destinations on the Peninsula. If you want to be close to the buzz of the city, it's possible to surf at Glen Beach, a tiny beach between Camps Bay and Clifton; if you need nerves of steel head to Dungeons off Hout Bay, which can produce waves of up to 25 feet when conditions are right.

If you don't mind traveling some distance out of the city, Elands Bay (West Coast) is considered surfing heaven, although this too can get very crowded, and the time taken to get there means it's most suitable for a two-day outing (locals are also not very friendly).

There's a telephone hotline with the

daily surf report (tel: 082 234 6340) and you can get the lowdown on Cape Town's many and varied surf hotspots at www.wavescape.co.za. The outfits below will rent equipment and offer tuition. If all you need is equipment or advice, call Matthew Moir (tel: 083 444 9442).

Downhill Adventures,
Tel: 021 422 0388
www.downhilladventures.com

Catering to a wide range of outdoor activities, Downhill Adventures also operates a surf school and provides all necessary equipment. A full day's surf outing costs R655, including transfers from the city and lunch.

Gary's Surf School
Beach Road, Muizenburg
Tel: 021 788 9839
www.garysurf.com

Operating since 1989, Gary's is the oldest surf school in the country and popular amongst both locals and internationals looking for beginner and professional coaching. A two-hour lesson (with equipment for the entire day) costs R500; lessons happen every day at 9am, 11am, and 2pm. They also rent equipment to non-students.

Swimming

If the icy waters of the Atlantic don't appeal, you may be interested to join the crowd that flocks to Sea Point's public baths, or the historic indoor complex on Long Street.

Long Street Baths
Long Street, City Centre
Tel: 021 400 3302

Built in 1908, this complex includes a heated pool for swimming and there are Turkish baths, too. Not the most salubrious changing rooms you've ever encountered.

Sea Point Pavilion
Beach Road, Sea Point
Tel: 021 434 3341

There's an Olympic-size public swimming pool filled with seawater, although temperatures are a few degrees warmer than you'll find in the ocean, which is just on the other side of the barrier. There's also a diving pool and a children's pool, so be warned that it's very popular with families and can get crowded and noisy.

Whale Watching

The Cape's southern coast is a Southern Right whale nursery, with whales migrating to its shallow coastal basin to calve from mid-July to November; the Whale Hot Line (tel: 083 910 1028) will key you in on what's happening along the coast. The city's best whale-spotting is along the False Bay side, with boats launching from Simons Town (see Cruises & Boat Trips). But for some of the best land-based whale-watching in the world you need to head to Hermanus, which can be reached in 90 minutes to an hour (depending on traffic). Hermanus has the only 'whale crier' in the world; from 10am to 4pm

Pasika blows his kelp horn to keen everyone up to speed on the whereabouts of the whales; alternatively take a boat trip with a local Hermanus company such as Ivanhoe Sea Safaris (tel: 082 926 7977).

info...

Holidays

If you are traveling during the South African school holidays (check exact dates on www.southafrica.net but usually four weeks over Dec/Jan, two weeks in April, three weeks June/July, one week in September), make sure you book your accommodations well in advance. Banks, government offices, post offices, and most museums are closed on the following national holidays: January 1 (New Year's Day), March 21 (Human Rights Day); Good Friday, Easter Sunday and Monday; April 27 (Founders/Freedom Day); May 1 (Workers Day); June 16 (Soweto/Youth Day); August 9 (Women's Day); September 24 (Heritage Day); December 16 (Day of Reconciliation); Christmas Day; and December 26 (Boxing Day).

Money

South Africa has a sophisticated financial infrastructure. ATMs and banks are ubiquitous, although the in-bank experience can be frustrating; try to make use of cash machines for all money withdrawals. The rand (denoted by the symbol R before the amount, available in R10, R20, R50, R100, R200 notes) is divided into 100 cents (c).

Smoking

All restaurants have a mostly non-smoking policy, although most will have a designated area for smokers. Bars are by and large non-smoking but if you see ashtrays and others lighting up, you can pretty much assume that it's fine to go ahead and join in. Clubs, too, are a mixed bag; it's assumed that smoking will be banned in all public places, but currently there are some joints that either ignore the law or seem to have special permits to allow smoking to continue.

Taxis

From the airport: Centurion (tel: 021 934 8281; centuriontours@telkomsa.net), offers an efficient door-to-door service in minibuses – ideally you should book this two days in advance. From the airport to the city centre costs around R150 for the first person and R20 per person thereafter. Mail or call them and they'll be waiting at the airport arrivals area with your name on a sign board; note that there's an early morning (before 6:30am) and late-night (after 10:30pm) surcharge.

In the city: metered taxis don't cruise the streets looking for fares; you'll have to phone. Most charge upwards of R10 per km. Cab Co. (tel: 082 580 9030) is a small, personal operation we like supporting; alternatively Sea Point Taxis (tel: 021 434 4444). Much cheaper than a metered taxi are Rikkis, London-style cabs which keep prices down by continuously picking up and dropping off passengers on a vaguely circular route, so it takes slightly longer to get to where you're going, but you may meet some interesting people en route. You pay according to city zones, priced from R20 to R35 (after 7pm a R5 surcharge applies). These are operational 24/7 and will drop you off anywhere in the centre, City Bowl suburbs, the Waterfront, or Camps Bay (tel: 086 174 5547; www.rikkis.co.za; you can also contact Rikkis from dedicated telephones they have set up in locations around the city).

Car hire: Cape Town is a great city to explore in your own car; aside from the usual suspects (Avis, Hertz, etc) independent outfits offering a cheaper deal include Penny K's (tel: 072 736 6957; www.pennyks.co.za; from R170 per day) and Value (tel: 021 386 7699; www.valuerentalcar.com; from R189 per day). If you want to tool around with the wind in your hair, rent a classic convertible, with or without chauffeur, from Motor Classic (tel: 021 461 7368 or 072 277 5022; www.motorclassic.co.za; from around R1,300 per day self-drive).

Telephone

Landlines are reliable and cellphone reception is generally excellent given how mountainous the Cape is. If you are using a landline, call directory assistance at tel: 1023 for numbers in South Africa; to track down a service, call tel: 10118. If you plan to use your phone a lot it's definitely worth bringing your cell phone and purchasing a local SIM card (between R1 and R20, depending on where and when you buy it), and purchasing pay-as-you-go airtime (available in bundled minutes that cost upward of R20). You will find retailers selling SIM cards and airtime throughout metropolitan areas; look for signs on shop windows. You can rent a phone (as well as purchase a SIM card and airtime) at a Vodafone or Vodacom outlet; there is a 24-hour desks at Cape Town international airport, as well as in all the big malls (including the Waterfront).

Tickets & Timetables

Computicket (www.computicket.com; tel: 083 915 8000) is a free national booking service that covers cinema and concert seats, as well as intercity bus tickets; payment can be made over the phone by credit card. Also look at www.webtickets.co.za.

Tipping

Be generous if you feel the service warrants it; this is the best way to redistribute wealth into what remains a very poor country. Add 10% and upwards to your restaurant bill, 10% to your taxi. Porters get around R5 to R10 per bag. There are no self-serve garages, or gas stations; when filling up with fuel, tip the person around R5; this is also what you tip informal car guards (identified by their neon bib) who look after cars on the street (assuming you are not just stopping for a few minutes). You do not need to tip the informal car guards if you don't have any change but it's a bit churlish to refuse to do so if you have.

index...

notes...

notes...

Hedonism /hedoniz'm/

"The philosophy that pleasure is the highest good and proper aim of human life."